ABSTRACTS OF CHANCERY COURT RECORDS OF MARYLAND 1669-1782

Debbie Hooper

HERITAGE BOOKS
2008

HERITAGE BOOKS
AN IMPRINT OF HERITAGE BOOKS, INC.

Books, CDs, and more—Worldwide

For our listing of thousands of titles see our website at
www.HeritageBooks.com

Published 2008 by
HERITAGE BOOKS, INC.
Publishing Division
100 Railroad Ave. #104
Westminster, Maryland 21157

Copyright © 1996 Debbie Hooper

All rights reserved. No part of this book may be reproduced or transmitted in any form or by any means, electronic or mechanical, including photocopying, recording or by any information storage and retrieval system without written permission from the author, except for the inclusion of brief quotations in a review.

International Standard Book Numbers
Paperbound: 978-1-58549-331-9
Clothbound: 978-0-7884-7613-6

CONTENTS

Introduction v
Chancery Court Records, 1671-1782 ... 1
Index 129

INTRODUCTION

Marylanders in the seventeenth century were served by a number of courts: 1) an appellate court, made up of the Governor and Council, 2) the Provincial Court, which heard general law cases, 3) the Court of Chancery, which heard equity cases, 4) the individual county courts, and 5) the manorial or leet courts, which functioned on the larger manors.[1]

Before 1668 the records of the Chancery and Provincial Courts were recorded in the same volumes because the two courts had the same judges, and the same clerk. Beginning in 1669 the records were kept separately even though the same individual kept the records.

The bulk of the material recorded in the chancery proceedings had to do with inheritance of land. These cases contain writs of *diem clausum extremum* and *mandamus*, which were orders to investigate ownership of land by someone who was supposed to have died without lawful heirs. Lord Baltimore had an interest in such cases as the land might have reverted to him. An *inquisition post mortem* would be held and a jury, usually of 12 men, would investigate the facts of the case.[2] Inquisitions post mortem were held in England when someone who held land directly from the crown died. An inventory of the land would be given, along with names of anyone who had a claim on the property along with the name and age of the next heir. In Maryland such a jury was often convened to investigate the boundaries of land. In the county court these investigations were often called land commissions.[3]

Other legal terms found in the records of the Chancery and other courts include:[4]

Ad quod damnum: an order to a sheriff to summon a jury to determine what damage might occur of private property were to be taken for public usage.

Audita querila: an order for a court to reconsider the

---

[1] J. Hall Pleasants, editor, Samuel K. Dennis, and John M. Vincent, Committee on Publication, "Letter of Transmittal," *Archives of Maryland, LI: Proceedings of the Court of Chancery, 1666-1679: Court Series (5)* (Baltimore: The Maryland Historical Society, 1934), p. ix.

[2] Pleasants et al, *op. cit.*, p. xvi.

[3] Carroll T. Bond, "Introduction to the Legal Procedures," *Archives of Maryland, LI: Proceedings of the Court of Chancery, 1666-1679: Court Series (5)* (Baltimore: The Maryland Historical Society, 1934), pp. xxvi, xxvii.

[4] Bond, *op. cit.*, pp. xxiii, ff.

action to be taken, as such action already provided for, would be unduly harsh or extreme.

Benefit of clergy: in colonial Maryland, the right of a felon to escape punishment if he could prove he was literate. The right could only be claimed once, and to show that the felon had used this right, he was burnt in the hand.

Certiorari: an order to send records of a case from a lower court to a higher court; used when one of the parties felt aggrieved by the decision of the lower court.

Habeas corpus: an order for an official to bring another person into court at a specified time.

Praecipe: an order to a defendant to perform a specific act, such as paying a debt.

Si te fecerit securum: a writ used if a plaintiff gave a sheriff some security to prosecute his claim.

Subpoena: an order issued to private individuals to perform a specific action, such as to appear in court.

Supercedas: an order to postpone execution of a judgment pending an appeal or other further proceeding.

The present volume of Abstracts of Chancery Court Records summarizes the proceedings of that court from 1671 to 1784. It contains the names of the parties of the case, as well as names of others mentioned in the testimony. Material for the years 1666 to 1679 was originally published in *The Archives of Maryland, LI: Proceedings of the Court of Chancery, 1666-1679: Court Series (5)* (Baltimore: The Maryland Historical Society, 1934). It is summarized in this book on pp. 1-10.

The book contains many depositions made by colonial Marylanders. These depositions not only addressed the facts of the case, but often gave autobiographical data about the deponent.

References to remarriages of widows and widowers are found. In addition, there are some clues to the European origins of Marylanders.

It should be noted that colonial clerks often misspelled names and/or with the passage of time, old handwriting has become faded and difficult to read. Therefore, researchers will want to check the index for variant spellings. For example, Hutchinson may have appeared as Hitchinson, Hoskins as Hopkins, and Whiteley as Wrightly.

Robert Barnes
29 March 1996

CHANCERY COURT RECORDS
1671-1782

Utie, Coll. Nathaniel. 18 Jan 1667. Indenture with John Carter, Lancaster Co., Virginia. That Nathaniel Utie shall marry Elizabeth, dau. of said John Carter, if she will consent before the last day of Feb. next. (Arch. of MD, v. LI, p. 4). Baltimore Co. (?)

Oversee, Simon. Died in the beginning of Feb 1659 possessed of 1000 ac. on east side of Portobacco Creek and other acreage. His land called *St. John's Freehold* and the 800 ac. adjoining was occupied by his widow Elizabeth for one year after his death. (Arch. of MD, v. LI, p. 12, 66, 120, 333, 370). Charles Co.

Hambleton, William, aged aet 33. 22 Dec 1669. Deposition. Lived at Capt. Giles Brent's in Potomack River for 9-10 months; also living there was William Green, carpenter, and his wife. (Arch. of MD, v. LI, p. 18).

Rousby, Christopher, and his wife Elizabeth against John Peirce. 12 Apr 1670. (Arch. of MD, v. LI, p. 22, 331).

Parrott, William. Devised to his son Henry Parrott a parcel of land called *Poppingay*. Henry Parrott on 26 Feb 1669 conveyed to Samuell Chew of AA Co. said tract. (Arch. of MD, v. LI, p. 40). Talbot Co.

Bonner, Henry and his wife Elizabeth, widow and admx. of Walter Storey. Defendants in Chancery case, John Long complainant (1670). Elizabeth saith that she was left a widow and a child. That Storey died on his return from England. (Arch. of MD, v. LI, p. 44). 10 Jan 1672. Reference to Walter, son of Walter Storey, decd. (Arch. of MD, v. LXVI, p. 231). Charles Co.

Johnson, Peter. Died ca. Apr 1660, with his brother James Johnson as heir. (Arch. of MD, v. LI, p. 68). Calvert Co.

Batten, William. Died ca. last of Oct 1662, leaving widow Margery who m. John Bowles. (Arch. of MD, v. LI, p. 70). Charles Co.

Kilborne, Francis and his wife Elizabeth, guardian of Daniell Johnson, infant. Defendant, 16 Sep 1672. (Arch. of MD, v. LI, p. 84). Francis Kilborne and his wife Margaret, admrs. of Donnell Johnson, late of Charles Co., decd. (Arch of MD, v. LI, p. 379). Charles Co.

Andrews, Christopher and his wife Mary, late wife of William Standley. At the suit of Robert Chapman in a plea of slander and defamation. 7 Oct 1672. (Arch. of MD, v. LI, p. 85). Kent Co.

Beedle, Henry and his wife Sophia. Against George Wells. 25 Sep 1672. (Arch. of MD, v. LI, p. 85).

Wright, John and his wife Mary, admrs. of Bartholomew Glevin. [John Wright died prior 29 Dec 1675.] Defendants, Tobias Wells, complainant. 7 Feb 1672, 29 Dec 1675. (Arch. of MD, v. LI, p. 95, 165). Mary Wright and Tobias Wells are dead by 2 May 1677; Tobias Wells left his wife Mary a widow who later married Lewis Blangy. 2 May 1677. (Arch. of MD, v. LI, p. 217, 442). Kent Co.

Hatton, John, formerly of London and now merchant of Maryland, died in 1663 in Maryland, seized of divers tracts, 600 ac. in Baltimore Co., 350 ac. called *Mt. Harmour*, 400 ac. of James Rigby in Rumley Creek, a parcel on Chester River called *Whiteclifts*. His brother, Thomas Hatton, of Tewksbury in Gloucester Co., England is heir. (Arch. of MD, v. LI, p. 101). Baltimore Co.

Eaton, Jeremy and his wife Mary, adrs. of Thomas Ingram. 17 Nov 1673. (Arch. of MD, v. LI, p. 106). Mary Easton, extx. of Jeremiah Eaton, late of Kent Co. to answer Mary Roe, widow, extx. of Edward Roe [of Talbot Co.] (Arch. of MD, v. LXVIII, p. 211). Kent Co./Talbot Co.

Pritchett, John. Died Sep 1656. His son, William Pritchett, is now 21-22 yrs. of age. (Arch. of MD, v. LI, p. 111, 443). St. Mary's Co.

Claugh, William and his wife Sarah. Summoned to appear. 18 Apr 1674. (Arch. of MD, v. LI, p. 113).

Ellenor, Andrew (a Spaniard) died seized of 1/2 of the land called *Stoopley Gibson* in the manor of Baltimore; he died Jun 1660; his two daughters, Sarah the wife of William Joyner is aged ca. 17 and Ann, wife of Lawrence Arenold is aged ca. 15. His widow m. Macom Mehenny and after his death the widow m. John Dabb. 10 Apr 1674. (Arch. of MD, v. LI, p. 113). Kent Co.

Glevin, Bartholomew, died ca. 1667 without issue. (Arch. of MD, v. LI, p. 118). Anne Arundel Co.

Sanford, Alice, servant to Pope Alvey was killed by divers blows from Pope Alvey, cooper, in Britton's Bay, St. Mary's Co. 29 Feb 1663 at St. Winifred's in St. Clements Hundred. (Arch. of MD, v. LI, p. 122). St. Mary's Co.

Aspinall, Henry. Refers to statement on 25 Dec 1665 by his father in law, Walter Pake. (Arch. of MD, v. LI, p. 125). St. Mary's Co.

Hammond, Daniell aged 17, makes statement regarding Pope Alvey, his father in law. (Arch. of MD, v. LI, p. 125). St. Mary's Co.

Bateman, Mary of London, spinster, dau of John Batemen, decd., late of London, haberdasher, otherwise called John Bateman, late of Patuxent River, planter. 7 Aug 1674. Mary Bateman, widow of John Bateman conveyed to Henry Scarborough of North Waltham, county of Norf and Richard Perry of Patuxent, Maryland, merchant, for 100 lbs. *Resurrection Manor*. (Arch. of MD, v. LI, p. 130, 446). Calvert Co.

Stringer, James, died seized of divers lands which ought to descend to Mary Williams, his dau and only apparent heir, and wife of Lodowick Williams. 23 Aug 1674. (Arch. of MD, v. LI, p. 135, 154). Anne Arundel Co.

Lewis, Lieut. William. Died with right to 3000 ac. without heirs. (Arch. of MD, v. LI, p. 139). Charles Co.

Strong, Leonard. 28 Oct 1674. Owned 2 parcels of land in Calvert Co. About 19 yrs. ago he went to England and died there leaving a dau Elizabeth, at the time 2 yrs. old. She later married Charles James by whom she had a son or dau. She and the child are now dead. No other heirs are known. (Arch. of MD, v. LI, p. 140). Anne Arundel Co./Calvert Co.

Liget, Bridgett, widow of John Leget; he died without issue, possessed of 400 ac. (Arch. of MD, v. LI, p. 147). Charles Co.

Woolchurch, Henry and his wife Elizabeth. To answer John Beamont. 4 Mar 1674. (Arch. of MD, v. LI, p. 149).

Foxum, Richard, son of Richard Foxum, decd. and William Chadborne and his wife Susanna, to answer complaint of Edward Skidmore. (Arch. of MD, v. LI, p. 150). Baltimore Co.

Bland, Thomas and Damocis, his wife, extx. of Nicholas Wyatt. Complainants against Edward Dorsey of Anne Arundel Co. Anne Arundel Co.

Beson, Capt. Thomas, aet 58. 10 Mar 1674/5. Deposition regarding James Stringer. (Arch. of MD, v. LI, p. 155). Anne Arundel Co.

Beckwith, George and his wife Frances, in right of said Frances, was seized of a parcel of land, the land of Nicholas Harvey father of the said Frances, called *St. Joseph's Manor*, who conveyed same to Emporer Smith and Abdelo Martin Feb 1658. (Arch. of MD, v. LI, p. 156). George Beckwith had died by 11 Feb 1679. (Arch. of MD, v. LXIX, p. 116). Calvert Co.

Martin, Abdelo, died ca. 1667-1668, leaving three daughters which are believed to be still living and the eldest of them is 17 yrs. old. Abdelo Martin and Emperor Smith became seized of 165 ac. but were alianes [aliens] and died without being naturalized. The land was escheated. 9 Feb 1674. (Arch. of MD, v. LI, p. 155). Calvert Co.

Little, John, died Sep 1666, possessed of a parcel on the north side of the Patuxent River on the south side of Hunting Creek, 250 ac., and other land; made a will with his wife Mary as extx. She afterwards m. Joseph Tilly who held the land after her death. (Arch. of MD, v. LI, p. 157). 4 May 1675. Calvert Co.

Bird, Margaret, widow of Charles Bird who purchased two parcels of land of 160 ac. adjoining *Calverton Manor*. She now petitions to have land for her child by a former husband. ca. Jul 1675. (Arch. of MD, v. LI, p. 162). Calvert Co.

Turner, Robert. Died intestate and without heir ca. 20 Feb 1675. (Arch. of MD, v. LI, p. 170, 194). Kent Co.

Hitchinson, John. Died 18 of 19 Dec 1668, possessed of 300 ac. at Nanjemy in Charles Co. (Arch. of MD, v. LI, p. 172). Charles Co.

Cressy, Samuel. Died seized of land in right of his wife Susanna, formerly Susanna Robinson, relict of William Robinson. Susanna died 20 Jan 1675. George Robinson, son and heir of William Robinson, died 26 Jan 1675 without heirs. (Arch. of MD, v. LI, p. 181, 184). Reference to two poor orphans Mary and Susanna by the exr. of Samuel Cressey's estate, Richard Edelen. 1679. (Arch. of MD, v. LI, p. 237, 478). Charles Co.

Peircy, Thomas. Died 5 Nov 1666, possessed of 150 ac. in Charles Co. In his will he mentions sole heir Jeremiah Long, exr. (Arch. of MD, v. LI, p. 186). Charles Co.

Gardner, William. Died 25 Dec 1674 intestate and without heirs. (Arch. of MD, v. LI, p. 188). Charles Co.

Horsley, Joseph. Died 25 Feb 1670, leaving widow Rosamond, now wife of Richard Ladd. No heirs found. (Arch. of MD, v. LI,

p. 190, 380). (Arch. of MD, v. LXVIII, p. 95). Calvert Co.
Young, Elizabeth, relict of Edward Parker, died seized of a parcel of land called *Fresh Pond Neck* in St. Michaels Hundred, St. Mary's Co., by virtue of a devise to her made by Edward Packer, son of said Elizabeth by his last will. William Claw and John Smallpiece were exrs. She had no apparent heirs. Shortly after proving the will Smallpiece died. Afterward said William Clawe was slain before the Susquahannough fort having made his will, and his wife Sarah sole extx. Said Elizabeth conveyed land previously belonging to her son, Edward Packer, to John Reignolds who by his last will dated 24 Aug 1673 directed the land be sold. Edward Jolly during his life and his wife Margaret, and John Stevens who m. said Margaret Jolly still hold the land. (Arch. of MD, v. LI, p. 192, 310). 17 Sep 1679. (Arch. of MD, v. LI, p. 310). St. Mary's Co.
Bland, Thomas and his wife Demoras, admrs. of estate of Nicholas Wyatt. (Arch. of MD, v. LI, p. 197). Anne Arundel Co.
Walton, Elizabeth. Killed by Thomas Curre, under the age of 21, "by misadventure." 25 Apr 1677. (Arch. of MD, v. LI, p. 202). Kent Co.
Hooper, Sarah and Elinor Hooper, infants, daughters of Ruth Hooper, decd. [represented] by Thomas Clagett and his wife Mary, their guardians, at the suit of Henry Hooper and Ruth Hooper; Henry is the son of Henry Hooper. (Arch. of MD, v. LI, p. 204).
Peterson, Andrew, son of Peter Mounts of Cecil Co., and George Oldfield, to answer a bill in chancery at the suit of John John Browning . (Arch. of MD, v. LI, p. 205). Cecil Co. Andrew Peterson, son of Peter Munse, decd., under the age of 21. 29 Oct 1679. (Arch. of MD, v. LI, p. 288).
Blangy, Lewis and his wife Mary, admrs. of Disborah Bennett against Thomas Brite. 17 Oct 1677. (Arch. of MD, v. LI, p. 205). She was also admx. of Tobias Wells. 1677. (Arch. of MD, v. LXVII, p. 108). Lewis Blangy, tailor, late of Kent Co. 1678. (Arch. of MD, v. LXVIII, p. 2). Kent Co.
Okaine, Martha, wife of Rickart Okaine, pardoned by His Lordship, for the remission of the corporal punishment due unto her for stealing a hog of property of Samuell Mattox. (Arch. of MD, v. LI, p. 206, 211). St. Mary's Co.
Haselwood, John, and his wife Mary, exrs. of the last will of John Avery, complainants against Benjamin Granger. 5 Jan 1677. (Arch. of MD, v. LI, p. 208). Reference to Mary, wife of Benjamin Granger and Ann, wife of John Haselwood. 25 Mar 1679. (Arch. of MD, v. LI, p. 236). Benjamin Granger had married the dau of said John Avery. Mary Haselwood was the widow of John Avery. John Avery had a son named John Avery in England to be brought up by his brother, James Avery in England. John Avery, son of John Avery, died at sea. (Arch. of MD, v. LI, p. 526). Dorchester Co.
Hooper, Sarah and Elinor Hooper, infants, daughters of Richard Hooper, decd. [represented] by Thomas Clagett and his wife Mary, their guardians. Henry Hooper commanded to pay to Thomas and Mary Clagatt the sum of 800 lbs. of tobacco adjudged them as afsd. by our court of chancery 4 Oct last in

a cause depending between the said Henry Hooper and Richard Hooper, son of said Henry. 27 Oct 1677. (Arch. of MD, v. LI, p. 208).

Durant, Eagle, killed by Thos. Floyd, "by misadventure," who was convicted 20 Jun 1677. (Arch. of MD, v. LI, p. 210). Anne Arundel Co.

Barrett, John, died intestate and without issue, possessing 100 ac. *Ebdons Rest*. (Arch. of MD, v. LI, p. 212).

Smith, Thomas, died intestate and without issue, possessing *Batchellors Delight*, 260 ac. (Arch. of MD, v. LI, p. 212).

Dorsey, Edward and his wife Sarah, and Richard Hill to answer a bill in chancery from Thos. Bland and Damaras, his wife. 17 May 1678. (Arch. of MD, v. LI, p. 219).

Beck, Elizabeth, Mary Beck, and Margaret Beck, daughters of Richard Beck and Elizabeth Beck, daughters under the age of 21; in a suit against George Godfrey. 16 May 1678. (Arch. of MD, v. LI, p. 219). 24 Oct 1679. (Arch. of MD, v. LI, p. 290). Nicholas Emerson of Charles Co., decd. having married Elizabeth the mother of Richard Beck, father of above, by whom there was an estate in Virginia and this province. Richard had a brother named John Beck. (Arch. of MD, v. LI, p. 535). Charles Co.

Elliott, Henry who married Jane, relict of John Halfhead. Petitions that the land of John Halfhead be escheated in that he died intestate and without issue. John Halfhead died by the fall of a tree 6 Jan 1678. (Arch. of MD, v. LI, p. 221). 10 Mar 1678. (Arch. of MD, v. LI, p. 250). St. Mary's Co.

Jowles, Henry of Calvert Co., and his wife Sibel (Sybill), exrs. of last will of William Groom against Job Nutt, grocer in London and Michael Towney of Calvert Co. 8 Oct 1678. (Arch. of MD, v. LI, p. 224). 1678. (Arch. of MD, v. LXVII, p. 454). 16 Oct 1678. (Arch. of MD, v. LXVIII, p. 52). Calvert Co.

Roe, Mary, widow and extx. of Edward Roe, to answer bill in chancery, Nicholas Hackett complainant. Mar 1679. (Arch. of MD, v. LI, p. 233). Talbot Co.

Pascall, James of Calvert Co. Petitions that William Paggett, late of Anne Arundel Co., decd. died possessed of 300 ac. and devised same to his two sons, William and Thomas, who died as orphans, intestate. Petitioner is son of Sarah, a sister of said Pagett, and conceives himself to be heir of William Paggett. 3 May 1679. (Arch. of MD, v. LI, p. 234). Anne Arundel Co./Calvert Co.

Pascall, J---, son of James Pascall, is next heir to Wm. and Thomas Pagett, he being the son of James Pascall, brother of Amy Pagett, the late wife of said William Pagett, the mother of the said two sons, William and Thomas Pagett. Said heir is now 22 yrs. of age. George Pascall was the guardian of said William Paggett, the younger. Edward Thorley and his wife Mary held a lease on the land. His widow, Mary Thorley, was left at this death in possession of 400 ac. (Arch. of MD, v. LI, p. 263). [See above.]

Smith, Edward. Died 13 Feb 1676. Joint partner with John Arding [Harding] in taking up a parcel of land in Baltimore Co. (Arch. of MD, v. LI, p. 240, 316). Baltimore Co.

Breed, John, of Charles Co. His wife and her son, Ignatius

Mathews were present when he was served with a subpoena on 3 Oct 1678. (Arch. of MD, v. LI, p. 242). Charles Co.

Sallers, John. Petitions that Jeremiah Shulivant of Anne Arundel Co., late husband of Ann [now wife of Sallers?] died leaving a will dated 24 Feb 1675 by which he devised certain land to his wife, Ann. (Arch. of MD, v. LI, p. 248). Anne Arundel Co.

Acheson, Robert, son of Vincent and Hannah Acheson, decd. John Baker of St. Mary's City, claimant against Samuell Tovey admr. of Vincent Acheson and Robert Acheson. Samuell Tovey is guardian of Robert Acheson. 3 Jul 1679. (Arch. of MD, v. LI, p. 249). St. Mary's Co.

Thomas, Macum, of Somerset Co., and his wife were murdered by their man servant Henry Parratt in their beds at their dwelling house in Pocomoke at his plantation called *King's Neck* ca. 18 Feb 1675. Hugh Marinx, son of Hugh Marinx, late of Nansemum, Virginia, decd. born of Katherine his wife at Nansemum, 15 Mar 1665, to be the right heir to Macum Thomas. When Macum Thomas died he was possessed of 300 ac. called *King's Neck* of the manor of Nanticoke. Sold by Jenkin Price and Matthew his wife [sic] on 26 Mar 1667 to said Macum Thomas. (Arch. of MD, v. LI, p. 256). Somerset Co.

Tucker, John. Died Mar 1670. John Burges and his wife Amy, relict of said John Tucker, occupied the land possessed by said Tucker. (Arch. of MD, v. LI, p. 258). Calvert Co.

Caplin, Henry, was seized of 400 ac. at his death, called *Oatleys Choice*. He died in 1658 leaving a dau named Elizabeth who married Thomas Watkins; she died in 1672 without issue. (Arch. of MD, v. LI, p. 262). Anne Arundel Co.

Mascall, Richard. Departed the province in 1673, possessed of 230 ac. in Baltimore Co., but formerly in Anne Arundel Co. He died in Carolina in 1675 and no heir can be found. (Arch. of MD, v. LI, p. 264). Baltimore Co.

Diniard, Thomas. Died ca. 5 Nov 1659 without heirs, seized of 500 ac. of the manor of *West St. Mary's*. (Arch. of MD, v. LI, p. 265).

Hall, Thomas. Died Nov 1655, seized of 20 ac. called *Hall's Land* near Anne Arundel River in Todd's Neck. He had one son named Christopher Hall who died aged 26 without issue in Jan 1676, who by his will appointed his mother Elizabeth Hall, alias Record, aged ca. 46 his sole heir. (Arch. of MD, v. LI, p. 266). Anne Arundel Co.

Holloway, Oliver. Died No 1676 without issue, seized of 450 ac. in Anne Arundel Co. called *Hollaways Increase*, and 100 ac. called *Olivers Neck*. Both parcels have been occupied by his relict, Dianah, and Thomas Lunn who married said Dianah. (Arch. of MD, v. LI, p. 268). Anne Arundel Co.

Medley, William, son of John Medley. Heir of Mill Land. He is age 26 and upwards. 4 Jun 1679. (Arch. of MD, v. LI, p. 269). St. Mary's Co.

Sheale, Robert. Died 5 Mar 1662 without issue leaving his widow, Bridgett Sheale, in possession of 50 ac. She later married Gregory Rowse. She died ca. Mar 1679/80.

Lurke, John and Nicholas, orphans. Their mother, Mary Lurke, was given 150 ac. late in the tenure of John Potter for which

Nicholas Lurke, their father, hath paid rent. 1679. (Arch. of MD, v. LI, p. 276).

Drury, William. Died 28 Aug 1676 without heirs. William Drury married Christian Meriken, relict of John Meriken; she had by her right 50 ac. She died sometime before said William Drury. Petitions of her son Hugh Merrikin regarding the 50 ac. on the north side in Anne Arundel Co. which descended to petitioner's brother after the death of his mother who sold the land to William Drury. Christian Drury, dau of William and Christian Drury, died in her minority. (Arch. of MD, v. LI, p. 277, 300). Anne Arundel Co.

Patent of Mr. Hewitt who sold it to William Resbrooke who was drowned and afterwards his wife died and Francis Lumbard, who lives with her was possessed of the land and he mortgaged it to Thomas Marsh who sold it to Thomas Hynson who sold it to Henry Carline who left it to his widow and she married William Head. After she died William Head married Elizabeth Cash who survived him and survived the petitioner, William Rawles. ca. 5 Jun 1679. (Arch. of MD, v. LI, p. 277). Kent Co.

Evans, William. Died Mar 1669 seized of a parcel of land on the east side of St. Clements Bay. He left a will dated 10 Feb 1667 in which he left his wife, Elizabeth Evans, all his lands. She married Capt. John Jordain. John Jordain died ca. 8 Sep 1678. She married 28 Oct 1678 Cuthbert Scott. 4 Jun 1679. (Arch. of MD, v. LI, p. 283). St. Mary's Co.

James, Richard, gives to his master, John Browning, a parcel of land called *Jone's Adventure*, 200 ac; if his brother William Jones does not come into this country to settle, then his master to have it. 12 Feb 1669. (Arch. of MD, v. LI, p. 287). Baltimore Co.

Venall, John. Died ca. 1675 without issue. (Arch. of MD, v. LI, p. 296). Anne Arundel Co.

Heard, Bridgett, relict of William Heard. Patent granted to Coll. John Douglas, late of this co. decd., exr. of Bridgett Heard. William Heard died 4 Jan 1664 possessed of 1000 ac. called *Beach Neck*. (Arch. of MD, v. LI, p. 297). Charles Co.

Lindsey, James, Jr. Died Dec 1676, seized of 600 ac. on the west side of St. Thomas Creek, leaving no heirs. (Arch. of MD, v. LI, p. 299). Charles Co.

Williams, David, alias David Williamson, died Feb 1677, seized of 200 ac., having been killed by Indians, without heirs. His wife was killed by Indians at the same time. He was possessed of a parcel called *Long Acre*. (Arch. of MD, v. LI, p. 302). Somerset Co.

Ascombe, John, and his wife Winifred conveyed 400 ac. to Richard Wadsworth, Andrew Hinderson, and David Read. Said Wadsworth and his wife Susan released his third part to the joint tenants, Hinderson and Read, on 20 Sep 1664. On 23 Jan 1671 said Hinderson made his will, making his wife Elizabeth his extx., leaving her all but 100 ac. which he left to her son, Roger Moore, "if he comes into this country..." Andrew Hinderson died Jan 1671. The petitioner, Nicholas Buttram, married Elizabeth, relict of said Hinderson and she made her will on 4 Jan 1676 and bequeathed her estate. (Arch. of MD,

v. LI, p. 303, 314). Calvert Co.

Hollis, Henry and his wife Elizabeth, late relict of John Grammer of Calvert Co. John Grammer, Apr 1678, died without heirs possessed of two parcels of land on the Patuxent River called the School House and in 1677 made his last will and bequeathed the land to his wife Elizabeth. After the death of John Grammer said Elizabeth married the petitioner, Henry Hollis. 2 Dec 1679. (Arch. of MD, v. LI, p. 305, 317). Calvert Co.

Fowke, George, aet 21, Charles Co. 11 Nov 1679. Deposition in the chancery case of heirs of Richard Beck. [See earlier.] (Arch. of MD, v. LI, p. 311, 317).

Jenifer, Daniell and his wife Mary, extx. of William Smith, late of St. Mary's Co. against John Brooke and his wife Katherine, later Katherine Stevens admr. of Robt. Stevens. 1669. (Arch. of MD, v. LI, p. 326). Calvert Co.

Dorrington, William of Calvert Co., father of Sarah Dorrington, age 12 yrs., in her behalf against Thomas Manning, whereas Thomas Manning did beat and evil intreat the said Sarah. (Arch. of MD, v. LI, p. 332). Calvert Co.

Blomfield, John and his wife Elizabeth lately called Elizabeth Barbier, admx. of Luke Barbier of Newtown of St. Mary's Co. (Arch. of MD, v. LI, p. 334). St. Mary's Co.

Richardson, John, Tred Avon, Talbot Co., killed his wife Mary "by misadventure." 13 Dec 1670. (Arch. of MD, v. LI, p. 346). Talbot Co.

Harris, George and his wife Sarah and Morgan Williams subpoenaed at the suit of John Ingram and his wife Hannah. 1670. (Arch. of MD. v. LI, p. 351).

Thompson, George and his wife Margaret... 10 Feb 1670. (Arch. of MD, v. LI, p. 355).

Lewis, Lieut. William. Died 29 Mar 1656, seized of 3000 ac. in Charles Co. called Lewis's Neck without heirs. At the time of his death 2000 ac. of the land was in the possession of Job Chandler and Symon Oversee. The land is now in the possession of Mrs. Ann Fowke widow of Col. Gerrard Fowke, Edmund Lindsey, Benjamin Rozer, Mrs. Elizabeth Johnson relict of Daniell Johnson, and Philip Brown; to say 100 ac. now in the possession of Mrs. Ann Fowke, relict of Job Chandler, the other 1000 ac. in possession of Edmund Lindsey by virtue of a lease from Mrs. Elizabeth Oversee, relict of Symon Oversee, for 21 yrs. (Arch. of MD, v. LI, p. 369). Charles Co.

Chaffe, John and his wife Mary, and James Smith to appear at Chancery Court. 30 Jun 1671. (Arch. of MD, v. LI, p. 374). Talbot Co.

Hopewell, Hugh of Sackawit in Patuxent, aet 57, 18 Feb 1668. Deposition regarding chancery case between John Halfhead, plaintiff and Joseph Edloe, defendant. Believed Barnaby Edloe was the eldest son of said Joseph Edloe, decd. living at the time of said Joseph Edloe's death. William Abeston of St. Michael's Hundred, St. Mary's Co., aged 43 yrs., deponent. (Arch. of MD, v. LI, p. 400).

Hopewell, Hugh, aet 60, saith that Barnaby Edloe, son of Joseph Edloe, decd. if he had lived until his present time would have been about 28 yrs. of age. 10 Jul 1671. (Arch. of MD, v. LI, p. 401).

Beane, Ellinor, widow of Walter, appeared by her son in law, Mathew Hill of Charles Co., who surrendered the grant of land called *Durham*. (Arch. of MD, v. LI, p. 433). Charles Co.

Gerard, Thomas, son of Thomas Gerard, decd. To appear in Chancery Court. 14 Apr 1674. (Arch. of MD, v. LI, p. 439). St. Mary's Co.

Hatton, Richard and his wife Ann, dau of John Price, decd. against Thomas Dent, William Hutton, George Mecall, and Daniel Clocke, defendants. John Price died ca. 1660. (Arch. of MD, v. LI, p. 445, 450). St. Mary's Co.

Cole, Robert, left orphans. (Arch. of MD, v. LI, p. 457). St. Clement's Bay, St. Mary's Co.

Foxon, Richard, son of Richard Foxon of Baltimore Co. Bill of Complaint from Edward Skidmore. William Chadborne and his wife Susanna. (Arch. of MD, v. LI, p. 474). Cecil Co.

Jacobson, Peter, a Swede, who died and left 80 ac. of land on the north side of the Sassafras River to his son, Jeffrey Peterson. The land was taken up by Francis Smith and sold to John Brown of New England, and by him to Marquis Seaerton, a Swede, and by him to Peter Jacobson. 29 Nov 1676. (Arch. of MD, v. LI, p. 479). Cecil Co.

Legatt, Bridget, widow of John Legatt. Regarding land sold by William Smoote and his wife Grace to Humfrey Atwicks and Richard Smoote. Humfrey Atwicks and his wife Elizabeth assigned their rights to Thomas Peircy. 14 Apr 1676. (Arch. of MD, v. LI, p. 481). Charles Co.

Cornelius, Mathias. Died ca. 1666, seized of 50 ac. on the north side of Sassafrax. (Arch. of MD, v. LI, p. 484). Cecil Co.

Trueman, Thomas, brother of Nathaniel Trueman, now decd. Defendant in case with Thomas Sprigg, complainant regarding 1000 ac. 1677. (Arch. of MD, v. LI, p. 484). Calvert Co.

Mathews, Ignatius, infant son of Thomas Mathews, the younger, decd. who was the son of Thomas Mathews, the elder. Defendant represented by William Boarman, Gent., his guardian, Wm. Guyther, complainant, son of Nicholas Guyther. Nicholas Guyther was taken prisoner at Severne by the enemies of the Lord Proprietary and condemned to be shot to death but escaped. His wife's name was Mary. (Arch. of MD, v. LI, p. 496). St. Mary's Co.

Gerard, Justinian, son of Thomas, decd. 17 Jun 1678. (Arch. of MD, v. LI, p. 505). St. Mary's Co.

Dermott, Edmond, aet 26. Deposition in the case of the will of John Deery who died ca. 2 Dec 1677; he lived in the house of John Deery, St. Mary's City, innholder. Deposition also given by Richard Dalton, aet 25 who was servant to Capt. John Quigley. Reference to Ellinor Deery and Owen Quigley, sister and brother of John Deery. 1678. Elizabeth Manning, aet 35, testifies regarding the mentioning in the will of John Quigley, of Virginia, merchant, cousin of the decd, John Deery. (Arch. of MD, v. LI, p. 510). St. Mary's Co.

Letchworth, Elizabeth, widow of Thomas Letchworth and guardian to the orphans of said Thomas, claimed his land in right of her children. (Arch. of MD, v. LI, p. 522). Joseph Letchworth, son and heir of Thomas Letchworth. (Arch. of MD, v. LXVII, p. 422). Tobitha Blanford, deponent, aet 30, former wife of William Mills decd. Roger Brooke of Calvert Co. aet 40. Ambrose Biggs of Calvert Co., deponent, aet 53. Andrew Tenehill of Calvert Co., merchant, aet 36, deponent. Ninian Beale of Calvert Co. aet 48, deponent. 15 Jun 1678. (Arch. of MD, v. LXVII, p. 422). (Arch. of MD, v. LXVIII, p. 57). Calvert Co.

Coates, Leonard and his wife Martha, admx. of William Russell. (Arch. of MD, v. LI, p. 539). 1679. "...said Martha since his [Wm. Russell] during her widdowhood." (Arch. of MD, v. LXVIII, p. 208). Anne Arundel Co.

Bland, Thomas and his wife Damoras (Damoris), relict of Nicholas Wyatt of Anne Arundel Co., decd, exhibited their Bill of Complaint against Edward Dorsey and his wife Sarah. (Arch. of MD, v. LI, p. 544). 18 Mar 1673. (Arch. of MD, v. LXVI, p. 247). Anne Arundel Co.

Atchinson, Vincent, decd. late of Kent Co., and his wife Hannah were seized of a tract called *Colchester* in Talbot Co. and now in Kent Co. on the north side of the Chester River. Hannah died 10 Oct 1676 leaving Robert, her son, under the age of 21; soon afterwards Vincent Atchinson also died being indebted to Samuel Tovey of the Island of Kent who obtained admin. of the estate of said Atchinson and guardianship of Robert Atchinson. (Arch. of MD, v. LI, p. 554). (Arch. of MD, v. LXVII, p. 270). Kent Co.

St. Mary's Co. 11 Feb 1679. Elizabeth Beck, Margaret Beck, and Mary Beck, infants, by their guardian vs. George Godfrey. (Liber PC, p. 173).

St. Mary's Co. 14 Oct 1679. Thomas Bland and Damoras, his wife, vs. Edward Dorsey and Sarah, his wife. Damoras was the relict and extx. of Nicholas Wyatt of Anne Arundel Co., deceased. (Liber PC, p. 175).

May 1679. Mentions Mary Tilley, late wife of Joseph Tilley, deceased. (Liber PC, p. 223).

Docket. 30 Apr 1681. Thomas Penroy, brother of John Penroy. (Liber PC, p. 243).

1679. John Hudson, the younger son of John Hudson, the elder of Dorchester Co., deceased. (Liber PC, p. 244).

Docket. 30 Apr 1681. John Brown, the father of James Brown. (Liber PC, p. 246).

Docket. 30 Apr 1681. Thomas Medley vs. William Brook and Thomas Corden, his guardian. (Liber PC, p. 252).

Docket. 30 Apr 1681. Nicholas Parker and Judith, his wife vs. Samuel Louise. (Liber PC, p. 252).

Docket. 30 Apr 1681. William Harris and Jackaline, his wife vs. John Maning, Nathaniel Maning, and Walter Smith. (Liber PC, p. 258).

Docket. 30 Apr 1681. Thomas Medley vs. William Brooks, son of Robert Brooks, and Thomas Corden, his guardian. (Liber PC, p. 261).

Docket. 30 Apr 1681. Benjamin Parrott and Elizabeth, his wife, and Martha Keene, an infant by William Berry, her guardian vs. Susanna Keene and Susanna Hant, an infant by Susanna Keene, mother and guardian. (Liber PC, p. 274).

19 Apr 1689. Garret Vansweringen of St. Mary's Co. vs. Thomas Taylor of Dorchester Co., Gent., and Edward Day, who married the relict and extx. of Thomas Walker, deceased of Somerset

Co. (Liber PC, p. 278).
5 Jan 1688. Edward Saunders of Charles Co. and Jane, his wife, one of the daughters of John Ocane, late of the same county, deceased vs. Robert Thompson of same county and Mary, his wife and extx. of Giles Blizard, Merchant, deceased, her former husband and Susanna Blizard, daughter and heir of said Giles and Susanna, his wife, the other daughter of said John Ocane, and infant by said Robert and Mary, her guardians. (Liber PC, p. 282).
22 Jul 1695. Deposition of George Oldfield of Cecil Co., age ca. 46, regarding the ownership and possession of a tract of land lying on Elk River in dispute. (Liber PC, p. 299).
23 Jul 1695. Deposition of Casparus A. Herman, age ca. 38, regarding the possession of a tract of land lying on Elk River. (Liber PC, p. 300).
23 Jul 1695. Deposition of John Hyland, age ca. 57, regarding the possession of a tract of land lying on Elk River. (Liber PC, p. 300).
23 Jul 1695. Deposition of Owen Howes, age ca. 46, regarding the possession of a tract of land lying on Elk River. (Liber PC, p. 301).
23 Jul 1695. Deposition of Joseph Moor, age ca. 50, regarding the possession of a tract of land lying on Elk River. (Liber PC, p. 301).
23 Jul 1695. Deposition of Alexander Campbell, age ca. 39, regarding the possession of a tract of land lying on Elk River. (Liber PC, p. 301).
23 May 1695. William Nichols, Merchant of Calvert Co., vs. John Sunderland, son and heir of John Sunderland, late of Calvert Co., deceased, an infant under 21 years by Margaret Sunderland, his mother and guardian. (Liber PC, p. 302).
13 Nov 1694. John Anderson of Dorchester Co., planter, vs. John Rawlings, son and heir of John Rawlings of said county, planter, deceased. (Liber PC, p. 302).
9 Oct 1695. Robert Mason of St. Mary's Co., Gent., vs. Joseph Spernon that Thomas Hinton of Cecil Co. sold a tract of land in St. Mary's Co. ca. 1681. After the decease of Thomas Hinton, Joseph Spernon married his widow and relict and admx. of his estate. (Liber PC, p. 316).
11 May 1695. Samuel Houldsworth of Calvert Co., Merchant, and Helena, his wife, the relict and extx. of Thomas Parslow, late of same county, Ship Carpenter, deceased vs. Charles Ashcomb, Mary Ashcomb, and Richard Gallaway and his wife regarding the division of a tract of land called *The Deserts* in Calvert Co. Charles Ashcomb is brother and heir and executor to Samuel Ashcomb. Mentions Benjamin, Lawrence, Nathaniel, and Mary Ashcomb. (Liber PC, p. 322).
19 Mar 1695. Thomas Dafforn of London, Merchant, vs. John Newman and Rebecca, his wife, extx. of John Bearcroft of St. Mary's Co., deceased.] (Liber PC, p. 341).
[No date] Richard Smith of Patuxent, Gent., purchased of James Bowling and Mary, his wife, and Baker Brooks, Gent., a parcel of land called *Brook's Partition*. (Liber PC, p. 346).
[No date] Mentions William Lowry and Hester, his wife. (Liber PC, p. 349).
9 Oct 1695. Deposition of John Richardson, age ca. 67,

regarding the bounds of a tract called *Westmoreland*. (Liber PC, p. 373).

1695. Steven Longman, heir and brother of Daniel Longman, lives in England. (Liber PC, p. 377).

24 Aug 1698. St. Mary's Co. Deposition of Peter Smith, Carpenter, age ca. 41, that after the death of Col. Lloyd, Madam Lloyd employed him to finish a chapel belonging to Col. Sayor. (Liber PC, p. 383).

14 Dec 1696. John Stanley of Anne Arundel Co. vs. Ann Brent, admx. of Henry Brent, deceased, and Richard Marsham, who intermarried with Ann Brent, and George Brent, brother and heir of Henry Brent. (Liber PC, p. 387).

Mentions James Bodkin, deceased, and his uncle, Dominick Bodkin. (Liber PC, p. 389).

Docket. Feb 1697. Frances Harison, Joseph James, and John Bell vs. Robert Smith, Esq., guardian of James Marks, son and heir of John Marks. (Liber PC, p. 393).

May 1697. Mentions John Ingram, father of John Ingram of Talbot Co. (Liber PC, p. 394).

24 Aug 1698. Charles Co. Deposition of Lydia Newman of Charles Co., widow, relict of George Newman, late of Charles Co., and now Lydia Manner by marriage to John Manner, now of Charles Co., that her father-in-law, Mr. William Ballin, and Thomas Thomas had a tract of about 1000 ac. around the Patapsco River in Baltimore Co. Mentions her mother, Margery Ballin. (Liber PC, p. 395).

2 Sep 1698. Deposition of William Gary, age ca. 59, regarding bounds of a tract called *Champingham* near St. Michaels River. (Liber PC, p. 396).

19 Nov 1698. Deposition of Woolfren Hunt of Anne Arundel Co., Chirurgeon, age ca. 44, that in 1681 he was a servant to Col. Philemon Lloyd, and that the wife of Capt. Hemsly was named Judith. (Liber PC, p. 396).

12 Sep 1698. James Brown of St. Mary's Co. vs. Mary Denton, wife of Henry Denton of Anne Arundel Co., deceased. Henry died intestate leaving Vachel Denton, his son, an infant about 2 years old and Mary Denton, his relict. (Liber PC, p. 401).

10 Dec 1698. Deposition of John Newman of Talbot Co., planter, age ca. 56, in perfect health regarding the bounds of a tract lying near the St. Michaels River. (Liber PC, p. 403).

29 Nov 1698. Charles Co. Deposition of Maj. William Dent, age ca. 38, that Howard Hawkings and Elizabeth, his wife, had a tract called *Locust Thicket*, lying formerly in Charles Co., now in Prince George's Co. (Liber PC, p. 404).

29 Nov 1698. Deposition of Capt. William Barton, age ca. 64, regarding bounds of tract called *Locust Thicket*. (Liber PC, p. 405).

29 Nov 1698. Deposition of Richard Harrison, age ca. 38, regarding bounds of tract called *Locust Thicket*. (Liber PC, p. 405).

29 Nov 1698. Deposition of Cleoburn Lomax, age ca. 55, regarding bounds of tract called *Locust Thicket*. (Liber PC, p. 405).

4 Oct 1698. Calvert Co. Deposition of Charles Hollingsworth, age ca. 60, regarding bounds of a tract called *Maiden Poynt*.

(Liber PC, p. 415).
4 Oct 1698. Calvert Co. Deposition of Richard Rattcliff, age ca. 37, regarding bounds of a tract called *Maiden Poynt*. (Liber PC, p. 415).
3 Mar 1698/9. Deposition of Phillip Connaway Sr., an inhabitant of Maryland and Virginia, age ca. 79, that about 32 years ago he lived with Jenkin Price at his plantation at the entrance at the northwest side of the Pocomoke River. (Liber PC, p. 416).
9 Oct 1699. Deposition of Thomas Larkin that Daniel Longman and Gabriel Parrott met at the house where the deponant's father, John Larkin, now lives; regarding a dispute of payment between Gabriel Parrott and Stephen Longman, heir to Daniel Longman. (Liber PC, 428).
9 Oct 1699. Deposition of John Dicks of Anne Arundel Co., planter, that he knows Samuel Galloway and Gabriell Parrott, both of Anne Arundel Co., and he was a servant boy of Daniel Longman. He further states that when servants complained to Longman, he said to be patient until he had fully paid his father, Parrott, to whom he had to pay all his tobacco. (Liber PC, p. 430).
6 Dec 1699. Deposition of Elizabeth Lockwood in which she refers to Gabriel and Susanna [Parrott]. (Liber PC, p. 432).
8 Apr 1699. John Biggin, late of Calvert Co., presents his Bill of Complaint against George Gray in which he states that he was persuaded by Joakim Giorslead to become bound to pay several hundred pounds of lawful money to Margaret Taney, the younger, on the day of her marriage or on her arrival of 21 years. Giorslead then died, leaving his then wife Margaret, formerly the widow of Michael Taney who since married George Gray. (Liber PC, p. 433).
15 Apr 1700. Docket. Elizabeth Baker, relict and admx. of John Baker, vs. Gerrard Slye. (Liber PC, p. 435).
15 Apr 1700. Docket. Gerrard Slye vs. John Bayne and Ann, his wife. (Liber PC, p. 435).
14 May 1701. Docket. Robert Gundry vs. Barbara Hutton, relict and admx. of John Hutton. (LIber PC, p. 435).
14 May 1701. Docket. Gerard Slye vs. Robert Sinclair and Priscilla, his wife. (Liber PC, p. 452).
8 May 1703. Docket. Cecilus Button and Margaret, his wife vs. Alexander Doliomiosia. (Liber PC, p. 473).
29 Nov 1700. St. Mary's Co. John Cood Sr., of St. Mary's Co., Gent., states in his Bill of Complaint vs. Giles Hill and Elizabeth, his wife, that he received land in deed from Justinian Tomoson, Jr. of said county and Elizabeth, his wife. After his death, Elizabeth married Giles Hill. (Liber PC, p. 474).
8 May 1703. Docket. John Sanders vs. Thomas Mudd, son and heir of William Boseman. (Liber PC, p. 480).
8 May 1703. Docket. Charles Beckwith and Ann, his wife vs.---. (Liber PC, p. 481).
8 May 1703. Docket. John Grooniff and Ruth, his wife, admx. of Edward Dorsey Jr. vs. John Dorsey. (Liber PC, p. 482).
8 May 1703. Docket. John Norton and Mary, his wife; Ann Tod, an infant; and James Tod, her guardian vs. Charles Merryman. (Liber PC, p. 483).

8 May 1703. Docket. Edward Wolfcomb and Rachel, his wife, extx. of Thomas Dally vs. Alexander Carlyle, administrator of William Carlyle. (Liber PC, p. 483).

1 --- 1702/3. Depositions about land for Col. John Addison filed 1st --- 1702/3. (1) John Middleton, age ca. 25; (2) George Athey, age ca. 60; (3) John Snuggs, age ca. 42; (4) John Wankins, age ca. 38; (5) Alexander Harbert, age ca. 31; (6) John Norris, Sr., age ca. 50; (7) William Dent, age ca. 34; (8) William Glover, age ca. 28; (9) Daniel Connell, age ca. 52; (10) William Tannehill, age ca. 49; (11) John Norris, Jr., age ca. 22; (12) Capt. George Thompson of St. Mary's Co., age ca. 65. (Liber PC, p. 484).

1 Apr 1703. Deposition of Col. Ninian Beale, age ca. 70, regarding bounds of tract called *Churtsy* for Col. William Holyday of Prince George's Co. (Liber PC, p. 492).

28 Jun 1703. Deposition of Robert Middleton, age ca. 53, regarding the bounds of a tract called *Blue Plain*. (Liber PC, p. 493).

8 Sep 1702. Deposition of Robert Goodrick of Charles Co., age ca. 70, regarding the bounds of a tract in Charles Co. held by Benjamin Rozer, deceased, which descended to his son, Notty Rozer. Deponent states that George Thompson married his sister, Margaret Goodrick also Jackson's widow, about 20 or 30 years ago. Col. Rozer purchased 100 ac. from Francis Gunby, but before the sale could be acknowledge, Gunby ran away leaving one daughter who married a Burges. (Liber PC, p. 494).

10 Feb 1702/3. Depositions taken for Cheffey Land for Hugh Ryley, filed 2 Mar 1702/3: (1) John Domall, age ca/ 45; (2) Thomas Addison, age ca. 3 [sic]; (3) James Mallikin, age ca. 40. (Liber PC, p. 495).

9 Oct 1702. Deposition of John Nunam of Talbot Co., planter, age ca. 50, regarding the bounds of *Enfield Chase, Edlington,* and *Howarton's Range* for Col. Henry Ridgley. (Liber PC, p. 498).

10 Jul 1701. Decree. John Gladstone of Dorchester Co. vs. John Stevens and Ann, his wife, extx. of Thomas Cook. (Liber PC, p. 504).

5 Apr 1706. Baptism. Mary, daughter of John Payn and Mary, his wife, was baptized at the house of Christopher Rousby in Patuxent River. (Liber PC, p. 512).

20 Oct 1704. Docket. Sarah Trindon alias Lumley, relict of Alexander Lumley vs. William Chew. (Liber PC, p. 515).

20 May 1706. Docket. Samuel Gurcham and his wife, Ann Congo vs. ----. (Liber PC, p. 523).

8 Jun 1706. Depositions to prove conveyance of land to Charles Rye from John Rye, his father. (1) Robert Taylor of Dorchester Co., age ca. 25, said that John Rye of Dorchester Co. by his will conveyed to his son, Charles Rye of Calvert Co., land in Dorchester Co. called *Bath's Addition* in June 1705. (2) Roger Woolford, age ca. 33. (3) Walter Campbell, age ca. 40. (Liber PC, p. 525).

17 Jun 1706. Further depositions in above case: (1) Christian Swornifield of Calvert Co., age ca. 44; (2) Thomas Hinton of Calvert Co., age ca. 62; (3) Robert Hoigh of Calvert Co., age ca. 38. (Liber PC, p. 525).

2 Aug 1705. Decree. Philemon Hemsley, executor of William Hemsley during the minority of William's daughter, Elizabeth Hemsley. The extx. of William Hemsley was Jane, the wife of Robert Friley, who was the widow of William and mother of Elizabeth. (Liber PC, p. 535).

4 Oct 1705. Decree. Martha Jones of Somerset Co., admx. of Thomas Jones of Somerset Co., who died intestate. (Liber PC, p. 537).

17 Aug 1705. James Heath states his Bill of Complaint against Thomas Tracy of Ann Arundel Co., planter, and Susanna, his wife. He states that John Sivick died leaving land called *Pascall's Purchase* to Susanna, his wife and her heirs. Susanna then married Augustine Hawkins. She afterwards sold 85 ac. to John Willson and 40 ac. to Jonathan Jones. Hawkins died, upon which Susanna married Thomas Tracy. They then sold 30 ac. to Christopher Vernon and 21 ac. more to Jonathan Jones. Thomas Tracy left, leaving Susanna with several small children. The following depositions were taken: (1) Benjamin Thorley of Calvert Co., age ca. 25, that his mother lived as the owner of *Pascall's Purchase*. (2) Susannah, wife of Thomas Tracy and relict of John Sivick (son of William Sivick), age ca. 36, that Mary Trundel was the mother of Benjamin Thurley by a former husband. (3) Jonathan Jones of Anne Arundel Co., planter, age ca. 32, that he was put to live with William Sivick as an orphan child of about 3 years of age. 9 Jul 1705. (Liber PC, p. 538).

7 Jul 1705. Depositions taken to examine evidences in a cause pending between John Rogers, Barronet, plaintiff, and John Danzey, Gent., defendant. (1) Abraham Peters, age ca. 49; (2) John Coade, Sr., age ca. 56; (3) William Coode, age ca. 26; (4) John Slye, age ca. 62; (5) Samuel Grafty, age ca. 41; (6) John Rogers, age ca. 22. (Liber PC, p. 546).

12 Aug 1705. Deposition of Joshua Guybert of St. Mary's Co., Gent., age ca. 60, regarding the ship, Rogers, in the cause between John Rogers and John Danzey. (Liber PC, p. 558).

12 Aug 1705. Deposition of Matthew Sanders, age ca. 60, regarding the ship, Rogers. (Liber PC, p. 561).

22 Jun 1704. Deposition of Capt. John Davis, age ca. 60, regarding the bounds of a tract of land in Talbot Co. called *Nathaniel's Point*. (Liber PC, p. 565).

22 Jun 1704. Deposition of Henry Coffin, age ca. 60, regarding the bounds of *Nathaniel's Point*. (Liber PC, p. 565).

30 Apr 1707. Deposition of William Hambleton of Talbot Co., planter, age ca. 44, regarding the bounds of *Wade's Point* for John and Edward Leeds. (Liber PC, p. 570).

30 Apr 1707. Deposition of William Leeds of Talbot Co., age ca. 42, that his father, Capt. William Leeds, told him the bounds of *Wade's Point*. (Liber PC, p. 570).

30 Apr 1707. Depositions taken regarding the bounds of *Wade's Point* for John and Edward Leeds. (1) Edward Elliot, Sr., age ca. 68; (2) Edward Hambleton of Talbot Co., planter, age ca. 36; (3) Hugh Sherwood of Talbot Co., Gent., age ca. 75. (Liber PC, p. 571).

13 Oct 1707. Margarett McNamara petitioned the court to live separately from her husband, Thomas McNamara, due to his inhuman treatment towards her. (Liber PC, p. 579).

13 Oct 1707. Depositions taken regarding the bounds of a tract called *Pascal's Purchase*. (1) Elizabeth, wife of John Wilson, age ca. 39, that about 6 years ago, John Wilson, son of her husband, John Wilson, showed her the bounds of said land, 3 Aug 1706; (2) Jonathan Jones, age ca. 33; (3) John Atwood, age ca. 66; (4) Robert Orme, age ca. 57. (Liber PC, p. 582).
13 Jul 1708. Docket. Samuel Weeks, guardian of the orphans of Joseph Weeks vs. Thomas Bruffe. (Liber PC, p. 604).
13 Jul 1708. Docket. James Haddorf and Sarah, his wife, extx. of William Barton vs. Ninian Beale. (Liber PC, p. 604).
13 Jul 1708. Docket. James Heath vs. Joseph Adderton and Mary, his wife, admx. of Charles Edgerton and James Neale. (Liber PC, p. 605).
13 Jul 1708. Docket. Henry Green vs. Ann Smith, relict and extx. of Edward Smith, alias Ann Marshall, now wife of Charles Marshall. (Liber PC, p. 605).
13 Jul 1708. Docket. George Young vs. Edward Batson and Ann, his wife, admx. of Ja. Martin. (Liber PC, p. 605).
26 Nov 1708. Docket. Mathias Vanbibber vs. Ephraim Augustus Herman and his guardian, John Gerrard. (Liber PC, p. 609).
26 Nov 1708. Docket. Benjamin Hall vs. Giles Hill and his guardian, Cornelius White. (Liber PC, p. 609).
26 Nov 1708. Docket. John Israel, admr. de bonus non of Edward Dorsey vs. Joseph Dorsey, guardian of Michael Dorsey and against the other guardians of Edward Dorsey's children. (Liber PC, p. 611).
12 Feb 1708/9. Depositions taken regarding the cause pending between Elizabeth Proctor and Mrs. Margarett Freeman regarding a lot in Annapolis. (1) William Blade, Gent., age ca. 38; (2) William Taylard, age ca. 47, that about 1694 in Annapolis, he met with Elizabeth Proctor, late of St. Mary's Co., and she told him that she and Mrs. Margrett Freeman, widow of John Freeman, had taken up a lot in Annapolis, which Mrs. Freeman wished to build upon. (3) Mary Vanswearingen, widow, age ca. 48. (Liber PC, p. 613).
16 Aug 1708. Deposition of Col. Ninian Beale, age ca. 83, regarding the bounds of a tract called *Stott's Lott* formerly surveyed for Daniel Cunningham. (Liber PC, p. 625).
16 Aug 1708. Deposition of James Moore, age ca. 62, that Charles Boteler, surveyor, and his brother Ninian Beale both went with the deponent to the same bounded tree of *Stott's Lott*. (Liber PC, p. 626).
5 Oct 1706. Depositions taken to examine evidences touching the pretended will of Richard Beards of Anne Arundel Co. (1) Walter Phelps of Anne Arundel Co., age ca. 67; (2) George Green, age ca. 65. (Liber PC, p. 648).
29 Sep 1709. Depositions taken regarding the bounds of a tract called *Mollington Happ*. (1) John Linn (Lunn?), age ca. 55; (2) Samuel Mollington, age ca. 70. (Liber PC, p. 649).
3 May 1710. Talbot Co. Depositions taken on behalf of William Louthis to prove lineage. (1) William Willowby of Dorchester Co., planter, age ca. 86, that about 34 years ago John Garnish of St. Mary's Co. said that Jane Garnish (now Jane Southes) was his brother William's child, and that she would be his heir. (2) Mary Camper, age ca 36, that Catherine

Catterton dwelt in Oxford on the lotts and houses now in possession of Robert Grundy. (3) John Ryan of Dorchester Co., planter, age ca. 48, that he was bookkeeper to Catherine Catterton of Oxford, and that her former husband named Garnish had satisfied her that Jane Garnish was his brother's child. (Liber PC, p. 651).

16 Nov 1709. Dorchester Co. Depositions taken on behalf of Col. Thomas Ennalls regarding the bounds of a tracted called *Phillip's Borrough*. (1) Henry Hooper of Dorchester Co., age ca. 63, planter. (2) William Smith of Dorchester Co., age ca. 42. (3) Phillip Shapley of Northumberland Co. in the Colony of Virginia, age ca. 61. (Liber PC, p. 653).

No date. James Heath of Anne Arundel Co. presented his Bill of Complaint against James Neale of Charles Co., Gent.; Jeremiah Adderton of St. Mary's Co., Gent., and Mary, his wife, daughter of said James. James Neale of Charles Co. and Elizabeth, his wife, 10 Apr 1702 by deed made over to Charles Edgerton of St. Mary's Co., deceased, a tract of land lying at Piscattaway in Prince George's Co. containing 600 ac. On 15 Jan 1703, Charles Edgerton and Mary, his wife, by deed conveyed to James Heath and his heirs with General Warranty the said 600 ac. The land was originally patented to William Calvert of St. Mary's Co., deceased, and upon his death descended to his eldest son, Charles Calvert, and was made over to his brother, Richard Calvert. Mary, the wife of Charles Edgerton, was the daughter of James Neale. (Liber PC, p. 659).

9 Feb 1709/10. Depositions taken regarding the last will and testament of Robert Smith, late of Queen Anne County. (1) Mary Malson was present when Robert Smith, Esq., deceased, had communication with Edmond Prior and Catherine, his wife, regarding Smith's purchase of land from Edmond and Catherine which descended to her upon the death of her father, Michael Paul Vanderford. (2) Deposition of Col. Robert Finley and Jane, his wife. (Liber PC, p. 665).

4 Jul 1710. Depositions taken to examine evidence of the will of Richard Beards the Elder recorded in Anne Arundel Co. records and afterwards was supposed to be cut out of the books and destroyed by his son, Richard, after Col. Burgesse's death. Interrogatories were posed to Walter Phelps of Anne Arundel Co. to which he replied that he knew Elizabeth Carrington that lived with him and Elizabeth Mash who married a Jones. He also stated that George Green had served his time with Richard Beards the elder. He also stated he knew John Rutter and his wife, Alice. (Liber PC, p. 668).

Interrogatories posed to Anne Bradley of Anne Arundel Co., a servant to Richard Beards [she is later referred to as Anne Barley]. She answered that she came to this country in the fall of the hard year. Her husband, John Stopkins, was a witness to Richard Beards' will. (Liber PC, p. 668).

Interrogatories of Mrs. Mahitable Peirpoint of Anne Arundel Co. were answered that about 26 years ago she heard that Richard Beard made a will which was recorded in Anne Arundel Co. records, that Henry Bonner (then clerk) was absent so said records were committed to the care of Otho Holland, her then husband. Her husband told her that Beard the younger had spent much time with the books one day and that the page with his father's will was missing. (Liber PC, p. 668).

22 Jul 1710. Depositions taken for James Haddock concerning Warren's estates in Prince George's Co. (1) Col. Ninian Beale, age ca. 84, that he was in the company of Maj. William Barton, deceased, and William Selby, deceased, when Selby came to the house of William Barton to give him bills of exchange for a tract bought by Selby of said Barton. Barton said he would not take the bills of exchange from Selby there, but would pass them at this father, Mr. Richard Marsham's, house to pay Marsham the money due the orphans of Bazill Warrens meaning Marsham Warrens and Bazill Warrens estates then in hands of Barton. (Liber PC, p. 673).

18 Oct 1710. Deposition of John Christian, age ca. 49, regarding bounds of a tract called *Padgett*. (Liber PC, p. 674).

19 May 1710. Deposition of Robert Coverthought about his land called *Barkett*. (Liber PC, p. 675).

13 Nov 1710. Deposition of John Bigger, age ca. 52, that in 1671 he lived at the house of John Adderson in Calvert Co. and Adderson was then married to the relict or widow of Robert Coverthought, Sr. of Calvert Co. (Liber PC, p. 675).

19 May 1710. Deposition of Jane Miller, age ca. 53, regarding land called *Barkett*. (Liber PC, p. 675).

15 Mar 1709. Docket. Robert Fondale vs. Elizabeth and Edward Digges, ext. of William Diggs and Charles Diggs. (Liber PC, p. 679).

8 Jan 1710. Calvert Co. Depositions taken regarding the bounds of a tract or parcel called *Ceader Branch* commonly called *Chaplain's Land*. (1) Raphael Hawood, age ca. 70, taken 20 Jan 1710/11. (2) Peter Sawell of Calvert Co., a Quaker, age ca. 39, that about 29 years ago his father, John Sawell, had a warrant of resurvey on land called *Ceador Branch*. (3) Thomas Arnoll, age ca. 77, that about 40 years ago Raphael Hawood lived on a plantation at Clements Bay in St. Mary's Co. and then he moved to a plantation in Calvert Co. called *Simon Reader's*. (Liber PC, p. 692).

29 Nov. 1710. Somerset Co. Deposition of Levin Denwood, age ca. 64, regarding a tract called *Almodington*. Also examined were (1) John Bozman, age ca. 61, and (2) Peter Elzey, age ca. 71. (Liber PC, p. 699).

28 Nov 1710. Interrogatories posed to Charles Calvert by James Neale and Jerome Adderton in a pending cause between James Neale and Jerome Adderton vs. Richard Calvert. Charles Calvert answers that he was a witness to his father's covenant and promise to give James Neale 600 ac. of land in marriage with the deponent's sister and that Mary Adderton was his niece. (Liber PC, p. 700).

5 Apr 1711. Calvert Co. Depositions taken on behalf of John Brooke regarding the bounds of a tract called *Brooke Adventure*. (1) Raphael Haywood, age ca. 70; (2) Rebecca Noakes of Calvert Co., age ca. 53, that about 39 years ago her father, William Pritchett, showed her a bounded tree of his land. (3) Gilbert Deavour, age ca. 44, (4) George Lyne, age ca. 23; (5) George Noakes of Calvert Co., age ca. 20.

(Liber PC, p. 709).
16 Jan 1710/11. Depositions taken regarding the bounds of a tract called *Westwood Lodge* in Charles Co. (1) James White, age ca. 67, that about 35 years ago he was a servant to Richard Edlen, Sr. (2) John Brayford, age ca. 34, that about 18 years ago he was a servant to Richard Edlen, Sr. (Liber PC, p. 714).
17 Aug 1710. Depositions taken regarding the bounds of a tract called *Lady's Delight* in Cecil Co. laid out 21 June 1683 for Col. Vincent Lowe. (1) William Boyer of Kent Co., age ca. 42. (2) Job Evans, aged ca. 55, a Quaker, that about 25 years ago he and his wife were oystering and fishing with William Sivick at Herring Creek (taken in Anne Arundel Co. 22 May 1711). (3) Robert Orin, age ca. 60. (Liber PC, p. 716).
24 Apr 1711. Depositions take regarding the bounds of a tract called *Hard Travel* in Calvert Co. (1) Thomas Tucker, aged ca. 60, that he heard William Harbert say that the oak was a bounded tree of *Hard Travell* taken up by Harbert's father. (2) James Aling, age ca. 48. (3) Joshua Sedwick, age ca. 38, that he heard his father, Thomas Sedwick, talk of the bounded trees of land formerly belonging to John Bigger and he believed it to be called *Hard Travel*. (Liber PC, p. 731).
19 Jun 1711. Interrogatory of Thomas Trott of Anne Arundel Co. He answers that he saw a deed porporting a conveyance of *Marshes Seal* from Thomas Knighton and Dorothy, his wife, to Christopher Vernon dated 19 Nov 1701. This testimony was regarding a tract called *Gadhill* for Christopher Vernon in a cause pending between John Hall and Christopher Vernon. (Liber PC, p. 733).
Interrogatory of Samuel Guichard. He answered he was born in Geneva and came to Maryland at age 16 and has been here 28 years. He served his time with Thomas Knighton the elder. He knew George Knighton, son of Thomas Knighton, but did not know if he died underage or not. He knew Sarah Knighton, daughter of Thomas, and she died at about 6 months old around 25 years ago. (Liber PC, p. 733).
Interrogatory of Thomas Knighton, age ca. 26, son and heir of Thomas Knighton of Herring Creek, Gent., deceased. After 5 years after his father's death, he went to England and enquired of his father's three brothers, James, John and George, if they knew of his father's will. George Simons offered his sister Elizabeth Simmons, wife of said George Simons, a deed for conveyance of *Gadhill* to sign. (Liber PC, p. 733).
11 June 1711. Depositions taken regarding a tract called *Gadhill*. (1) John Chappell, age ca. 61. (2) Samuel Guichard, age ca. 45, that about 25 years ago Thomas Knighton made a will which bequeathed to his son, George Knighton, a parcel called *Gadhill*. (Liber PC, p. 739).
5 June 1711. Decree in cause of James Haddock vs. Ninian Beale. James Haddock and Sarah, his wife, widow and extx. of William Barton, Gent., deceased. Humphrey Webb fled this province and is reputed to live in Virginia. (Liber PC, p. 740).
13 Jul 1711. Depositions taken regarding William Walker being heir at law of William Joffs. Deposition of William Walker,

Sr., aged ca. 64, that William Walker, Jr. is son to William Walker, son of Mary Walker alias Jophs and sister to Williams Joffs and was formerly possessed of said 300 ac. lying near Maryland Point. (Liber PC, p. 744).

28 May 1711. Depositions taken regarding the bounds of a tract called *Hard Travel*. (1) Thomas Tucker, age ca. 60, that about 20 years ago William Harbert, son of William Harbert, asked the deponent about a bounded tree of *Hard Travel*. (2) James Allen, age ca. 50. (3) George Young, Sr., age ca. 60. (Liber PC, p. 748).

6 Sep 1711. Prince George's Co. Deposition of Col. Ninian Beale, age ca. 86, regarding the bounds of *Free School Farm* lying in Calvert Co. (but now in Prince George's Co.) laid out for Francis Livingston. (Liber PC, p. 749).

28 Sep 1711. Depositions taken regarding the bounds of land of Richard Vowles on St. Clements Bay in St. Mary's Co. (1) John Novett of St. Mary's Co., planter, age ca. 70, that said land was part of lands owned by his father, Richard Novett. (2) Elizabeth Gough, age ca. 28, that she formerly the wife of George Medcalf, deceased, who was possessed of land on the east side of St. Clements Bay called *Rocky Point*. (Liber PC, p. 751).

11 Oct 1711. Deposition of Nicholas Cooper, age ca. 60, regarding the bounds of a tract called *Roizer's Refuge* lying in Charles Co. (Liber PC, p. 753).

11 Oct 1711. Depositions taken regarding the bounds of *Gadhill* and *Marshes Seal*. (1) John Chappell, age ca. 60; (2) Thomas Knighton, age ca. 35. (Liber PC, p. 754).

20 Sep 1711. Depositions taken regarding the bounds of *Miles End* and *Wobley* in Talbot Co. (1) Francis Bullock of Talbot Co., planter, age ca. 70, says that he heard William Webb say that he heard his father, Edmund Webb, talk of a bounded tree of *Wobley*. (2) Ennion Williams of Talbot Co., age ca. 40; (3) John Kemp, age ca. 30, regarding the bounds of *Miles End*; (4) Robert Sands of Talbot Co., planter, age ca. 50, that when he was a servant to John Cooper about 30 years ago, he saw a bounded pine tree of *Miles End*; (5) Charles Bridges of Talbot Co., planter, age ca. 48, that about 23 years ago Susannah Cooper showed him a gum tree that was the partition tree between the land of John Cooper and John Fuller; (6) John Cooper of Talbot Co., planter, age ca. 30; (7) George Hadaway, Sr. of Talbot Co., age ca. 53. (Liber PC, p. 755).

10 Dec 1711. Depositions taken regarding the bounds of *Barnes Neck* and *Barnes Neck Addition*. (1) Robert Peirson of Talbot Co., age ca. 77; (2) Jasper Hall of Talbot Co., planter, age ca 89. (Liber PC, p. 759).

22 Oct 1711. Depositions taken regarding the purchase and payment of a tract called *Smith's Ridge* lying in Queen Anne Co. bought by Henry Price of Robert Atkinson. (1) Richard Moon of Queen Anne Co., age ca. 39, that about 22 years ago he was living with his father-in-law, Henry Price. (2) Henry Williams of Queen Anne Co., age ca. 43, that about 12 or 13 years ago he was living at the house of Henry Price, his father-in-law. (3) Stephen Rich, age ca. 39, of Queen Anne Co. (Liber PC, p. 763).

17 Oct 1711. Dorchester Co. Deposition of William Willoughby

of Dorchester Co., bricklayer, age ca. 88, regarding the bounds of a parcel called *Calf Pasture*. (Liber PC, p. 764).

20 Oct 1711. Prince George's Co. Depositions taken regarding the bounds of a tract called *Marsham's Point*. (1) Luke Gardner, age ca. 31; (2) John Smith of Charles Co., age ca. 73; (3) John Rook, age ca. 47. (Liber PC, p. 766).

1711. Samuel Dorsey brought his Bill of Complaint against John Israel and William Bladen. Dorsey states that Edward Dorsey, late of Anne Arundel Co., Gent., father of Samuel Dorsey, was seized and possessed of several houses and lotts in the town of Annapolis. Edward and Margaret, his wife, mother of Samuel, granted and conveyed to John Dorsey of Baltimore Co., brother to Edward, several lotts of land in the town of Annapolis. Edward Dorsey's eldest son was Edward Dorsey, who died without issue. His second son was Samuel Dorsey. (Liber PC, p. 779).

12 Feb 1711. Deposition of William Willoughby, age ca. 88, regarding the bounds of a tract called *Nansonum Woods*. (Liber PC, p. 797).

1 Mar 1711/12. John Edmondson, father of Thomas Edmondson, was possessed of a tract called *Mount Hope* in Talbot Co. The tract descended to his eldest son James and his heirs. (Liber PC, p. 809).

1 Mar 1711/12. John Hall vs. Christopher Vernon. Bill of Complaint states that John Hall possessed a tract called *Marshes Point* which he sold to Thomas Knighton and his heirs. Christopher Vernon purchased it from Thomas Knighton, son and heir of Thomas Knighton and Dorothy, wife of the first named Thomas. Millicent Knighton, daughter of Thomas Knighton, died in her minority without issue. Thomas Knighton went to England and died there. Mentions George Simons and Elizabeth, his wife. (Liber PC, p. 816).

4 Mar 1711. John Beale, guardian of Andrew Norwood vs. Charles Kilburne of Anne Arundel Co. and Elizabeth, his wife, extx. of Andrew Norwood. Bill of Complaint states that Andrew Norwood, a minor under 21 years, was one of the children of Andrew Norwood, late of Anne Arundel Co., deceased. Andrew Norwood of Anne Arundel Co. ca. 1701 lay on his death bed with a lingering sickness and made his last will and testament to make equal distribution of his estate to his children-said Andrew and four daughters. Andrew Norwood died about 1 Mar 1701. Elizabeth Kilburne was the widow of Andrew Norwood, who upon his death married Andrew Wolply, and after his death married Charles Kilburne. One of the 4 sisters of Andrew Norwood, was Elizabeth, who was the eldest of the 5 children. Elizabeth, the sister of Andrew Norwood, married John Beale of Annapolis. (Liber PC, p. 825).

3 Jun 1712. Edmond Pryor of Queen Anne Co. vs. Robert Smith. Bill of Complaint states that Edmond Pryor and his wife, Katherine, daughter and heir of Michael Pinnell [also shown as Paul] Vanderford was entitled to lands in Talbot Co. in descent from her father. Anthony Ivy's wife, Anne, was heiress at law of Esq. Smith. (Liber PC, p. 839).

10 Aug 1710. Depositions taken regarding the bounds of a tract called *Swansons Lott* in Prince George's Co. (1) Col. Ninian Beale, age ca. 84; (2) Francis Collier, Sr., age ca. 65; (3)

Hugh Ryley, age ca. 60. (Liber PC, p. 844).

27 Nov 1711. Depositions taken regarding the bounds of a tract called *Mt. Hope*. (1) Francis Neale, age ca. 60; (2) John Newman, age ca. 66; (3) Thomas Smithson, age ca. 60. (Liber PC, p. 846).

25 Feb 1711. Depositions taken regarding the bounds of a tract called *Mt. Hope*. (1) Francis Neale, age ca. 60; (2) Thomas Sockwell, age ca. 41; (3) John Hendrix, age ca. 41; (4) Abraham Morgan, age ca. 46; (5) Nicholas Lowe of Talbot Co., age ca. 49. (Liber PC, p. 848).

7 Nov 1710. Depositions taken regarding the bounds of a tract in Talbot Co. upon Treadhaven Creek called *Griffith*. (1) Peter Stoakes, age ca. 80, that he was well acquainted with Richard Howard in Virginia before he moved to Maryland to live upon the tract called *Griffith*. (2) William Willoughby, age ca. 87, that about 44 years ago he lived with Richard Howard, Gent., as a boarder and that William Taverns was an overseer for Richard Howard. (Liber PC, p. 851).

29 Apr 1712. Depositions taken regarding the bounds of a tract called *Gill's Land* and the dividing line of *Wooliston Mannor* in Charles Co., and the bounds of a tract called *Neale's Gift*. (1) Anthony Neale, age ca. 53, that about 40 years ago his brother, James Neale, showed him the first bounded tree of *Gill's Land* which their father, Capt. James Neale, owned. (2) William Compton, age ca. 52. (3) George Newman, age ca. 53. (Liber PC, p. 854).

1 Jun 1712. Depositions taken regarding the bounds of a tract called *Whites Ford* alias *Aquousock* in Charles Co. (1) John Clements, age ca. 63; (2) Patrick Maggatee, age ca. 60. (Liber PC, p. 856).

25 Oct 1712. Depositions taken regarding a tract called *Stockeley* in possession of Henry Clarke and Elizabeth Hutchins. (1) John Tauman, age ca. 70, that about 48 years ago John Hannat, John Winnall, John Daniel, and William Allinge were servants on the plantation of Woodman Stockley. (2) Peter Sewell, age ca. 40. (3) William Williams, age ca. 70. (4) John Godsgrace, age ca. 50. (5) Thomas Edmonds, age ca. 51. (Liber PC, p. 857).

1 Jun 1712. Deposition of James Pattison, age ca. 53, regarding the bounds of a tract called *Taylor's Folley* in Dorchester Co. (Liber PC, p. 860).

2 Aug 1712. Deposition of William Roby(?), Sr., age ca. 70, regarding the bounds of a tract called *Taylor's Folley*. (Liber PC, p. 860).

22 Nov 1712. St. Mary's Co. Depositions taken regarding land in possession of John Dansey. (1) John Fosieg(?), age ca. 73, that he heard Augustinian Warren, son of John Warren, say that the pear tree was the bound between John Bayley and his father. (2) Mrs. Mary Dent, age ca. 65, that her father, John Schertilife (Shatteless?); her mother, Ann Schertilife; and her uncle, Henry Spinck often said her father and uncle sold the tract to Edward Cotten. (Liber PC, p. 861).

30 Dec 1712. St. Mary's Co. Deposition of John Burroughs, age ca. 68, that he lived with Thomas Truman about 7 years ago. John Morris bought the land that James Keech now claims of Cornelius Canidey, and said Morris died and his heir became

an orphan who was brought up from a child by Thomas Trueman. Deposition was regarding the bounds of a tract called *Trent Neck*. (Liber PC, p. 863).

3 Sep 1712. Docket. Thomas Trueman Greenfield vs. Elizabeth Keech, extx. of James Keech, and James Keech, heir at law of James Keech. (Liber PC, p. 865).

3 Sep 1712. Docket. Dennis Kerney vs. Mary, the relict of Dennis Dwane. (Liber PC, p. 866).

31 Mar 1713. Depositions taken regarding Piscattaway Mannor. (1) Francis Malbury, age ca. 50; (2) Richard Conner, age ca. 51; (3) John Hendall, age ca. 39; (4) Phillip Lowing, age ca. 60. (Liber PC, p. 871).

17 Mar 1713. Depositions taken regarding a deed or conveyance made from John Clements to Christopher Wise. (1) Caleb Eastgate, age ca. 72, (2) Abigail Wise, age ca. 69, said that about 38 years ago she and her husband, Christopher Wise, bought said land of Christopher Peak. (Liber PC, p. 872).

12 Sep 1712. Depositions taken regarding bounds of a tract in Calvert Co. called *Goodluck* belonging to Capt. Henry Cox. (1) John Lawfell of Calvert Co., age ca. 60; (2) Mary Gold, age ca. 50; (3) John Leach of Calvert Co., age ca. 50; (4) Joseph Strickland, age ca. 60; (5) Col. Ninian Beale, age ca. 88; (6) William Whittenton, Sr, age ca. 63 (1 Oct 1712); (7) Jacob Stallons, age ca. 33 (12 Oct 1712). (Liber PC, p. 874).

9 Apr 1713. Depositions taken regarding the bounds of a tract called *Trent Neck*. (1) Richard Marsh of Prince George's Co., age ca. 79; (2) Thomas Greenfield, age ca. 64, that about 25 years ago Cornelius Watkinson was a next neighbor to land called *Trent Neck* and he bought his land from Maj. Thomas Trueman; (3) Mrs. Martha Danzey of St. Mary's Co., age ca. 44, that her former husband was Charles Ashcome; (4) John Burroughs of St. Mary's Co., age ca. 70. (Liber PC, p. 877).

26 Mar 1713. Depositions taken regarding the bounds of a tract called *Wolfsford* in Somerset Co. belonging to Roger Wolford of Dorchester Co. (1) Livin Denwood, Sr, a Quaker. (Liber PC, p. 879).

9 Dec 1712. Depositions taken regarding the bounds of a tract in Dorchester Co. called *Towneneck*. (1) Henry Hooper, age ca. 70, that about 43 years ago he was present at a survey of land called *Towneneck* for his brother, Richard Hooper. (2) Phillip Shapley of County of Northumberland in the Colony of Virginia, Gent., age ca. 67 (13 Oct 1712). (Liber PC, p. 881).

17 Apr 1713. Deposition of John Coffer, age ca. 23, that about 5 years ago he was living at the house of James Maddox of Charles Co., and that Maddox and William Doynes agreed about the price of a negro man named Robin Couler. (Liber PC, p. 883).

5 Jun 1713. Deposition of George Cowley of Talbot Co., Gent., age ca. 81, regarding the bounds of a tract called *Old Towne* in Queen Anne Co. near the head of the Choptank River. (Liber PC, p. 883).

19 Jun 1713. Deposition of Henry Tanner of Charles Co., aged ca. 55 yrs. regarding the bounds of a tract in St. Georges in St. Mary's Co. belonging to Thomas Hebb which he purchased of

the heir of Giles Glover. About 26 yrs. ago he lived as a boarder in the house of Elizabeth who was the mother of William Glover, the son of Giles Glover, which son was the sole son and heir of said Giles, who sold 100 ac. to said Thomas Hebb, formerly the land of Hutton Corbett and which said Elizabeth was then the widow of Kenelm Macloughlin and lived at Maryland Point. Elizabeth gave the patent to the land to said William when he was about 16 yrs. of age and told him it belonged to him which William was then under the care and as a servant of Francis Meek, who married a sister of the said William and was sold by his said mother for 1500 lbs. of tobacco to said Francis for ca. 5 yrs. To the best of this deponent's remembrance, James Mackey, Mary the now wife of Richard Wade and then the wife of Francis Meek, were both present. (Liber CL, p. 15).

19 Jun 1713. Deposition of Mary, the now wife of Richard Wade of Charles Co., planter, age ca. 50 yrs. that she heard her mother Elizabeth, widow and relict of Giles Glover, say and showing a writing to this deponent's brother, Wm. Glover when he was under the care of Francis Meek her then husband... (Liber CL, p. 15).

6 Jul 1714. Deposition of Col. John Bigger, aged ca. 56 yrs. regarding the bounds of a tract called *Magruder*. (Liber CL, p. 18).

6 Jul 1714. Deposition of Bryan Macdaniel, aged ca. 59 yrs. regarding the bounds of a tract called *Magruder*. (Liber CL, p. 18).

6 Jul 1714. Deposition of Margarett Thompson, aged ca. 46 yrs. regarding the bounds of a tract called *Magruder* recalls that her first husband, John Howell, went with her to a white oak... (Liber CL, p. 18).

6 Jul 1714. Deposition of George Waide, aged ca. 53 yrs. regarding the bounds of a tract called *Magruder*. (Liber CL, p. 18).

25 Jul 1713. Deposition of George Young, the elder of Calvert Co., Gent. aged ca. 60 yrs. that when he was a boy he knew a Benjamin Brasheur who then lived at the upper end of the Clifts in Calvert Co. on a plantation on a tract called *Upper Bennett* and often heard people say the said Brashier was a Frenchman borne. (Liber CL, p. 19).

25 Jul 1713. Deposition of David Morgan, the elder of Calvert Co., planter aged ca. 70 yrs. that about 53 yrs. ago he knew Benjamin Brashear who lived at the upper end of the Clifts in Calvert Co., and that about the time of this deponent's coming into the country the said Brashear brought some of the servants that came in the shipp with this deponent, and it was generally reported that he was a Frenchman borne. (Liber CL, p. 19).

5 Aug 1713. Joseph Chew, Sr. of Ann Arundel Co., aged ca. 76 yrs. recalls that upwards of 50 yrs. ago he knew Benjamin Brashears who lived at the upper end of the Clifts in Calvert Co. being the first year of his seating the plantation he bought of Gov. Bennett who all that time was reputed to be a Frenchman, and that he likewise knew his brother Robert who lived in Virginia, being a new neighbor to him and was always reputed to be a Frenchman likewise. (Liber CL,

p. 19).
5 Nov 1712. Chancery case regarding a tract called *Hebden Hole* in St. Mary's Co. in which the land was divided between Ignatius Fenwicks and his wife Ellen of the one part and John Reed and his wife Hannah of the other part. (Liber CL, p. 20).
3 Mar 1712. Talbot Co. Examining the evidences of the bounds of a tract called *Crosse Doyer (Cross Door, Cross Dower)*. (Liber CL, p. 21).
27 Mar 1713. Talbot Co. Deposition of John Dickenson aged ca. 79 yrs. regarding the bounds of a tract called *Cross Doyer (Cross Door, Cross Dower)*; recalls he heard his brother, Walter Dickenson, say ... (Liber CL, p. 21).
27 Mar 1713. Talbot Co. Deposition of Richard White aged ca. 80 yrs. regarding the bounds of a tract called *Crosse Doyer (Cross Door, Cross Dower)*. (Liber CL, p. 21).
27 Mar 1713. Talbot Co. Deposition of John Mullakin aged ca. 54 yrs. regarding the bounds of a tract called *Crosse Doyer (Cross Door, Cross Dower)*, recalls his father Patrick Mullakin told him ... (Liber CL, p. 22).
27 Mar 1713. Talbot Co. Deposition of Richard Holmes aged ca. 49 yrs. regarding the bounds of a tract called *Crosse Doyer (Cross Door, Cross Dower)*. (Liber CL, p. 22).
9 Jul 1713. Talbot Co. Deposition of Joseph James, Sr. aged ca. 66 yrs. regarding the bounds of tract called *Crosse Doyer (Cross Door, Cross Dower)*. (Liber CL, p. 22).
9 Jul 1713. Talbot Co. Deposition of John Reston aged ca. 68 yrs. and his wife Jane aged ca. 60 yrs. regarding the bounds of a tract called *Crosse Doyer (Cross Door, Cross Dower)*, that they lived with Walter Dickenson about 45 yrs. ago. (Liber CL, p. 22).
9 Jul 1713. Deposition of Anne Lowe, dau of John Preston, aged ca. 22 yrs. that her father told certain parties that the bounded tree of the land of his master, Walter Dickenson, was... (Liber CL, p. 23).
9 Jul 1713. Deposition of Jasper Hall aged ca. 90 yrs. that about 45 yrs. ago when he was a servant to Walter Dickenson... (Liber CL, p. 23).
15 Apr 1714. Deposition of Grace Mitchell aged ca. 72 yrs. that she knew Gabriell Goulden who lived and died at the head of St. Leonards Creek and owned the land the John Broughton lives on. Gabriell Boulden had a wife named Mary who was with child when the said Golden died and the child died soon thereafter. Later John Holeings (Hollins) married the widow Mary and had a dau. by her and no other child that lived to age. The said dau. married John Wadnior (?) and by him bore a child the now wife of afsd. John Brouton. The deponent further says that before she knew Gabriel Goulden she was acquainted with Daniel Phiggett in Virginia who married the aunt of the said Mary, wife of Gabrell Goulden which said Phiggett, as she heard, had a son by said wife, named Daniel Phiggett; it has been about 20 yrs. since the mother of Daniel Phiggett had been to her house. She had two or three sons by her husband Phiggett. (Liber CL, p. 24).
16 Apr 1714. Deposition of Isaac Baker aged ca. 67 yrs. that he knew Gabriel Goulden about 40-50 yrs. ago. He recalls

talking to a young man named Walker out of Virginia to see Mary Hollings as he had heard say was the first wife of Gabriel Goulden and called her Aunt. (Liber CL, p. 25).

14 Jun 1714. Prince George's Co. Deposition of Robert Tyler, Gent. aged ca. 42 yrs. regarding the bounds of a tract called *Essington*. (Liber CL, p. 26).

14 Jun 1714. Prince George's Co. Deposition of Hugh Ryley, carpenter, aged ca. 61 yrs. regarding the bounds of a tract called *Essington*. (Liber CL, p. 27).

14 Jun 1714. Prince George's Co. Deposition of Thomas Wells, Sr. aged ca. 61 yrs. regarding the bounds of a tract called *Essington*. (Liber CL, p. 27).

14 Jun 1714. Prince George's Co. Deposition of James Mullakin aged ca. 51 yrs. regarding the bounds of a tract called *Essington*. (Liber CL, p. 27).

14 Jun 1714. Prince George's Co. Deposition of Charles Walker, aged ca. 46 yrs. regarding the bounds of a tract called *Essington*. (Liber CL, p. 27).

ca. 1714. Talbot Co. Joan Preston aged ca. 60 yrs. withdraws her statement [regarding Dickenson land in Talbot Co.]. (Liber CL, p. 29).

26 Jan 1713. Talbot Co. Deposition of Thomas Brown of said co. planter, aged ca. 43 yrs. regarding a tract called *Cattlins Plains*, recalls the time when he was a servant to Samuel Abbott about 25-26 yrs. ago and Mrs. Jane Abbott carried him and some others into the old field where the said Samuel then dwelt. About 18 yrs. ago Anthony Cox called to his father in law Samuel Abbott regarding a stump which his uncle Anthony Dawson told him was the second tree of *Catlins Plains*. (Liber CL, p. 29).

26 Jan 1713. Talbot Co. Deposition of John Mullakin of said co. aged ca. 54 yrs. regarding a tract called *Cattlins Plains*. (Liber CL, p. 30).

20 Jul 1695 [filed with depositions of 1713]. Deposition of Samuel White, regarding the bounds of a tract called *Cattlins Plains*. (Liber CL, p. 30).

20 Jul 1695 [filed with depositions of 1713]. Deposition of Anthony Cox aged ca. 35 yrs. regarding the bounds of a tract called *Cattlins Plains*. (Liber CL, p. 31).

27 Jan 1695 [filed with depositions of 1713]. Deposition of John Cox aged ca. 60 yrs. regarding the bounds of a tract called *Cattlins Plains*. (Liber CL, p. 31).

5 Apr 1714. Deposition of John Cox aged ca. 80 yrs. regarding the bounds of a tract called *Rich Neck* now in the possession of James Lord. (Liber CL, p. 31).

5 Apr 1714. Deposition of Abraham Beasly of Talbot Co., planter, aged ca. 60 yrs. regarding the bounds of a tract called *Rich Neck* now in the possession of James Lord; says that about 23 yrs. ago he lived near a plantation now in the possession of Alexander Boyce on Dividing Creek and upward and across the creek lived Thomas Martin (late decd.) on a tract which James Lord now claims part of called *Rich Neck*. (Liber CL, p. 31).

5 Apr 1714. Deposition of William Smith of Talbott Co., planter aged ca. 60 yrs. regarding the bounds of a tract called *Rich Neck* now in the possession of James Lord; says

that about 30 yrs. ago he was a servant to Capt. Henry Alexander, late of said co. decd. (Liber CL, p. 32).

5 Apr 1714. Deposition of John Cliff of Talbot Co., aged ca. 33 yrs. regarding the bounds of a tract called *Rich Neck* now in the possession of James Lord; recalls being in company with William Martin who claimed part of a tract called *Shoreditch* on Dividing Creek and the remainder thereof was also claimed by James Lord on behalf of Thomas Martin, son and heir of Samuel Martin, decd. (Liber CL, p. 32).

5 Apr 1714. Deposition of John Burneat of Talbot Co., weaver, aged ca. 21 yrs. regarding the bounds of a tract called *Rich Neck* now in the possession of James Lord; sometime in Nov last he was in the company of William Martin. (LIber CL, p. 32).

ca. 1714. Talbot Co. Deposition of John Cox, planter, aged ca. 79 yrs. concerning the uppermost bounded tree of a tract called *Patricks Plains*. (Liber CL, p. 33).

11 Jul 1713. Talbot Co. Deposition of James Auld of Talbot Co., aged ca. 48 yrs. relating to the first bounded tree of a tract called *Fairplay*. (Liber CL, p. 34).

15 Jul 1713. Talbot Co. Deposition of Elizabeth Elliott wife of Edward Elliott, Sr. aged ca. 72 yrs., formerly the wife of Henry Frith the purchase of the land called *Lankester*. The commission also reports finding a receipt from the papers of Richard Feddeman, decd. to land called *Lankester*, dated 26 Apr 1673 from John Darby [see p. 34]. In 1669 her decd. husband, Henry Frith, purchased from William Hambleton of Talbot Co., decd. a parcel called *Lankashire* containing 1000 ac. (Liber CL, p. 35).

11 Jul 1713. Talbot Co. Deposition of Edward Elliott Sr. of Talbot Co. aged ca. 72 yrs. regarding the bounds of a tract called *Fairplay*. (Liber CL, p. 35).

20 Aug 1713. Somerset Co. Deposition of Walter Lane of Somerset Co., Gent. aged ca. 63 yrs. regarding a tract called *Bleakes Hope*. (Liber CL, p. 36).

20 Aug 1713. Somerset Co. Deposition of Griffith Thomas of said co. aged ca. 67 yrs. regarding a tract called *Bleakes Hope*. (Liber CL, p. 36).

20 Aug 1713. Somerset Co. Deposition of John Pirkins of said co. aged ca. 70 yrs. regarding a tract called *Bleakes Hope*. (Liber CL, p. 36).

20 Aug 1713. Somerset Co. Deposition of Mr. Allexander Mattucks aged ca. 60 yrs. regarding a tract called *Blakes Hope*. (Liber CL, p. 37).

20 Aug 1713. Somerset Co. Deposition of John Russell aged ca. 90 yrs. regarding a tract called *Williams Hope*. (Liber CL, p. 37).

13 Apr 1714. Charles Co. Deposition of Mary Hager, aged ca. 64 yrs., wife of Thomas Hagar regarding 650 ac. that joined Wm. Boarman's land. (Liber CL, p. 38).

13 Apr 1714. Charles Co. Deposition of William Borman aged ca. 60 yrs. regarding a tract called *Lanternum*. (Liber CL, p. 38).

13 Apr 1714. Charles Co. Deposition of Abraham Lancaster aged ca. 77 yrs. regarding a tract called *Lanternum*. (Liber CL, p. 38).

3 Apr 1714. Talbot Co. Deposition of Francis Porter aged ca. 46 yrs. regarding the tract called *Fair Play*. (Liber CL, p. 39).

3 Apr 1714. Talbot Co. Deposition of James Spencer aged ca. 47 yrs. regarding the bounds of a tract called *Fair Play*. (Liber CL, p. 39).

3 Apr 1714. Talbot Co. Deposition of Laurence Porter aged ca. 33 yrs. regarding the bounds of a tract called *Fair Play*; states about 15-16 yrs. ago he lived with his brother, Francis Porter, on a tract adjoining the land called *Fairplay*. (Liber CL, p. 39).

Somerset Co. Deposition of William Whittington aged ca. 64 yrs. regarding a tract called *Cow Quarter*. (Liber CL, p. 41).

Somerset Co. Deposition of Walter Reed aged ca. 65 yrs. regarding a tract called *Cow Quarter*. (Liber CL, p. 41).

6 Oct 1712. Deposition of Col. Ninian Beale aged ca. 87 yrs. regarding the bounds of a tract in Prince George's Co. called *Beales Chance*. (Liber CL, p. 42).

4 Oct 1712. Deposition of Richard Jones aged ca. 50 yrs. regarding the bounds of a tract in Prince George's Co. called *Beales Chance*. (Liber CL, p. 42).

1 Jun 1714. Talbot Co. Deposition of Thomas Browne of Talbot Co., planter, aged ca. 44 yrs. regarding the bounds of *Cattlins Plains*; says about 20 yrs. ago he was a servant to Samuel Abbott of the same co. (Liber CL, p. 42).

1714. Statement of Ninian Beall about the destruction of Calvert Co. records. "after he heard of the Destruction of the Records of Calvert County..." (Liber CL, p. 45).

29 Apr 1714. Talbot Co. Deposition of Richard White, planter, aged ca. 80 yrs. regarding the bounds of a tract called *Scotland*; recalls Henry Alexander and his children say ... (Liber CL, p. 45).

29 Apr 1714. Talbot Co. Deposition of John Mullakin, planter, aged ca. 54 yrs. regarding a bounded tree at the head of Dividing Creek. (Liber CL, p. 46).

29 Apr 1714. Talbot Co. Deposition of Mary Harrahave, wife of John Harrahave of said co., planter, aged ca. 50 yrs. regarding the bounds of a tract called *Scotland*. (Liber CL, p. 46).

3 Mar 1714. Chancery case to examine evidences produced by William Clayland in a cause depending in the Provincial Court between the said William Clayland and Daniel Peirce. Nathaniel and Wm. Comegys, Do you know Anne the resent wife of Wm. Clayland?
Answer: Yes, she is the dau. of Edward and Elizabeth Fry.
Question: Whose dau. was Elizabeth Fry?
Answer: She was the dau. of my father Cornelius Comegys, late of Kent Co.
Question: Had Edward Fry any more children?
Answer: No. (Liber CL, p. 46).

1714. Petition of Francis Barnes of Kent Island to examine evidences touching the first bounded tree of a tract on Kent Island called *Potts Gift*. (Liber CL, p. 47).

6 Oct 1714. Deposition of Francis Benton of Kent Island regarding the bounds of a tract called *Potts Gift*, says he

formerly lived a freeman with Francis Barnes late of Kent Island, decd. (Liber CL, p. 47).
20 Oct 1714. Deposition of Thomas Smith regarding the bounds of a tract called *Potts Gift*. (Liber CL, p. 47).
1 Sep 1712. Deposition of Col. Ninian Beale aged ca. 87 yrs. regarding the third bound tree of *Croome*. (Liber CL, p. 49).
1 Sep 1712. Deposition of Francis Pile aged ca. 52 yrs. regarding the third bound tree of *Croome*. (Liber CL, p. 49).
9 Aug 1714. Talbot Co. Deposition of Henry Costin of Queen Anne's Co. aged ca. 72 yrs. concerning a tract called *Woolmans Inheritance*. (Liber CL, p. 50).
9 Aug 1714. Talbot Co. Deposition of John Nunam aged ca. 68 yrs. concerning a tract called *Woolmans Inheritance*. (Liber CL, p. 50).
St. Mary's Co. Deposition of Samuel Williamson aged ca. 55 yrs. regarding the bounds of a tract called *Hillylee* on the branches of the Chaptico. (Liber CL, p. 51).
St. Mary's Co. Deposition of Thomas Barber aged ca. 53 yrs. regardng the bounds of a tract called *Hillylee* on the branches of the Chaptico; heard his brother Edward Barber say... (Liber CL, p. 52).
30 Sep 1714. St. Mary's Co. Deposition of Thomas Trottman of Prince George's Co. (Liber CL, p. 52).
30 Sep 1714. St. Mary's Co. Deposition of John Burroughs of St. Mary's Co. aged ca. 70 yrs. (Liber CL, p. 53).
13 Oct 1714. Deposition of John Smith aged ca. 38 yrs. recalled about 17 yrs. ago coming with John or Thomas Tasker, sons of Thomas Tasker, Sr. decd., down towards Halls Creek. (Liber CL, p. 53).
13 Oct 1714. Deposition of Col. Ninian Beale aged ca. 88 yrs. recalls about 48 yrs. ago when he was a servant to Mr. Rd. Hall. (Liber CL, p. 54).
Deposition of John Vadry of Charles Co., planter, aged ca. 70 yrs. regarding the bounds of a tract called *Norwood* in Charles Co. (Liber CL, p. 55).
Deposition of Joshua Holdsworth of St. Mary's Co., planter aged ca. 61 yrs. regarding the bounds of a tract called *Norwood* in Charles Co. (Liber CL, p. 55).
Deposition of Capt. Thomas Love of St. Mary's Co. aged ca. 53 yrs. regarding the bounds of a tract called *Norwood* in Charles Co., recalls hunting with Robert Slye who married one of his sisters. (Liber CL, p. 55).
Deposition of John Noe of Charles Co., planter, aged ca. 64 yrs. regarding the bounds of a tract called *Norwood* in Charles Co. (Liber CL, p. 56).
19 Oct 1714. Deposition of John Burroughs of St. Mary's Co., planter aged ca. 70 yrs. recalls his former master, Mr. Thomas Trueman. (Liber CL, p. 56).
19 Oct 1714. Deposition of George Godfrey aged ca. 70 yrs. regarding a tract called *Millerne*. (Liber CL, p. 57).
1714. It appears to the court that John Richardson, brother to the complainant James Richardson, was not at the time of his making his will in his senses and afterward confessed himself to be mad and denied the said will. Opinion of the court that the will is null and void. (Liber CL, p. 77).
11 Mar 1714. Came into court, Sarah Brice, widow, relict and

devisee of John Brice, late of Anne Arundel Co., merchant, decd. (Liber CL, p. 87).

23 Sep 1714. Commission appointed to examine the bounds of several tracts of Randolph Brant, minor, under the age of 21. (Liber CL, p. 97).

20 Nov 1714. Deposition of Henry Tanner aged ca. 58 yrs. regarding the bounds of land of Randolph Brant, minor. (Liber CL, p. 98).

20 Nov 1714. Deposition of John Marlo aged ca. 42 yrs. regarding the bounds of land of Randolph Brant, minor. (Liber CL, p. 98).

10 Nov 1714. Deposition of Anthony Neale of Charles Co. aged ca. 55 yrs. regarding the bounds of land of Randolph Brant, minor, son of Capt. Randolph Brant. (Liber CL, p. 98).

Last day of Nov 1714. Charles Co. Deposition of Thomas Hagen aged ca. 31 yrs. regarding the bounds of the land of James Hagen. (Liber CL, p. 99).

Last day of Nov 1714. Charles Co. Deposition of William Carter aged ca. 60 yrs. regarding the bounds of the land of James Hagen. (Liber CL, p. 99).

Last day of Nov 1714. Charles Co. Deposition of John Burross aged ca. 70 yrs. regarding the bounds of the land of James Hagen. (Liber CL, p. 100).

Last day of Nov 1714. Charles Co. Deposition of Thomas Lawson aged ca. 65 yrs. regarding the bounds of the land of James Hagen. (Liber CL, p. 100).

Last day of Nov 1714. Charles Co. Deposition of John Hagathe aged ca. 40 yrs. regarding the bounds of the land of James Hagen. (Liber CL, p. 100).

Last day of Nov 1714. Charles Co. Deposition of Henry Mudd aged ca. 29 yrs. regarding the bounds of the land of James Hagen. (Liber CL, p. 100).

Last day of Nov 1714. Charles Co. Deposition of William Lawson aged ca. 21 yrs. regarding the bounds of the land of James Hagen. (Liber CL, p. 100).

Last day of Nov 1714. Charles Co. Deposition of James Nuttwell aged ca. 35 yrs. regarding the bounds of the land of James Hagen. (Liber CL, p. 100).

Last day of Nov 1714. Charles Co. Deposition of Thomas Davis aged ca. 24 yrs. regarding the bounds of the land of James Hagen. (Liber CL, p. 100).

25 Feb 1714. Deposition of Nicholas Clouds aged ca. 63 yrs. regarding a discussion he had with Andrew Skinner at his house in St. Michaells River, regarding a tract he laid out for Joseph Churnell in the forks of the Eastern Branch on the south side of Chester River then in Talbot Co. [now Kent] called *Churnells Neck*, the land on which John Hollingsworth was then seated. [Also refers to John Hollingsworth, son of afsd. John Hollingsworth.] (Liber CL, p. 101).

25 Feb 1714. Deposition of William Hackett aged ca. 67 yrs. regarding a tract in now Kent Co. of Joseph Churnell. (Liber CL, p. 101).

25 Feb 1714. Deposition of Thomas Hinds aged ca. 69 yrs. regarding a tract in now Kent Co. of Joseph Churnell. (Liber CL, p. 101).

25 Feb 1714. Deposition of Richard Iagoe (Jagoe?) aged ca. 47

yrs., who was guardian to John Hollingsworth's orphan; refers to Thomas Hollingsworth, son of John Hollingsworth. (Liber CL, p. 101).

2 Aug 1714. Deposition of John Tanman of Calvert Co. aged ca. 70 yrs. regarding the bounds of a tract called *The Ordinary* now in possession of Charles Sewell and his wife Elianor, the relict of John Tasker, decd. (Liber CL, p. 102).

2 Aug 1714. Deposition of Major Henry Cox of Calvert Co. aged ca. 51 yrs. regarding the bounds of a tract called *The Ordinary*. (Liber CL, p. 102).

7 Aug 1711. Deposition of Thomas Cades of Calvert Co. aged ca. 77 yrs. regarding the bounds of a tract called *The Ordinary*. (Liber CL, p. 102).

1714. Baltimore Co. Deposition of Stephen Bentley aged ca. 57 yrs. regarding the bounded tree of *Upper Spring Neck*. (Liber CL, p. 103).

1714. Baltimore Co. Deposition of Michaell Young aged ca. 50 yrs. regarding a bounded tree. (Liber CL, p. 103).

30 Dec 1714. Baltimore Co. Deposition of Joseph Gostwick aged ca. 55 yrs. regarding the bounds of Wm. Pearl's land. (Liber CL, 104).

3 Jan 1714. Deposition of Sarah Perigoy aged ca. 42 yrs. regarding the bounds of Wm. Pearle's land; recalls seeing her father Edwd. Maurford told her... (Liber CL, p. 104).

20 Nov 1714. St. Mary's Co. Deposition of Henry Tanner aged ca. 58 yrs. regarding the bounds of a tract called *Tattershalls Gift*. (Liber CL, p. 104).

11 Jan 1714. Queen Anne's Co. Deposition of Nicholas Clouds ca. 60 yrs. regarding the bounds of a tract called *Delmore End*. (Liber CL, p. 105).

11 Jan 1714. Queen Anne's Co. Deposition of Mr. John Whittington aged ca. 60 yrs. regarding the bounds of a tract called *Delmore End*. (Liber CL, p. 105).

11 Jan 1714. Queen Anne's Co. Deposition of Daniel Perry aged ca. 50 yrs. regarding the bounds of a tract called *Delmore End*. (Liber CL, p. 105).

14 Jul 1714. Deposition of Mary Gringoe of St. Mary's Co. aged ca. 76 yrs. regarding the purchase of a tract called *Jones's Woods*; says her husband, Wm. Gringoe, bought the said land of Robt. Jones and after a brief period sold the land to Francis Cole, father of Valentine Cole [the petitioner]. (Liber CL, p. 106).

13 Jan 1714. Prince George's Co. Nicholas Coop(?) aged ca. 70 yrs. regarding a tract in Charles Co. called *Rotterdam*. (Liber CL, p. 107).

13 Jan 1714. Prince George's Co. Robert Taler aged ca. 50 yrs. regarding a tract in Charles Co. called *Rotterdam* recalls being in company with Thomas Craxson late of Charles Co., decd. (Liber CL, p. 107).

19 Jan 1714/15. Baltimore Co. Deposition of Charles Gorsuch, Sr. aged ca. 60 yrs. regarding the bounds of a tract called *Wilkinson Spring*; states he bought the land called *Upper Spring Neck* of one Walter Dickinson and sold it to Wm. Pearle. (Liber CL, p. 108).

19 Jan 1714/15. Baltimore Co. Deposition of Philip Pitstoe aged ca. 30 yrs. regarding the bounds of Wm. Pearle's land.

(Liber CL, p. 108).

19 Jan 1714/15. Baltimore Co. Deposition of Philip Washington aged ca. 50 yrs. regarding the bounds of Wm. Pearle's land. (Liber CL, p. 109).

19 Jan 1714/15. Baltimore Co. Deposition of John Mackartee aged ca. 35 yrs. regarding the bounds of a tract called *Wm. Pearle's land*. (Liber CL, p. 109).

19 Jan 1714/15. Baltimore Co. Deposition of Thomas Biddyson aged ca. 40 yrs. regarding the bounds of a tract called *Wm. Pearle's land*; says he has lived in these parts about 30 yrs. (Liber CL, p. 109).

19 Jan 1714/15. Baltimore Co. Deposition of Thomas Smith aged ca. 45 yrs. regarding the bounds of a tract called *Wm. Pearle's land*; he has lived in these parts 21 yrs. (Liber CL, p. 109).

19 Jan 1714/15. Baltimore Co. Deposition of Stephen Bentley aged ca. 57 yrs. regarding the bounds of a tract called *Wm. Pearle's land*; he has lived in these parts 21 yrs; he the said Bentley lived on the said land of *Upper Spring Neck* and was possessed with it and he married Willm. Pearle's mother. (Liber CL, p. 109).

10 Feb 1714/5. Baltimore Co. Deposition of John Norton aged ca. 37 yrs. regarding the bounds of a tract called *Wm. Pearle's land*; he has lived thereabouts 17 yrs. (Liber CL, p. 110).

22 Dec 1714. Deposition of Thomas Reves (Reeves) of St. Mary's Co., planter, aged ca. 70 yrs. regarding the bounds of a tract called *Clear Doubt*; says he was a servant to Mr. Robt. Slye. (Liber CL, p. 110).

18 May 1715. Reference to Rachel, widow of Charles Greenberry. (Liber CL, p. 228).

27 9ber 1714. Affirmation of Elisha Hall of Calvert Co. aged ca. 51 yrs, a Quaker, regarding the bounds of a tract called *Broughton Ashley*; recalls his father, Richard Hall, say that ... (Liber CL, p. 233).

27 9ber 1714. Deposition of Danll. Brown of Calvert Co., carpenter, aged ca. 58 yrs. regarding the bounds of a tract called *Broughton Ashley*. (Liber CL, p. 233).

1 Dec 1714. Deposition of Elizabeth Saunders, wife of Joseph Saunders of Anne Arundel Co., aged ca. 59 yrs. regarding the bounds of a tract called *Broughton Ashley*; recalls hearing her former husband Jno. Franton say... (Liber CL, p. 234).

1 Mar 1714. Deposition of Edward Ming aged ca. 76 yrs. regarding the bounds of a tract in Charles Co. on Potomack River in Nanjemy Parish. (Liber CL, p. 234).

20 Feb 1714. Talbot Co. Deposition of Alexr. Mecotter of said co. aged ca. 54 yrs. regarding the bounds of a tract called *Sutton Grange*. (Liber CL, p. 234).

20 Feb 1714. Talbot Co. Deposition of Charles Harbert of said co. aged ca. 47 yrs. regarding the bounds of a tract called *Sutton Grange*. (Liber CL, p. 235).

26 Feb 1714. St. Mary's Co. Deposition of Thomas Barber of St. Mary's Co., Gent. aged ca. 60 yrs. regarding the bounds of a tract called *Westham*. (Liber CL, p. 235).

26 Feb 1714. St. Mary's Co. Deposition of Samll. Williamson of St. Mary's Co. aged ca. 55 yrs. regarding the bounds of a

tract called *Westham*. (Liber CL, p. 235).
21 Mar 1714. Talbot Co. Deposition of Alexander Mecotter of afsd. co. aged ca. 54 yrs. regarding the bounds of a tract called *Woolsey Mannor*. (Liber CL, p. 236).
21 Mar 1714. Talbot Co. Deposition of John Eason of said co., planter, aged ca. 50 yrs. regarding the bounds of a tract called *Woolsey Mannor*. (Liber CL, p. 236).
21 Mar 1714. Talbot Co. Deposition of William Carr of said co., planter, aged ca. 54 yrs. regarding the bounds of a tract called *Woolsey Mannor*. (Liber CL, p. 236).
16-20 Jun 1715. Deposition of Nathaniel Cooper of St. Mary's Co. aged ca. 42 yrs. regarding the bounds of a part of *Fenwick Mannor*; says that about 26 yrs. ago he was then a servant to Mr. Michael Taney and dwelling on a tract of land of his formerly in the tenure of John and Anne Sawell now in the possession of Mr. John Taney. Paul Peacock was then Mr. Michl. Taney's overseer. Reference is made to land in the possession of Col. Henry Lowe in right of his dau. in law, Darnall [sic]. (Liber CL, p. 237).
16-20 Jun 1715. St. Mary's Co. Deposition of Anne Head aged ca. 45 yrs. regarding the bounds of a part of *Fenwick Mannor*; states that during her minority her uncle and guardian had in possession the land now in possession of Mr. Taney, then belonging to her [dau. of John Darnall?]. (Liber CL, p. 237).
16-20 Jun 1715. St. Mary's Co. Deposition of Martin Yates aged ca. 49 yrs. regarding the bounds of a part of *Fenwick Mannor*; was a servant to Mr. Henry Darnall about 30 yrs. ago who leased land from Mr. Richard Fenwick as guardian of his niece, now called Mrs. Anne Head. (Liber CL, p. 238).
16-20 Jun 1715. St. Mary's Co. Deposition of Adam Head, husband of Anne Head, aged ca. 40 yrs. regarding the bounds of a part of *Fenwick Mannor*. (Liber CL, p. 238).
16-20 Jun 1715. St. Mary's Co. Deposition of Simon Gerling aged ca. 50 yrs. regarding the bounds of a part of *Fenwick Mannor*. (Liber CL, p. 238).
16-20 Jun 1715. St. Mary's Co. Deposition of Peter Joy aged ca. 50 yrs. regarding the bounds of a part of *Fenwick Mannor*. (Liber CL, p. 238).
16-20 Jun 1715. St. Mary's Co. Deposition of John Hall aged ca. 50 yrs. regarding the bounds of a part of *Fenwick Mannor*. (Liber CL, p. 238).
16-20 Jun 1715. St. Mary's Co. Deposition of Levin Haseler aged ca. 65 yrs. regarding the bounds of a part of *Fenwick Mannor*. (Liber CL, p. 238).
20 Dec 1714. St. Mary's Co. Commission to examine the evidences of the bounds of a tract called *Revill* on Brittains Bay in St. Mary's Co. formerly conveyed by Luke Barber and his wife Elizabeth to William Battershall and now in possession of James Tant. Luke Barbar and Margarett Tant possessors of the residue of the said tract. (Liber CL, p. 239).
13 Apr 1715. St. Mary's Co. Deposition of Cornelius Marley aged ca. 53 yrs. regarding the bounds of a tract called *Revill* in St. Mary's Co. (Liber CL, p. 239).
2 Sep 1714. Granting to David Evans, carpenter, 10 ac. on each

of Nicholls Runn of St. Mary's Co. for a mill. (Liber CL, p. 240).

5 Apr 1715. Deposition of Abraham Lemaster of Charles Co., planter, aged ca. 70 yrs. regarding the bounds of a tract called *Lantarnam*. (Liber CL, p. 253).

5 Apr 1715. Deposition of Thomas Hagan of Charles Co., planter, aged ca. 70 yrs. regarding the bounds of Manwaring's land. (Liber CL, p. 253).

5 Apr 1715. Deposition of Joseph Gardner [probably of Charles Co.] aged ca. 66 yrs. regarding the bounds of Manwaring's land. (Liber CL, p. 253).

Anne Arundel Co. Petition of John Cheny and his wife Elizabeth as guardian to --- Tilly, son and heir of Charles Tilly, of said co., decd. (Liber CL, p. 257).

18 Jul 1715. Anne Arundel Co. Deposition of Walter Phelps aged ca. 70 yrs. regarding the bounds of a division of *Timber Neck*. (Liber CL, p. 257).

18 Jul 1715. Anne Arundel Co. Affirmation of Aron Rawlings, a Quaker, regarding the bounds of a division of *Timber Neck*; states that Wm. Bateman, Christian Wheeler, relict of John Wheeler, and Leonard Wayman told him... (Liber CL, p. 258).

St. Mary's Co. Deposition of Henry Spink aged ca. 51 yrs. regarding the bounds of a tract called *Fibben (Fibnee)*. (Liber CL, p. 259).

St. Mary's Co. Deposition of Robert Ford aged ca. 51 yrs. regarding the bounds of a tract called *Fibben (Fibnee)*; recalls his father, Robert Ford, saying... (Liber CL, p. 260).

St. Mary's Co. Deposition of William Bayly aged ca. 32 yrs. regarding the bounds of a tract called *Fibben (Fibnee)*; recalls his father John Bayly showing him... (Liber CL, p. 260).

St. Mary's Co. Deposition of George Hayden aged ca. 60 yrs. regarding the bounds of a tract called *Fibben (Fibnee)*; recalls his father John Bayly showing him... (Liber CL, p. 260).

Queen Anne's Co. Deposition of Samuell Wright aged ca. 23-24 yrs. regarding the sale of slaves. (Liber CL, p. 262).

Queen Anne's Co. Deposition of John Atkinson aged ca. 27 yrs. regarding the sale of slaves. (Liber CL, p. 262).

Queen Anne's Co. Deposition of John Goff aged ca. 30 yrs. regarding the sale of 10 Negroes and a Mulatto by Mr. James Coursey to Mr. Jno. Hawkins, Jr. (Liber CL, p. 262).

6 Feb 1715/16. Deposition of Charles Kilburne aged ca. 55 yrs. states that within 50 feet from the northeast end of the house built by Mr. John Carpenter in the city of Annapolis stood a house built for Majr. Edward Dorsey and rented to Hester Gross, now Hester Warman, who kept ordinary for sometime and accommodated Governor Nicholson and after burnt out lived in the house where Willm. Brymer now lives. (Liber CL, p. 266).

6 Feb 1715/16. Deposition of George Valentine aged ca. 47 yrs. regarding a dwelling house in Annapolis. (Liber CL, p. 266).

6 Feb 1715/16. Deposition of Samuel Leatherwood aged ca. 34 yrs. regarding a dwelling house in Annapolis. (Liber CL, p. 266).

23 May 1715. Deposition of Jonathan Jones aged ca. 42 yrs. regarding the bounds of a tract called *Heath's Landing*, formerly a part of *Pascall's Purchase* at Herring Creek in Anne Arundel Co. (Liber CL, p. 267).
23 May 1715. Deposition of Samuel Guitchard aged ca. 51 yrs. regarding the bounds of a tract called *Heath's Land* formerly a part of *Pascall's Purchase* at Herring Creek in Anne Arundel Co.; recalls about 20-22 yrs. ago he was horse hunting and Henry Fish, a blacksmith, was then making a coal pit which was upon a spot of ground... (Liber CL, p. 267).
23 May 1715. Deposition of Saml. Maccubbins aged ca. 43 yrs. regarding the bounds of a tract called *Heath's Land*, formerly a part of *Pascall's Purchase* at Herring Creek in Anne Arundel Co. (Liber CL, p. 268).
23 May 1715. Deposition of Thomas Larkin aged ca. 40 yrs. regarding the bounds of a tract called *Heath's Land*, formerly a part of *Pascall's Purchase* at Herring Creek in Anne Arundel Co. (Liber CL, p. 268).
3 May 1716. Deposition of John Burroughs, Sr. of St. Mary's Co. aged ca. 70 yrs. regarding the bounds of a tract now in the possessin of Thomas Letchworth of Prince George's Co., the said land formerly lying in St. Mary's Co., but now in Charles Co. (Liber CL, p. 269).
3 May 1716. Deposition of Thomas Hunt aged ca. 40 yrs. regarding the bounds of a tract of Col. Beale. (Liber CL, p. 270).
8 May 1716. Dorchester Co. To examine the evidences of the bounds of a tract called *Sectar* and another called *Chamberley* in controversy between the heirs of William Seward and Thomas Hicks of Dorchester Co. (Liber CL, p. 270).
26 Jun 1716. Prince George's Co. To examine the evidences of the bounds of a tract called *Evan's Range*, 800 ac. and another tract called *Green's Delight*, 200 ac. (Liber CL, p. 271).
20 Mar 1715. Deposition of Robert Tyler of Prince George's Co., merchant, aged ca. 44 yrs. regarding the bounds of a tract called *Evan's Range*, 800 ac. and another tract called *Green's Delight*, 200 ac. (Liber CL, p. 272).
20 Mar 1715. Deposition of John Henry of Prince George's Co., planter, aged ca. 60 yrs. regarding the bounds of a tract called *Evan's Range*, 800 ac. and another tract called *Green's Delight*, 200 ac.; recalls being a chain carrier when they laid out Hugh Riley's land called *Riley's Range*. (Liber CL, p. 273).
20 Mar 1715. Deposition of John Turner of Prince George's Co., planter, aged ca. 44 yrs. regarding the bounds of a tract called *Evan's Range*, 800 ac. and another tract called *Green's Delight*, 200 ac. (Liber CL, p. 273).
20 Mar 1715. Deposition of Charles Walker of Prince George's Co., planter, aged ca. 48 yrs. regarding the bounds of a tract called *Evan's Range*, 800 ac. and another tract called *Green's Delight*, 200 ac. (Liber CL, p. 274).
20 Mar 1715. Deposition of Col. Ninian Beale of Prince George's Co., planter, aged ca. 90 yrs. regarding the bounds of a tract called *Evan's Range*, 800 ac. and another tract called *Green's Delight*, 200 ac. (Liber CL, p. 274).

Anne Arundel Co. To examine evidences touching two Negroes whereof Col. Charles Greenbury was possessed in right of his mother called Sampson and Judith, which Negroes are now in the possession of Charles Hammond of Anne Arundel Co., Gent. and his wife Rachel who was the widow and relict of said Charles Greenbury, decd. (Liber CL, p. 275).

26 Mar 1716. Deposition of Katherine Lamb of Anne Arundel Co. aged ca. 39 yrs. states that Anne Greenberry, on her death bed, gave the two Negroes, Sampson and Judith, to her son Charles Greenberry. (Liber CL, p. 276).

7 Dec 1715. Prince George's Co. To examine evidences touching a certain mare and her increase which John Bradford and his wife Joyce, admrs. of James Butler decd. replevied from Arthur Nelson of the county afsd. (Liber CL, p. 276).

20 Xber 1715. Deposition of William Prather aged ca. 45 yrs. regarding the branding of a mare for Arthur Nelson. (Liber CL, p. 277).

20 Xber 1715. Prince George's Co. Deposition of John Williams aged ca. 38 yrs. states he was with Majr. John Bradford when they came to the house of John Nelson to demand a mare. (Liber CL, p. 277).

20 Dec 1715. Prince George's Co. Deposition of Joseph Belt aged ca. 35 yrs. regarding a black mare. (Liber CL, p. 277).

20 Dec 1715. Prince George's Co. Deposition of Charles Beale aged ca. 43 yrs. regarding a mare in the possession of Arthur Nelson. (Liber CL, p. 278).

20 Dec 1715. Prince George's Co. Deposition of Walter Evans, Jr. aged ca. 23 yrs. regarding a mare in the possession of James Butler. (Liber CL, p. 278).

20 Apr 1716. To examine the bounds of a tract called *Friendship* in Calvert Co. (Liber CL, p. 278).

25 May 1716. Deposition of Ann Skinner of Calvert Co., widow, aged ca. 55 yrs. regarding the bounds of a tract called *Friendship* in Calvert Co.; recalls riding to church with her former husband, Andrew Tanihill; when he on several occasions showed her the Second Branch so called, it being the second branch from the old dwelling house of the said Tanihill and the deponent. (Liber CL, p. 279).

Anne Arundel Co. Deposition of Thomas Humphrey. That in June 1715 Capt. George Westgarth, mariner; Michael Hunt, the brother of Wornell Hunt, Esq. [at Annapolis]; and the deponent went from the house of Mr. Richd. Johns on board the ship Susannah in Chesapeake Bay and then proceeded on a voyage to England. And Michael Hunt left the ship at Margett Road in England. [Michael Hunt was indebted to Mr. Saml. Peel in a considerable sum.] (Liber CL, p. 279).

2 Jul 1715. Queen Anne's Co. Interrogatories to several persons touching a supposed defect in the law will of Col. Henry Coursey, regarding the devise of land called *Coursey's Choice* to James and Jane Coursey, children of said Henry. Deponents: (1) Col. Wm. Coursey; (2) Christopher Denny; (3) Mrs. Anne Denny says that Mrs. Anne Earle, decd., said the defect in the will was that of her husband, Michael Earle, who wrote the will, leaving out the words to them and their heirs for ever; (4) Briant Shield refers to Mr. Thomas Coursey, son of the said Henry, and Madm. Eliza. Coursey,

wife of the said Henry, and says that Henry Coursey mentioned his son Henry who was beyond seas, that the wife of the testator said in reference to son Henry, "my dear consider me and my four children for your son Harry Coursey has married a wife with an estate;" (5) James Earle, son of Michael and Anne Earle [dau. of the testator], recalled his mother and father talking about the defect in the will. (Liber CL, p. 281).

28 Apr 1716. Prince George's Co. To examine the evidences of the bounds of a tract called *Riley's Range*. (Liber CL, p. 284).

28 Apr 1716. Deposition of Richard Isaack of Prince George's Co. aged ca. 36 yrs. regarding the bounds of a tract called *Riley's Range*. (Liber CL, p. 285).

12 Apr 1716. Deposition of Hugh Riley, planter, Prince George's Co., aged ca. 63 yrs. regarding the bounds of a tract called *Riley's Range* at the head of Cheny's Marsh. (Liber CL, p. 285).

30 Apr 1715. Dorchester Co. To examine the evidences of the bounds of the land which William Ford, late of Dorchester Co., decd. possessed of. (Liber CL, p. 285).

12 Jul 1715. Dorchester Co. Deposition of John Hodson, Sr. aged ca. 62 yrs. relating to the bounded tree of a tract called *Hockety* (William Ford's land). (Liber CL, p. 286).

12 Jul 1715. Dorchester Co. Deposition of Francis Bullock of Talbot Co. aged ca. 76 yrs. relating to the bounded tree of a tract called *Hockety* (William Ford's land). (Liber CL, p. 286).

2 Dec 1715. Baltimore Co. To examine evidences touching the right of Peirce Welsh to a servant woman (Wealthy Taylor) lately by him replevied from Jonathan Tipton of said co. Deponents: William Welsh and Wealthy Taylor. (Liber CL, p. 287).

9 May 1715. Queen Anne's Co. To examine the evidences of the bounds of a tract called *Robinsons Farme* and the contiguous lands. Depositions of (1) Solomon Wright aged ca. 60 yrs. and (2) John Hacker aged ca. 60 yrs. regarding the tract called *Robinsons Farme* which Solomon Wright told him John Sergent bought of John Robinson. (Liber CL, p. 289).

11 7ber 1716. To examine the evidences of the boundsof a tract called *White Hall*, possessed by Mr. Samuel Gallaway and Mr. Gerard Hopkins of Anne Arundel Co. Deponents: (1) Neale Clarke of Anne Arundel Co., planter, aged ca. 49 yrs. recalls hunting with John Gaiter about 30 yrs. ago when they sat down to light their pipes... that said Gaiter was one of the first seators in these parts (meaning the head of South River). (2) John Gaitrell of Anne Arundel Co. aged ca. 53 yrs. (3) John Gaiter of Anne Arundel Co. aged ca. 37 yrs. says that his father was one of the seaters in them parts (meaning the head of South River). (Liber CL, p. 304).

21 Sep 1716. Somerset Co. To examine the evidences of the bounds of a tract called *Richardsons Ridge*, on the part and behalf of Edward Chapman and his wife Mary, plaintiffs against Thomas Powell, defendant. Deponents: (1) John Teague aged ca. 53 yrs. that he knew Richard Harris, father of afsd. Mary Chapman 5-6 yrs. before he died; that Richard

Harris departed this Province into North Carolina; that said Richard had issue living, a son and a dau. besides the plantiff Mary, before his departure for North Carolina [about 19 yrs. ago], but was informed by his widow after his decease upon her coming again into this Province, that they were dead and none then living but the plaintiff Mary. (3) John Evans of Virginia, planter, aged ca. 47 yrs. that Richard Harris died about 20 yrs. ago; the deponent married the widow of Richard Harris; that the dau. Mary was about 9 yrs. old at the time of her father's death. (Liber CL, p. 307).

30 Jun 1716. Depositions taken regarding the bounds of a tract in Calvert Co. called *Reserve* in possession of John Stinnett. (1) Thomas Edmonds, age ca. 56; (2) Robert Coverthought of Calvert Co., age ca. 55; (3) George Wade, age ca. 55. (Liber CL, p. 320).

14 Sep 1714. Kent Co. Depositions taken regarding the bounds of a tract in Kent Co. near Worton Creek belonging to Col. Nathaniel Hynson called *Buck Neck*. (1) Col. William Pearce, age ca. 73; (2) Joseph Hopkins, age ca. 36, stated that the same land belonged to him and he was at this place about a year ago with Philip Kennard, who is married to his mother, and Kennard showed him... (3) John Green, age ca. 50. (Liber CL, p. 322).

1 Nov 1716. Deposition of Edmund Norris, age ca. 61, regarding the bounds of a tract in Queen Anne Co. called *Chesterfield*. (Liber CL, p. 325).

12 Nov 1716. Depositions taken regarding the bounds of a tract in Baltimore Co. called *Beales Camp*. (1) Daniel Scott, Jr., age ca. 35; (2) John Huller, age ca. 35; (3) Symon Pearson, age ca. 56. (Liber CL, p. 326).

21 May 1716. St. Mary's Co. Depositions taken regarding the bounds of William Assistor's lands. (1) Edward Field, Sr., age ca. 64; (2) Edward Field, Jr., age ca. 25. (Liber CL, p. 328).

21 Sep 1716. Deposition of John Ramsey of Germantown in the county of Philadelphia, Pennsylvania, carpenter, age ca. 46, regarding the bounds of a tract called *Ryley's Range* in Prince George's Co. He stated that he served his apprenticeship with Hugh Ryley of North Branch of Patuxent River. About 1694, he and James Woodall, his fellow apprentice, carried the chain on the survey. (Liber CL, p. 330).

10 Jan 1716. Docket. Maurice Birchfield, Esq. vs. Michael Miller, exr. of Arthur Miller; and Arthur Miller; and William Haden, Esq.; and Philip Hemsley; and John Smith, son and heir of John Smith; and Michael Martin and et al. (Liber CL, p. 336).

5 Sep 1711. Queen Anne Co. Samuel Griffith of Calvert Co., planter, and Sarah, his wife, one of the daughters of Lewis Evans, late of Anne Arundel Co.; Katherine and Ann Evans, two other of the said Lewis' daughters present their Bill of Complaint against Christopher Vernon and Lois, his wife, extx. of said Lewis Evans. Soon after the death of Lewis Evans, his widow Lois married Christopher Vernon.
Christopher Vernon's father was in England. Interrogatories were put to William Vernon, son of the defendant; Edmund

Evans; and Elizabeth Anctill, eldest daughter of Lewis Evans and wife of Francis. (Liber CL, p. 340).

30 Apr 1717. St. Mary's Co. Depositions taken regarding the bounds of a tract in St. Mary's Co. called *Bashforde Mannor*. (1) Thomas Jameson of Charles Co., age ca. 38, and (2) Philip Tippett, age ca. 35. (Liber CL, p. 352).

29 Aug 1717. Kenelyn Cheseldyne vs. Audry Taylard, extx. of William Taylard. Deposition of Joseph Vansweringen, age ca. 35, that James Hayes paid Mary Vansweringen, widow, 9000 lbs. of tobacco. (Liber CL, p. 354).

28 Apr 1718. Deposition of Walter Phelps, age ca. 79, regarding bounds of a tract in Anne Arundel Co. called _old Land. (Liber CL, p. 356).

9 Jan 1717. Depositions taken regarding the bounds of two tracts of land-*Mearsgate* and *Nathaniel's Point*. (1) Henry Costin of Queen Anne Co., age ca. 73, that he was a servant to Edward Lloyd, grandfather of the Honorable Edward Lloyd, about 50 years ago. (2) John Newman of Talbot Co., age ca. 71, that in 1665 being newly free, became employed as an overseer by Mr. Henry Hawkins. He also stated that William Newbury lived on Mr. Hawkins' plantation. (3) James Steward, age ca. 60. (Liber CL, p. 357).

3 Aug 1717. Depositions taken regarding the birth and lineage of Edmund Plowden and Brent Nuthall of St. Mary's Co. (1) Rev. Mr. Nicholas Gulick, age ca. 70, that some 24 years ago he married John Nutthall, Jr. of St. Mary's Co. and Miss Mary Brent of Stafford Co., Virginia. (Liber CL, p. 362).

3 Aug 1717. Deposition of Susan Evans, age ca. 65, that 20 years ago this October, she was sent for as a midwife to Mrs. Mary Brent, sister to Margarett Brent and wife to John Nutthall, Jr., at the house of said Nutthall. She delivered a male child who is now known by the name of Brent Nuthall. The deponent always understood that Mary Brent was the wife of John Nutthall, and that Margaret Brent was the wife of George Plowden, late of St. Mary's Co. Both of them were sisters of William Brent of Stafford Co., Virginia, who lately died in Great Britain. The deponent further states that Brent Nuthall is the only surviving son of Mrs. Mary Brent. (Liber CL, p. 363).

6 Aug 1717. Deposition of Leonard Brooke of Allfaith's Parish, St. Mary's Co. states that Edmund Plowden has always been decreed as the legal issue of Margaret Brent and George Plowden. (Liber CL, p. 363).

23 May 1718. Depositions taken regarding the bounds of a trct in Anne Arundel Co. called *Dinah's Beverdam*. (1) John Harris, age ca. 73; (2) John Goldsberry, age ca. 52. (Liber CL, p. 363).

2 Aug 1717. Depositions taken regarding the bounds of 2 tracts in St. Mary's Co. called *Westbury Mannor* and *Bean's Creek*. (1) John Boomer, age ca. 56; (2) Richard Forest, age ca. 46; (3) Thomas Watts, age ca. 38; (4) George Clark, age ca. 25. (Liber CL, p. 365).

20 May 1718. Docket. Nathaniel Hynson, guardian of Nathaniel Hynson son of John Hynson vs. John Ward. (Liber CL, p. 412).

20 May 1718. Docket. Elsworth Bayne vs. Mary, wife of John Posey. (Liber CL, p. 413).

20 May 1718. Docket. John Smith, son of William Smith, one of many complainants against Michael Martin and Walter Storey, executors of Ann Lynes, extx. of Philip Lynes. (Liber CL, p. 418).

19 Oct 1719. Docket. James Lindow and Margaret, his wife, daughter and heir of Thomas Wilson vs. John Scott and Jane, his wife, extx. of Peter Dent. (Liber CL, p. 446).

2 Dec 1719. Deposition of Maj. Philip Briscoe, age ca. 72, regarding the bounds of a tract in St. Mary's Co. called *Luckland*. (Liber CL, p. 448).

18 Mar 1718. Queen Anne's Co. Deposition of John Hacker aged ca. 64 yrs, regarding the bounds of several tracts of land- *Nathaniel's Point* on the Wye River in Talbot Co., *Woolman's Hermitage*, *Woolman's Inheritance*, *Meer's Gate*, *Meer's Gate Addition*, and *Thrimby Grange*. (Liber CL, p. 450).

18 Mar 1718. Queen Anne's Co. Deposition of Henry Costin, age ca. 75, that he heard Col. Philemon Lloyd say that Joyce (Josie?) Cleave, wife to Nathaniel Cleave, was always buzzing him in the ears about her husband's rights to *Nathaniel's Point*. (Liber CL, p. 451).

18 Mar 1718. Queen Anne's Co. Deposition of Thomas Hinesley, age ca. 70, stated that about 40 years ago he married a daughter of Nathaniel Cleave and lived with his father-in-law. Joyce Cleave, in talking to Col. Phil Lloyd, stated her Boy Nalley and her Boy Neddy would have a pull for said land sometime or other. (Liber CL, p. 453).

20 Jul 1718. Depositions taken regarding the bounds of a tract called *The Field*. (1) James Collins of Cecil Co., age ca. 35. (2) Benjamin Cox of Cecil Co., age ca. 41, that his father, John Cox, was told by Robert Crook that he had cut down the bounded tree. About 18 years ago, he was with Thomas Cox, his elder brother by another mother, who showed him the beginning tree of a tract of land called *Sheffield*, which the aforesaid Robert Crook cut down the bounded tree. (Liber CL, p. 457).

19 Jul 1718. Depositions taken regarding the bounds of a tract called *Nathaniel's Point* in Talbot Co. (1) Henry Costin, age ca. 74; (2) Mary Sockwell, age ca. 79. (Liber CL, p. 459).

22 Sep 1719. Dorchester Co. Depositions taken regarding the bounds of a parcel called *Galerby*. (1) John Hudson, Sr. of Dorchester Co., age ca. 66; (2) John Brannock of said co. age ca. 55. (Liber CL, p. 461).

20 Nov 1718. Baltimore Co. Depositions taken regarding the bounds of a tract known as *Dickson's Neck*. (1) Andrew Anderson, age ca. 50; (2) Thomas Biddison, age ca. 44. (Liber CL, p. 463).

20 Nov 1718. Baltimore Co. Depositions taken regarding the bounds of a tract known as *Dicksons Neck*. (1) Alexander Keith, age ca. 37; (2) William Farfarr, age ca. 69; and (3) Thomas Cannon, age ca. 34. (Liber CL, p. 464).

20 Sep 1718. St. Mary's Co. Deposition of Edward Price aged ca. 54 yrs. regarding the bounds of a tract called *St. Lawrence* in St. Mary's Co. (Liber CL, p. 466).

20 Sep 1718. St. Mary's Co. Deposition of Mary Howard, daughter of Thomas Melton, age ca. 50; regarding the bounds of a tract called *St. Lawrence* in St. Mary's Co. (Liber CL, p. 467).

20 Sep 1718. St. Mary's Co. Depositin of Thomas Warren, age ca. 40, that he heard Cezar Mattingsly's wife say that she heard her mother say that she wished the land called *St. Lawrence* then purchased by John Greaves might not prejudice John Sattle, her brother. (Liber CL, p. 468).

1 Dec 1718. Depositions taken regarding the bounds of a tract called *St. Lawrence* in St. Mary's Co. (1) Cezar Mattingly, age ca. 64. (2) Nicholas Powers, son of Nicholas Powers (Liber CL, p. 468).

19 June 1716. Depositions taken regarding the bounds of a tract called *Kedger's Bite*. (1) Peter Watts, age ca. 47; (2) Thomas Watts, brother of Peter Watts, age ca. 31. (Liber CL, p. 468).

19 Jun 1718. Anne Arundel Co. Francis Lee declared an idiot who beats and abuses his own mother, wife, and children. His two children are Sarah Lee, age 4 1/2 years, and Mary Lee, age 2. (Liber CL, p. 470).

29 Jul 1718. Depositions taken regarding a lot in Doncaster Town at the mouth of the Wye River. (1) John Koss of Talbot Co., age ca. 59, that he was overseer at Col. Philemon Lloyd's, father of Edward Lloyd. (2) Edward Head of Queen Anne Co., age ca. 60 (27 Aug 1718). (Liber CL, p. 471).

15 Jul 1719. Depositions of Susannah Mackall of Calvert Co., daughter of said Gabriel Parrott, aged ca. 44 yrs. regarding the last will and testament of Gabriell Parrott of Anne Arundel Co. She stated she was present when her father was making a will about Feb. 1700, and at that time were then only living Gabrielle and Elizabeth Parker, children of said Susannah and George Parker. Four years later, when her father died, there were living besides the said Gabriell and Elizabeth Parker, aforesaid Susannah and Mary Parker--2 other daughters of the said Susannah and George Parker, and after that the deponent had another daughter by George who is now living: Sarah Parker. (Liber CL, p. 472).

15 Jul 1719. Deposition of Margaret Shaw, alias Turner, of Anne Arundel Co., age ca. 69; regarding the will of Gabriel Parrott. (Liber CL, p. 473).

26 Jun 1719. St. Mary's Co. Depositions taken regarding the bounds of a tract called *Bodle ats Knight* in St. Mary's Co. (1) Benjamin Reader, age ca. 52, declares that Margaret Philips, relict of Bartholomew Philips, should enjoy one part of the division. (2) Oswald Dar, Jr., age ca. 36, declares that he has heard his mother, who had been the relict of John McCart, say that after the death of Bartholomew Philips, his widow came over to said McCart's and used some hard words to him upon which McCarty took a tomahawk and marked a piece of land round the house of the Philip's surely to satisfy her. (Liber CL, p. 475).

26 Jun 1719. St. Mary's Co. Depositions taken regarding the bounds of a tract called *Bodle ats Knight* in St. Mary's Co. (1) John Greas__ (page torn), age ca. 53. (2) Thomas Chamberlain, age ca. 37, stated there was a jury or two upon the land called *Bodle* at the insistence of Thomas Allman, who claimed a part of same in right of his wife who was legatee of John Tongue, who was legatee of Bartholomew Philips. (Liber CL, p. 477).

16 Jul 1717. Deposition of Philip Hemsley mentions his brother,

William Hemsley, regarding the bounds of a tract called *Nathaniel's Point*. (Liber CL, p. 479).
14 Aug 1719. Depositions taken regarding the bounds of a tract called *End of Controversie*. (1) Elizabeth Mills, wife of William Mills, formerly Elizabeth Dawsey, widow of William Dawsey. (2) Joseph Kennerly of Dorchester Co., age ca. 47. (Liber CL, p. 480).
14 Aug 1719. Depositions taken regarding the bounds of a tract called *End of Controversie*. (1) Thomas Brannock of Dorchester Co., age ca. 43. (2) William Stoakes of Dorchester Co., age ca. 22. (Liber CL. p. 479).
16 Nov 1716. Cecil Co. Depositions taken regarding the bounds of a tract called *Bohemia Mannor*. (1) John Humbers, planter, age ca. 72; (2) John Bavington of Cecil Co., planter, age ca. 55; (3) Thomas Terry of Cecil Co., planter, age ca. 53. (Liber CL, p. 483).
16 Nov 1716. Cecil Co. Depositions taken regarding the bounds of a tract called *Bohemia Mannor*. (1) Thomas Mercer of Cecil Co., age ca. 53; (2) William Ward of Cecil Co., Gent., age ca. 70; (3) Herman Vanburkeloe of Cecil Co., Gent., age ca. 54. (Liber CL, p. 484).
16 Nov 1716. Cecil Co. Depositions taken regarding the bounds of a tract called *Bohemia Mannor*. (1) William Pearce, age ca. 70; (2) Benjamin Cox, age ca. 41; (3) Samuel Byard, Gent., age ca. 41; (4) Henry Slyter, age ca. 44. (Liber CL, p. 485).
29 Oct 1715. Depositions taken regarding the bounds of a tract called *Woolman's Inheritance* in Talbot Co. (1) John Newman, age ca. 71; (2) James Steward, age ca. 60; (3) Henry Costin, age ca. 73, mentions Richard Woolman, son of Richard Woolman. (Liber CL, p. 489).
Apr 1720. Docket. The Lord Proprietary vs. Edward Lloyd, a minor by Sarah Lloyd, his natural guardian. (Liber CL, p. 501).
Apr 1720. Docket. Thomas Bordley, Esq. and Rachel, his wife, admx. of John Beard vs. Margaret Macnemara, admx. of Thomas Macnemara, Esq., and Amos Garrett. (Liber CL, p. 502).
1 Jan 1716. Nathaniel Hynson of Kent Co., Gent., guardian and next friend of Nathaniel Hynson, son of John Hynson, late of Cecil Co. Case states that John Hynson in right of his wife, Mary the daughter of John Stoope, was seized of 500 ac. of land called *World's End* originally surveyed and patented in the name of Francis Childe about 1665. John Ward hoped to make himself master of the whole improvements which John Hynson had made and thereby oblige Benjamin Pearce and Mary, his wife, or Nathaniel the minor after her decease to purchase the said 50 ac. from him. (Liber CL, p. 502).
6 Nov 1719. Depositions taken regarding the bounds of *World's End* and *Urinson* in Hynson vs. Ward (above). (1) Otto Ottosen of Cecil Co., age ca. 53; (2) Thomas Prior of Kent Co., planter, age ca. 45. (Liber CL, p. 509).
6 Nov 1719. Depositions taken regarding the bounds of *World's End* and *Urinson* in Hynson vs. Ward (above). (1) Thomas Boyeth of Kent Co., planter, age ca. 50; (2) Benjamin Pearce of Cecil Co., Gent., age ca. 34; (3) John Adkey of Cecil Co., planter, age ca. 91. (Liber CL, p. 510).

26 Mar 1720. Cecil Co. Deposition of Francis Smith, age ca. 59, regarding land rents in Baltimore Co. (Liber CL, p. 513).
21 Jun 1720. Depositions taken regarding the bounds of a tract called *Cedarpoint*. (1) Josias Mace of Dorchester Co., age ca. 52; (2) Nicholas Mace of Dorchester Co., age ca. 53. (Liber CL, p. 516).
26 Jul 1720. Deposition of John Broome of Calvert Co., Gent. aged ca. 40 yrs. regarding the marriage of Basil Booth, late of Calvert Co., and the birth and lineage of John Booth. Deponent states that he was well acquainted with Basill Booth when he was courting the deponent's sister, Martha Broome now the wife of Jeremiah Sherredine. Not long after their acquaintance, Basill Booth told this deponent that he was lawfully married to said sister Martha. Basill Booth received 20,000 lbs. of tobacco from Henry Fernley, executor of Martha and John Broome's father. Booth had also made sale of a tract of land which he possessed by being lawfully married to Martha Broome. The deponent states he saw John Booth, son of Basill and Martha, 6 hours after his birth. The deponent stood Godfather at the baptism, which was published in Christ Church Parish in Calvert Co. and was requested by Basill Booth to take care of his son, John Booth, if he should be the longer liver. (Liber CL, p. 519).
26 Jul 1720. Deposition of Nathaniel Dare of Calvert Co., Gent., age ca. 60, regarding the birth and lineage of John Booth. Deponent states he has carried several letters overseas to Mrs. Booth, who lived at the Saracen head in Friday St. in London. He has often heard Mrs. Booth say that Basill Booth was her son and has sent him money several times at his request. (Liber CL, p. 521).
26 Jul 1720. Depositions taken regarding the birth and lineage of John Booth. (1) Mrs. Elizabeth Mauldin, age ca. 50. (4) Mrs. Grace Brooks, age ca. 58. (Liber CL, p. 522).
20 Jul 1720. Docket. Elsworth Bayne vs. John Mellor and Mary, his wife, and John Posey. (Liber CL, p. 535).
20 Jul 1720. Docket. James Lindow and Margaret, his wife, heir of Thomas Wilson vs. John Scott and Jane, his wife, extx. of Peter Dent. (Liber CL, p. 536).
20 Jul 1720. Docket. Rizdon Bozman and wife, extx. of Philip Sherwood vs. Thomas Ashcroft. (Liber CL, p. 537).
20 Jul 1720. Docket. Thomas Bordley, Esq. and Rachel, his wife, admx. of John Beard vs. Margaret Macnemara, admx. of Thomas Macnemara, Esq. and Amos Garrett, Esq. (Liber CL, p. 538).
20 Apr 1719. Depositions taken regarding the bounds of a tract called *Whitehaven* lying in Prince George's Co. (1) Robert Taylor, age ca. 51. (2) John Club, age ca. 57, states that about 11 years ago a division in the tract called *Whitehaven* was made by Philip Lee for his wife, Maj. Dent's relict, her dower in the same the beginning was from the above-mentioned fallen and rotten beech in Haines Branch. (Liber CL, p. 548).
8 Dec 1719. Depositions taken regarding the bounds of several tracts called *Borrough, Bowdle's Choice, Tyler's Discovery, Ridgley,* and *Tyler's Chance* in Prince George's Co. (1) Hugh

Rioly, age ca. 66; (2) John Demell, age ca. 62; (3) Humphrey Beckett, age ca. 44; (4) Mahitable Parpoint, age ca. 52. (Liber CL, p. 550).

8 Dec 1719. Depositions taken regarding the bounds of several tracts called *Borrough, Bowdle's Choice, Tyler's Discovery, Ridgley*, and *Tyler's Chance* in Prince George's Co. (1) Jane Mogbee, widow, age ca. 53, that her husband, Matt Mogbee, showed her... (2) Thomas Bennett, age ca. 44; (3) Richard Duckett and Elizabeth Bradley, who was told by her husband, John Anderson, deceased, that... (Liber CL, p. 551).

8 Dec 1719. Depositions taken regarding the bounds of several tracts called *Borrough, Bowdle's Choice, Tyler's Discovery, Ridgley*, and *Tyler's Chance* in Prince George's Co. (1) John Moberly, Sr., who married the widow of Robertson [space], deceased; (2) James Gladstone, age ca. 39; (3) Marren Duvall of Anne Arundel Co., son of Marreen Duvall, Sr. Thomas Harwood, son of Richard Harwood, was present when depositions were taken.

26 Aug 1720. Deposition of John Hacker of Queen Anne Co., age ca. 66, regarding the bounds of a parcel of land lying in Queen Anne Co. called *French Woman's* belonging to William Hiney of Talbot Co. (Liber CL, p. 557).

24 Feb 1720. Depositions taken regarding Richard Collins of Queen Anne Co. being the lawful and right heir of Thomas Collins, late of Talbot Co., deceased. (1) Edward Head of Queen Anne Co., age ca. 66, that he knew very well the grandfather of above Richard Collins in old England. He also knew Thomas Collins and Richard Collins, father of Richard Collins, Jr. aforesaid, in England and they were always taken to be brothers. The deponent came from England about 40 years ago, and the Collins brothers came over about 3 years ago. Richard Collins, Jr. was born after his mother and father were legally married. (2) John Witting, age ca. 70, declares that he knew Richard Collins was married to the widow Hampleton. (3) John Hamour, Sr., age ca. 66. (Liber CL, p. 573).

23 Jul 1721. Depositions taken regarding the bounds of a tract called *Taylor's Pride* lying in Talbot Co. (1) Joseph James of said county, age ca. 69; (2) Stephen Rushoon, age ca. 49; (3) Richard Burgesse, son of John Burgesse deceased, age ca. 32. (Liber CL, p. 575).

9 Feb 1721. Depositions taken regarding a tract of Richard Moy of St. Mary's Co., Gent. (1) Richard Moye of St. Mary's Co., planter, age ca. 23 states the land of Darby Carter, his brother-in-law... (2) Elizabeth Hlintifso of St. Mary's Co., spinster, age ca. 30. (Liber CL, p. 577).

9 Feb 1721. Depositions taken regarding a tract of Richard Moy of St. Mary's Co., Gent. (1) Thomas Ward of St. Mary's Co., age ca. 26, that William Maria Farthing sent for him by his brother, John Farthing, concerning the sale of land by Richard Moye; (2) James Farthing of St. Mary's Co., planter, age ca. 31. (Liber CL, p. 578).

10 Mar 1719. Deposition taken regarding the right of John Clements of Dorchester Co. to a lot of land in Cambridge. Deposition of Thomas Taylor of Dorchester Co., age ca. 32, that he had discourse with Col. Thomas Ennalls about a lot in

Dorchester Co. that formerly belonged to the deponent's grandfather, Maj. Thomas Taylor, Sr. of said county, which was then supposed to belong to John Clements. (Liber CL, p. 580).

10 Mar 1719. Deposition of Arthur Wrightly, age ca. 60, regarding the right of John Clements of Dorchester Co. to a lot of land in Cambridge. Depondent declares the Court House of Dorchester Co. now stands on the lot belonging to John Clements. (Liber CL. p. 581).

10 Mar 1719. Depositions taken regarding the right of John Clements of Dorchester Co. to a lot of land in Cambridge. (1) Arthur Smith of Dorchester Co., age ca. 40. (2) Charles Tomson of Dorchester Co., age ca. 39. (3) Thomas Brannock, age ca. 45. (Liber CL, p. 582).

21 Nov 1720. Depositions taken regarding Morgan Hart and Mary, his wife, and their right to a tract lying in Kent Co. called *Poplar's Neck*. Robert Down, Sr. was asked whether he knew if William Price's father had exchanged a tract which Philemon Lloyd, deceased, did possess which was commonly known by the name of *Woodland Neck* and is now in the possession of Morgan Hunt who married Mary Price, daughter of William Price, deceased. Robert Down, Sr. answered that he did not have direct knowledge, only by common report. He also stated that Mary Price was the only living child of William Price's first wife and believes her to be heir to the tract called *Poplar Neck* also known as *Woodland Neck*. (Liber CL, p. 584).

12 Feb 1721/2. Somerset Co. Deposition of Arnold Elzey, age ca. 60, says that before his mother, Sarah Ballard, would give consent that her daughter, Sarah Ballard, should be married to Randall Revell, Jr., Randall Revell (his father) should alionate and make over to the said Randall, his son, and Sarah Ballard and the heirs of their bodies 500 ac. of land which Revell's father promised to do. After Sarah's death, Randall Revell married a second wife. (Liber CL, p. 590).

12 Feb 1721/2. Somerset Co. Deposition of Charles Ballard, age ca. 50, that before his mother, Sarah Ballard, would consent that her daughter, Sarah Ballard, should be married to Randall Revell... (Liber CL, p. 591).

12 Feb 1721/2. Somerset Co. Deposition of Ann Jones, age ca. 60, says that sometime in 1683 she was at the dwelling of Robert King in Manokin with Randall Revell and Catherine, his wife, now deceased and Sarah Ballard, now deceased. Randall Revell, son of Randall Revell and Catherine (his wife), had married Sarah, the daughter of Sarah Ballard by her late husband, Charles Ballard. Edward Jones was her late deceased husband. (Liber CL, p. 592).

17 Mar 1720. John Brannock of Dorchester Co., Gent., vs. John Moll of Kent Co. regarding a dispute of the delivery of grain. John Brannock mentions his brother, Thomas Brannock, in his Bill of Complaint. Depositions from (1) Thomas Peeke, age ca. 41; and (2) Nehemiah Lecompt, age ca. 22. (Liber CL, p. 597).

27 Oct 1721. St. Mary's Co. Depositions taken regarding the bounds of a tract in St. Mary's Co. called *Watt's Lodge* and prove division of said land between Peter Rule and Thomas

Watts, both of said county. (1) Richard Forrest, age ca. 50. (2) William Thomas, age ca. 37. (Liber CL, p. 610).

27 Oct 1721. St. Mary's Co. Depositions taken regarding the bounds of a tract in St. Mary's Co. called *Watts Lodge* and to prove division of said land between Peter Rule and Thomas Watts, both of sd. co. (1) William Watts, age ca. 61. (2) Alexander Leeky, age ca. 40, declares that he was a tenant under William Wherell who married the person to whom the one moiety of said land called *Watt's Lodge* was bequested to... and showed him the dividing line between lands of Thomas Watts and his sister Wherrell. (Liber CL, 611).

17 May 1720. Prince George's Co. Deposition of Neall Clarke, age ca. 56, regarding a tract called *Ralpho* lying in Prince George's Co. bounding a parcel of land called *Happy Lott* in possession of Miss Jenifer. (Liber CL, p. 612).

11 May 1720. St. Mary's Co. Nicholas Sewell vs. John Baker, Gent. regarding the bounds of a piece of land called *St. Mary's Hill* in St. Mary's Co. The Bill of Complaint states that 200 ac. was surveyed for Capt. Cornwallis about 28 Jun 1654, which became the right of John Nuthall together with Barbara, his wife, by their deed dated about 14 Nov 1688. [Too dark to read] Elizabeth Baker, the defendent's mother who [too dark to read]. Said Elizabeth and all others that claimed the said *Cross Neck* under said Cornwallis had always peaceably and quietly enjoyed the land in dispute as part of *Cross Neck* until some short time before said Elizabeth's decease, who died about 1713. Robert Dowling and John Smith, tenant of said land under said Elizabeth and the defendant, made threats to dispose of the defendant. Depositions were taken of the following: (1) Hans Lawson of Dorchester Co., age ca. 96. (2) John Sanders of Charles Co., Gent., distinguished by the name of John Sanders of Pumfret, age ca. 50, states that 27 or 28 years ago he married Sarah Mathews, who he had been informed was heiress to part of the land where he now stands which was called *St. Mary's Hill*. (Liber CL, p. 655).

11 May 1720. St. Mary's Co. Depositions taken regardiing the bounds of a tract called *St. Mary's Hill*. (1) William Asbriton of St. Mary's Co., age ca. 51. (2) Charles Calvert of St. Mary's Co., Gent., age ca. 57, that he was told by his mother and father the hill on which he now stands was called *St. Mary's Hill*. (Liber CL, p. 656).

11 May 1720. St. Mary's Co. Depositions taken regarding the bounds of a tract called *St. Mary's Hill*. (1) Nicholas Guither of St. Mary's Co., Gent., age ca. 30, was informed by his father, William Guither, who was born in St. Mary's Co. and if now alive would be 73 years. (2) Daniel Clocker of St. Mary's Co., planter, age ca. 40. (3) Alice Clocker, wife of above Daniel Clocker, age ca. 50, testifies to a promise made by Mrs. Susannah Sewall, wife of complainant, and Henry Sewell, son of complainant. (Liber CL, p. 657).

11 May 1720. St. Mary's Co. Depositions taken regarding the bounds of a tract called *St. Mary's Hill*. (1) William Jones of St. Mary's Co., age ca. 38. (2) William Johnson of St. Mary's Co., taylor, age ca. 55. (3) John Smith of St. Mary's Co., age ca. 33. (4) John Squires of St. Mary's Co.,

carpenter, age ca. 44. (Liber CL, p. 658).
11 May 1720. St. Mary's Co. Depositions taken regarding the bounds of a tract called *St. Mary's Hill*. (1) William Chandler of Charles Co., age ca. 42. (2) Jacob Williams, age ca. 39. (3) Philip Evans, age ca. 27. (4) Joseph Fitz Jefferys, age ca. 29. (Liber CL, p. 659).
27 May 1720. Thomas Bordley, Esq. and Rachel, his wife, admx. of John Beard, Esq. vs. Margaret Macnemara, widow and admx. of Thomas Macnemara, Esq. and Amos Garrett, Esq. concerning the purchase of some houses and lotts in Annapolis known as Maj. Dent's lotts. Bill of Complaint refers to Michael, a minor son of Macnemara, who was left when Thomas Macnemara went to England and died there. (Liber CL, p. 665).
12 Jul 1720. Depositions taken regarding the bounds of a tract called *Mary's Mount* lying in Anne Arundel Co. now in possession of John Miles of Baltimore Co. (1) John Woodin of Anne Arundel Co., planter, age ca. 70. (2) Richard Wigg of Anne Arundel Co., planter, age ca. 60. (3) William Richardson, age ca. 52. (Liber CL, p. 675).
19 Sep 1721. Cecil Co. Depositions taken regarding the bounds of a tract called *Great Bohemia Mannor*. (1) Thomas Mercer of Cecil Co., planter, age ca. 58. (2) Benjamin Cox, age ca. 46, states that he and his brother, Thomas Cox, deceased... and there father, John Cox, was overseer that cleared the road to make it a Delaware Road. (Liber CL, p. 679).
19 Sep 1721. Cecil Co. Depositions taken regarding the bounds of a tract called *Great Bohemia Mannor*. (1) Samuel Byard of Cecil Co., Gent., age ca. 46. (2) Henry Slater of Cecil Co., Gent., age ca. 49. (3) Walter Scott of Cecil Co., age ca. 50.
(Liber CL, p. 680).
19 Sep 1721. Cecil Co. Depositions taken regarding the bounds of a tract called *Great Bohemia Mannor*. (1) Thomas Jerry of Cecil Co., planter, age ca. 58. (2) Obediance Obence of Cecil Co., age ca. 60. (3) John Beetle of Cecil Co., age ca. 60. (4) William Boyer of Kent Co., age ca. 55. (Liber CL, p. 681).
19 Sep 1721. Cecil Co. Depositions taken regarding the bounds of a tract called *Great Bohemia Mannor*. (1) Col. John Ward of Cecil Co., Gent., age ca. 55. (Liber CL, p. 682).
21 Sep 1721. Cecil Co. Depositions taken regarding the bounds of a tract called *Great Bohemia Mannor*. (1) Richard Ford of Cecil Co., age ca. 47. (2) Harman Van Burkelo of Cecil Co., Gent., age ca. 59, testified that Ephraim Harman, uncle to the present Ephraim Augustine Harman... (3) Thomas Boyer of Kent Co., planter, age ca. 50. (Liber CL, p. 683).
21 Sep 1721. Cecil Co. Depositions taken regarding the bounds of a tract called *Great Bohemia Mannor*. (1) Elizabeth Keys of Cecil Co., widow, age ca. 50, that about 9 years ago she lived with her husband, Henry Pennington, on Col. Thompson's old plantation upon north side of Bohemia Mannor, and she had occasion to go down to her father's, Richard Boyer, then in Cecil Co. (2) William Freeman of Cecil Co., age ca. 53. (3) Charles Bobt of Cecil Co., age ca. 18. (Liber CL, p. 684).
20 Feb 1720. Docket. William Stone of Charles Co., Gent.; Daniell Jenifer of Charles Co., Chirurgeon, and Elizabeth,

his wife, extx. of John Rogers, Gent. vs. Philemon Lloyd, Esq. (Liber CL, p. 691).

20 Feb 1720. Mordecai Hammond of Anne Arundel Co. and Frances, his wife vs. Carpendor Lillingstone of Queen Anne Co., Gent. The Bill of Complaint states that Frances, wife of Mordecai Hammond, was one of the daughters of John Lillingstone of Queen Anne Co., Clerk, deceased, and one of the legatees of Richard Marklin of Talbot Co., deceased, and that Richard Marklin left his personal estate to be divided among the 4 young children (a son and 3 daughters) of said John Lillingstone. Dr. Edward Chatham was appointed executor, who later renounced himself as executor. (Liber CL, p. 695).

28 Oct 1721. Charles Co. Depositions taken regarding a parcel of land lying in Charles Co. containing 170 ac. in possession of Philip Hoskins, Esq., deceased; and upon his death in possession of Oswald Hopkins, now deceased, brother of Bennett Hopkins, a minor. (1) William Thompson, age ca. 66, that John Cockshutt came into this county with his wife and 2 children and had rights for 2200 ac. Cockshutt died before he put up rights in execution. His widow later married Nicholas Causoon, reputed to be a French man, and said widow gave her husband Causoon rights to 1000 ac. of above mentioned land. The remainder she gave to her 2 daughters, Mary and Jane Corkshutt [also referred to as Ann and Jeane]. Nicholas Causoon died and left his widow and one son named Ignatius Causoon. Afterwards, his widow married a surveyor, John [or Robert?] Clark and shortly after died. Her son took possession of his father's lands. This deponent was married to Bennett Hoskins mother's sister and has a tract of land lying contiguous. (Liber CL, p. 706).

28 Oct 1721. Charles Co. Deposition of John Sanders, age ca. 51, taken regarding a parcel of land lying in Charles Co. containing 170 ac. in possession of Philip Hoskins, Esq. Deponent stated he knew of an Ignatius Mathis who is said to be the son of Jane Corkshutt. John Causeen was reputed to be the heir to the above-mentioned land. Ignatius Causeen married the daughter of this deponent. (Liber CL, p. 707).

28 Oct 1721. Charles Co. Depositions of William Mathis, age ca. 47, regarding a parcel of land lying in Charles Co. containing 170 ac. in possession of Philip Hoskins, Esq. Deponent stated he was the son of the daughter of the above-mentioned John Cockshutt, and that he sold part of the tract he had by his mother to Col. Philemon Lloyd, which land is now in dispute. (Liber CL, p. 708).

16 Mar 1720. Depositions taken regarding a tract called *Langley* in Talbot Co. (1) Caleb Ilgato of Talbot Co., planter, age ca. 80. (2) Francis Armstrong of Talbot Co., age ca. 30. (3) Hannah Tate of Talbot Co., age ca. 80, stated that Thomas Bartlett, father of present Thomas Bartlett, owned a plantation on which Mary Skillington, now the wife of Richard Cooper, lived. (4) Mary Cooper, wife of Richard Cooper, age ca. 82. (Liber CL, p. 710).

25 Jul 1721. Deposition of William Fenton, age ca. 70, that about 15 years ago he was informed by George Hathaway, son of Kowland Hathaway... regarding a tract lying in Baltimore Co. called *Ridby*. (Liber CL, p. 712).

12 Jun 1720. Deposition of James Hayes, age ca. 34, regarding a tract in Dorchester Co. called *Widow's Purchase*. (Liber CL, p. 714).

24 Apr 1722. Queen Anne's Co. Depositions taken regarding the right and title to a tract in Kent Co. called *Utreck* in dispute of Richard Cole of Queen Anne's Co. and William Clayland of Talbot Co. (1) Daniel Pearce, age ca. 44, that about 14 years ago he was with Anthony Ivy of Queen Anne's Co. and Anna Stevenson, relict of Edward Stevenson of Talbot Co. Ivy claimed the land in right of his wife by Robert Smith, Esq. of Talbot Co. He further stated that Anna knew Robert purchased said land for her husband. (2) John Sutton, age ca. 56. (Liber CL, p. 732).

24 Apr 1722. Queen Anne's Co. Deposition of Charles Hollingsworth, age ca. 61, regarding the right and title of a tract in Kent Co. called *Utreck* testified that William Comegys was the uncle of Anna Stevenson. (2) Deposition of Christopher Bateman, age ca. 64. (Liber CL, p. 733).

24 Apr 1722. Queen Anne's Co. Deposition of Elizabeth Salsbury, age ca. 57, regarding the right and title of a tract in Kent Co. called *Utreck* that she heard her husband, William Salsbury, say several times that he paid 80 lbs. to Edward Stevenson of Talbot Co., deceased, for Esq. Smith. (Liber CL, p. 734).

24 Mar 1721/2. Depositions taken regarding the bounds of a tract in Charles Co. called *Mudd's Rest*. (1) Bowling Speak, age ca. 48, that about 13 years ago he was purchasing a tract of land called *Mudd's Rest* from Barbary Mudd, daughter of Thomas Mudd. (2) Henry Mudd, age ca. 36. (Liber CL, p. 736).

9 Jun 1721. Depositions taken regarding the bounds of a tract called *St. Laurence's Freehold* and another tract called *Freehold of Land*. (1) Derrick Browne of St. Mary's Co., planter, age ca. 73. (2) John Greenwell of St. Mary's Co., Gent., age ca. 40. (3) John Heard of St. Mary's Co., planter, age ca. 40, that his mother was seized of a tract of land of Clement Hill. (Liber CL, p. 738).

4 May 1722. Depositions taken regarding the bounds of 3 tracts called *Waldridge, Broome,* and *Hoggneck* all in Anne Arundel Co. (1) Neale Clark, age ca. 58. (2) Thomas Reynolds, age ca. 60. (3) Joseph White, age ca. 35. (Liber CL, p. 740).

4 May 1722. Depositions taken regarding the bounds of 3 tracts called *Waldridge, Broome,* and *Hoggneck* all in Anne Arundel Co. (1) Alexander Warfield, age ca. 44. (2) Francis Hardesty, age ca. 44. (3) James Forrest, age ca. 28. (4) Orlando Griffin, age ca. 34. (5) Charles Griffin, age ca. 28. (Liber CL, p. 741).

4 May 1722. Depositions taken regarding the bounds of 3 tracts called *Waldridge, Broome,* and *Hoggneck* all in Anne Arundel Co. (1) Robert Tyler, age ca. 50. (2) Richard Warfield, age ca. 60. (3) Robert Hewett, age ca. 60. (4) Thomas Worthington, age ca. 30, that some time in January or February last, at the home of John Gatrell and Jane, his wife, ... (Liber CL, p. 742).

8 Oct 1721. Depositions taken regarding the right of Brent Nuthall to title of a tract in St. Mary's Co. called *Crop Mannor*. (1) Robert Clarke of St. Mary's Co., age ca. 71, that

he very well knew John Nuthall the elder, the grandfather of Brent Nuthall, and that he and the deponent were the same age, except that said John was as much older than the deponent as March til November. The deponent would be 71 on the fifth of November next. (2) Levina Twisden of St. Mary's Co., age ca. 71, that she knew John Nuthall, the great-grandfather of Brent Nuthall and father of John Nuthall, the grandfather of said Brent Nuthall. John the great-grandfather lived on land called *Crop Manor* about 54 years ago, when she came into this country, and where he died about 53 years ago last July. (3) William Combs of St. Mary's Co., age ca. 50. (4) Charles Calvert of St. Mary's Co., Gent., age ca. 59, who was son of William Calvert. (Liber CL, p. 748-750).

25 Jun 1722. Depositions taken regarding the birth and lineage of Gerrard Slye of St. Mary's Co., being the son and heir of Capt. Gerrard Slye of St. Mary's Co. and Jane Saunders of St. Mary's Co., sometime of Great Britain. Jane Saunders came into this province out of England about 40 or 50 years ago with the then Lady Baltimore, and that Jane soon after married Capt. Gerrard Slye. (1) Dorothy Gale of Charles Co., widow, age ca. 70, stated that Mr. Massey, a priest, and Mrs. Francis Rodes, wife to Abraham Rodes, came in the company with then Jane Saunders on the same ship from England about 51 years ago. Jane Saunders showed this deponent a key she was sent by her cousin Bouky from England. Gerrard Slye of Bushwood in St. Mary's Co. is the eldest son of Capt. Gerrard Slye and Jane, his wife, and that there was another son called Charles Slye. (2) Elizabeth Mahoney of St. Mary's Co., widow, age ca. 58, stated her mother, Susanna Cooksey, was nursemaid to Gerrard Slye. (3) James French of St. Mary's Co., age ca. 72. (4) Mrs. Elizabeth Cole of St. Mary's Co., widow, age ca. 53, that she was sister to Capt. Gerrard Slye by the same mother and father. To the best of her remembrance, she was 7 years old when Capt. Gerrard Slye was married to Miss Jane Saunders, an English Gentlewoman. About 3 years after their marriage, Jane Saunders went to England to look after her affairs and returned with goods and servants. (5) Edward Field of St. Mary's Co., age ca. 74, heard that Jane Saunders was from Worcestershire, England and that she asked her husband to name a tract of land called *Bushwood* after the name of *Piper's Hill* in remembrance of a tract called that name in Worcestershire where she claimed a right. Robert Slye of Bushwood, father of said Capt. Gerrard Slye, was married to Susanna, eldest daughter of Thomas Gerrard, Esq. formerly of New Hall in Lancashire, England. (6) George Keith, age ca. 90. (7) Maj. Nicholas Sewell of St. Mary's Co., age ca. 67, son of the Lady of the Lord of Baltimore, stated that Jane Saunders was big with child and while in London asked Lord Baltimore to be the godfather. She professed to be of the Church of England when first arriving in this county. (8) Mrs. Ann Duckworth, age ca. 70. (9) Daniell Henley, age ca. 70, that about 40 years ago, Capt. Gerrard Slye, his wife Jane, and their 2 sons went together to England. Thomas Gerrard had 3 sons, the eldest named Justinian, then Thomas and John, who are now dead

without issue. (Liber CL, p. 751-762).

17 Jul 1722. Maurice Birchfield, Esq. for his Majesty vs. Michael Miller, son and executor of Michael Miller; Arthur Miller; Thomas Smith; Edward Scott; Ann Miller; Edward Sweatnam; William Ashley; and Alice Weeks. The Bill of Complaint states that about 1698, Michael Miller died and in his will devised his estate to his sons, Michael and Arthur Miller, Alice Weeks his daughter, and Ann Miller his wife. (Liber CL, p. 763).

21 Jul 1722. Docket. Maurice Birchfield, Esq. for his Majesty vs. John Smith, son and heir at law of William Smith; Michael Martin and Walter Storey, executors of Ann Lynes and William Bladen's representatives. Philip Lynes died ca. 1709, leaving in his will his estate to his wife, Ann Lynes. William Bladen, Esq. and Mary Conlee, who was lately married with Philemon Hemsley of Queen Anne Co., Gent.. (Liber CL, p. 778).

21 Sep 1722. St. Mary's Co. Deposition of George Reed of St. Mary's Co., planter, age ca. 39. (Liber CL, p. 794).

19 Jul 1722. Thomas Larkin, admr. of John Leckie, deceased vs. Francis Campbell. Depositions from: (1) Mary Smith, age ca. 31, that while sick in bed, John Leckie gave her a purse to hold. (2) Edward Smith, age. ca 39, that his wife told him that John Leckie gave her a purse to hold. (3) Mary Stanton, age ca. 35. (Liber CL, p. 798).

4 Dec 1722. Docket. James Lloyd vs. David Robinson and Judith, his wife; Rebecca Tibballs; and John Robinson and Grace, his wife. (Liber CL, p. 804).

4 Dec 1722. Docket. Roger Boyce vs. Luke Howard and Grace, his wife. (Liber CL, p. 805).

4 Dec 1722. Docket. Lydia Reid, wife of James Reid vs. James Reid, her husband. (Liber CL, p. 805).

26 Jun 1722. Depositions taken regarding the bounds of a tract in Calvert Co. called *Gunmat(?)* and the right of Abraham Russell of Calvert Co. to it. (1) John Davis of Calvert Co., age ca. 80, that he knew John Russell, Sr. who was possessed of land where Grace Morgan now lives, and he knew of no one pretending rights to land during the lifetime of said John Russell, now deceased, or in the lifetime of his son, John Russell, now deceased. (2) John Taman of Calvert Co., age ca. 83. (3) William Davis of Calvert Co., age ca. 32. (4) William Morgan of Calvert Co., age ca. 37, that he heard his brother, David Morgan, say that John Russell, Sr. bought the land and that Grace Morgan was the widow of David. (Liber CL, p. 806, 807).

19 Feb 1722/3. Thomas Brooke, Esq. vs. John Rousby, Esq. Bill of Complaint states that the widow of George Plaiter of Calvert Co. married the defendant. (Liber CL, p. 808).

10 Jan 1720. Docket. Ann Frisby, extx. and widow of William Frisby of Kent Co. (Liber CL, p. 812).

26 Feb 1722. Docket. Ariana Frisby, extx. and relict of James Frisby of Cecil Co. and Peregrine Frisby, brother of said James. (Liber CL, p. 815).

10 Jan 1722. Docket. Henry Ennalls on behalf of his son, Thomas Ennalls vs. John Clements. (Liber CL, p. 831).

10 Jan 1722. Queen Anne Co. Depositions taken on behalf of

James Earle to prove that John Loydale or Lydall was an alien born and never naturalized. Bill of Complaint states that George Robier, Gent., was the son and heir of Thomas Robier, late of Talbot Co., Gent.. (1) Christopher Denny, stated that John Loydall was the commander of a vessel and died in Jamaica. He was said to be a Dutchman and married one of the deponant's sisters. (2) Ann Denny, that 20 odd years ago, Loydall was reported to be dead. He had married one of her sisters, and said sister removed to Carolina and sent letters that she had again married. (3) Elizabeth Parsons. (4) Anne Marshall stated that John Loydall and her mother were both born in Amsterdam. (Liber CL, p. 835-841).

20 Nov 1722. Depositions taken regarding the will of Col. Thomas Smithson, late of Talbot Co. (1) John Bradshaw, age ca. 63. (2) Jane Gray of Talbot Co., widow, age ca. 65, stated that Thomas Smithson died ca. Mar 1713. (3) William Woods of Talbot Co., age ca. 31. (4) Ambrose Woods of Talbot Co., planter, age ca. 24. (5) Abigail Wise, widow, of Talbot Co. age ca. 80. (6) John Carr of Talbot Co., Chyrurgion, age ca. 61. (Liber CL, p. 841-848).

27 Feb 1717. Depositions taken regarding the birth and lineage of Charles Somerset Smith of Calvert Co. (1) Sarah Clagett, age ca. 55, that she was acquainted with Capt. Richard Smith, late of Calvert Co. and Maria Johanna, his reputed wife, who went by the name and title of Madam Lowther. Within a year of their marriage, this deponant was present at the birth of Charles Somerset Smith, the youngest of Capt. Smith's children, and that she stood godmother at his christening. (2) Capt. Thomas Clagett, age ca. 40, that Capt. Richard Smith and Madame Lowther were reputed to be married at Christ Church in Calvert Co. by Mr. Hugh Jones, a clergyman of the Church of England. (3) Patrick Hepburne, Gent., age ca. 55, that Josiah Wilson, late of Prince George's Co. deceased, told his deponant he was present at the wedding of Capt. Richard Smith and Maria Johannah Lowther, relict of Col. Lowther. (Liber CL, p. 849).

6 Nov 1722. Depositions taken regarding a tract in Queen Anne Co. called *Camberwell* in the possession of James Gould of Queen Anne Co. (1) Charles Lowder of Queen Anne Co., age ca. 51, that the land was in the possession of Christopher Pindor about 14 years ago and that he gave it to his son, Alexander Pindor, who since sold it to James Gould. (2) Humphrey Wells of Queen Anne Co., age ca. 42. (Liber CL, p. 851).

18 Jan 1722. Depositions taken regarding a dispute involving the last will and testament of Michael Curtis, late of St. Mary's Co. (1) Gerrard Slye, age ca. 43. (2) Justinian Jordan, age ca. 37. (3) Robert Satt of St. Mary's Co., Clerk, age ca. 55. (Liber CL, p. 853).

27 May 1723. Depositions taken regarding a tract in Queen Anne Co. called *Poplar Neck* owned by William Berry, late of Talbot Co. who died and left it to Rebecca Ridley, his daughter. (1) Robert Merydith of Queen Anne Co., age ca. 61. (2) William Wheeler, age ca. 36. (3) Edward Richards, age ca. 44. (4) William Swift, age ca. 48. (Liber CL, p. 856).

8 May 1722. Depositions taken regarding the bounds of a tract in Dorchester Co. called *Hog Island*. (1) Amos Cahall of

Dorchester Co., planter, age ca. 52. (2) Robert Jones of Dorchester Co., planter, age ca. 39. (3) Thomas Sockwell of Talbot Co., age ca. 51. (4) John Hendrick of Talbot Co., age ca. 51. (Liber CL, p. 861).

13 Apr 1722. Depositions taken regarding the bounds of a tract in Charles Co. called *Christian Templemanor* owned by Thomas Bladen of London, Gent.. (1) Prior Smallwood, age ca. 42, that his father, Col. James Smallwood, showed him a red oak which was a bound tree of *Christian Templemanor*. (2) William Connell, age ca. 29. (Liber CL, p. 862).

17 Jun 1720. Deposition of John Hodson, Sr. age ca. 67, regarding the bounds of a tract adjoining a tract of John Jenkins' lying in Dorchester Co. (Liber CL, p. 863).

5 Dec 1722. Depositions taken regarding the bounds of a tract of William Young of Calvert Co. called *Hap*. (1) Matthew Gardner of Calvert Co., age ca. 45, that his father-in-law John Wilson and Thomas Bloomer were formerly the owners of land called *Hap at a Venture*. (2) Elizabeth Konifer of Calvert Co., age ca. 60, that her former husband was Thomas Bloomer. (3) Catherine Grover of Calvert Co., age ca. 65, that her former husband was John Winnall. (Liber CL, p. 865).

20 Apr 1723. Depositions taken regarding a tract called *Baltimore's Gift* in Charles Co. (1) Thomas Simpson, age ca. 60. (2) Phillip Scrivous, age ca. 50, that about 16 years ago he was overseet to Mr. Diggs on a plantation at Budd's Creek. (3) Edward Stonestreet, age ca. 50, that about 20 years ago his father, Thomas Stonestreet... (4) John Crane, age ca. 49. (Liber CL, p. 866).

18 Jul 1721. The Bill of Complaint in a case involving a dispute of land stated the following: William Calvert, Esq. about 1662 had a parcel of land lying then in Charles Co., now Prince George's Co., called *Pisscattaways* also known as *Elizabeth Manor* containing about 3000 ac. This was granted to him by the Honorable Cecilius Calvert, Proprietary of this Province. Calvert sold 2400 ac. reserving 600 ac. for his daughter, Elizabeth Calvert who married James Neale of Charles Co., Esq. Their daughter Mary married Charles Edgerton of St. Mary's Co. Charles Calvert, Gent., was a son and heir of said William Calvert. Richard Calvert was a younger brother of Charles Calvert. Richard Calvert died at the house of William Young. Charles Calvert resided in Stafford Co., Virginia at some time. The following depositions were taken between 1 May 1722 and 8 May 1722 at Prince George's Co. (1) Joshua Doyne of St. Mary's Co., Gent., age ca. 52. (2) James Neale, Jr., son of James Neale. (3) James Stoddart of Prince George's Co., Esq., age ca. 54. (4) Ann Nations of Prince George's Co., age ca. 38. (5) Walter Storey of Charles Co., Gent., age ca. 56. (6) Mary Van Sweringen of St. Mary's Co., widow, age ca. 39. (7) James Neale, Jr. of Charles Co., age ca. 27, that Richard Calvert came to his brother Charles and told him that James Neale was about settling the 600 ac. on his daughter Elizabeth in order to cheat his daughter Mary, who was the issue of the daughter of --- Calvert and asked him to transfer his right to him. He further said he would manage the said James Neale, upon which Charles Calvert told Richard Calvert, what would it

signify; he has already made over his right and claim to 600 ac. to James Neale. (8) Robert Bowling, age ca. 50. (9) David McGill, age ca. 40. (10) James Neale, Esq. (13 Sep 1722), stated that William Calvert by deed of settlement made between James Neale, father of deponent, and Ann his wife, and the said William Calvert and Elizabeth his wife of the one part; and this deponent and Elizabeth Calvert the daughter of the said Elizabeth Calvert of the other part... and that his daughter, Mary, by his wife Elizabeth Calvert married Charles Edgerton. (Liber CL, p. 868-888).

5 Sep 1718. A Bill of Complaint cites Joseph Brown, son of Peregrine Brown the elder, and Peregrine Brown, Jr., son of Peregrine Brown, Sr. (Liber CL, p. 889).

9 Jul 1723. Docket. John Taylor vs. Patrick Simpson, Richard Lancaster, James Lloyd Esq. and Ann his wife, John Oulcherlony, Samuel Chew, Elishar Hall and Elizabeth his wife, Ann Jones, and Ann Gordon. (Liber CL, p. 901).

9 Jul 1723. Docket. William Combes and Elizabeth, his wife vs. John Mills. (Liber CL, p. 901)

6 Sep 1723. Depositions taken regarding the bounds of a tract in Cecil Co. bordering on the Elk River called *St. John's Mannor* containing about 3000 ac. in possession of Herman Kenkie of Cecil Co. (1) John Renfro of Chester Co., Penn., farmer, age ca. 62, that about 40 years ago he lived with George Oldfield as an indentured servant for ten years on a plantation on the Elk River. (2) Sampson George of Cecil Co., planter, age ca. 58. (3) Ann Holy of Cecil Co., age ca. 48. (4) Ralph Rutter of Cecil Co., planter, age ca. 80. (Liber CL, p. 905)

13 Oct 1723. Baltimore Co. John Hall, Esq. vs. William Greenfield. Bill of Complaint states that William Greenfield, during his minority, was by his father, Thomas Greenfield. William Greenfield at age 12 or 13 was bound to Jonathan Hemson, a millwright and house carpenter. John Hall was placed as guardian to William Greenfield, who would receive a small estate at age 21. (Liber CL, p. 913).

27 May 1723. Ephraim Augustine Herman vs. Vachell Denton. Bill of Complaint states that in 1661 Augustine Herman, the complainant's grandfather whose heir at law the complainant is, had a certificate for a tract of land on the east side of the Chesapeake Bay in a branch of the Elk River called *Bohemia River*. Part of the tract came by assignment to Henry Denton, the defendant's father, in 1687. The defendant's father died 3 or 4 months after he was born ca. 1696. The complainant's father was Casparius Augustine Herman. Depositions taken: (1) Herman Van Burkelo of Cecil Co., Gent., age ca. 60. (2) Walter Scott, age ca. 51. (3) Humphrey Cahoon, age ca. 62. (Liber CL, p. 918).

27 May 1723. Depositions taken regarding a tract of land called *Bohemia River*. (1) John Smith of Cecil Co., age ca. 37. (2) John Cheek of Cecil Co., age ca. 41, that about 30 years ago his father-in-law John Evet came to settle on land called *Middle Neck*. The deponent and his 4 brothers used to go hunting. (Liber CL, p. 919).

27 May 1723. Depositions taken regarding a tract of land called *Bohemia River*. (1) Peter Bouchelse of Cecil Co.,

Gent., age ca. 28, asked his father-in-law Peter Sluyter also known as Vorsman about land he was surveying. He heard his father-in-law say he was 78 years sometime before he died, which was 1 Oct last. (2) Samuel Bouchell of Cecil Co., age ca. 41. (3) John Janart of Cecil Co., Gent., age ca. 53, that he had been told by the complainant's mother with whom he had married, that Casparius Herman had been her former husband. (Liber CL, p. 920).

1st Tues of Dec 1723. Docket. John Oldham, Sr. vs. Sibilla Coward, Charles Markland and Mary his wife. (Liber CL, p. 944).

14 May 1723. Depositions taken regarding the bounds of a tract called *St. Augustine's Mannor* in Cecil Co. (1) John Ward of Cecil Co., Gent., age ca. 52. (2) William Freeman of Cecil Co., age ca. 53. (3) Phillip Hollenger of Kent Co., planter, age ca. 51. (4) Stephen Onion of Cecil Co., planter, age ca. 50. (Liber CL, p. 949).

14 May 1723. Depositions taken regarding the bounds of a tract called *St. Augustine's Mannor* in Cecil Co. (1) Thomas Christian of Kent Co., planter, age ca. 55. (2) Walter Scott of Cecil Co., Cordwainer, age ca. 51. (3) 15 May 1723 - John Ryland of Cecil Co., planter, age ca. 50, that about 40 years ago he moved from the other side of the Sasafras River with his father-in-law Thomas Yorberry to Bohemia and settled a plantation there. Eleanor, wife of Simon Spear, went in place of her husband who was a lame man, getting his lameness in the Indian Wars. (Liber CL, p. 950).

14 May 1723. Depositions taken regarding the bounds of a tract called *St. Augustine's Mannor* in Cecil Co. (1) William Boulding of Cecil Co., planter, age ca. 57, that he heard his father-in-law Edward Jones say that Augustine Herman, by his cunning, would enlarge his mannor 3 or 4000 ac. (2) Allice Ryland of Cecil Co., age ca. 57, that 39 or 40 years ago Simon Sopear and Eleanor his wife came from Virginia to Bohemia and settled. She heard her brother, John Bavington, say that... (Liber CL, p. 951).

14 May 1723. Depositions taken regarding the bounds of a tract called *St. Augustine's Mannor* in Cecil Co. (1) Elizabeth Brockson of Cecil Co., age ca. 64, that her former husband was Thomas Yerberry. (2) Otto Ottoson of Cecil Co., Gent., age ca. 56, that his mother died about 51 years ago at Appoquininy to whose burying came his uncle Herman Othoson from Christien. (3) John Boomgardian of Cecil Co., age ca. 34. (Liber CL, p. 952).

14 May 1723. Depositions taken regarding the bounds of a tract called *St. Augustine's Mannor* in Cecil Co. (1) John Smith of Cecil Co., Gent., age ca. 37. (2) John Roe of Queen Anne Co., age ca. 59, that 34 years ago he lived on the head of St. George's Creek. (3) John Check of Cecil Co., age ca. 40, that about 20 years ago he lived with his father-in-law John Evitt who had a plantation on Back Creek. (Liber CL, p. 953).

14 May 1723. Depositions taken regarding the bounds of a tract called *St. Augustine's Mannor* in Cecil Co. (1) Daniel Pierce of Kent Co., Gent., age ca. 47, that he had ridden with his father, Col. William Pierce, on land in dispute. He and his brother, William Pierce, had occasion to travel over said

land. (2) Thomas Harper of Cecil Co., Farmer, age ca. 35. (3) James Van Bibber of Cecil Co., Gent., age ca. 32. (4) John Janart of Cecil Co., Gent., age ca. 53. (Liber CL, p. 954).

14 May 1723. Depositions taken regarding the bounds of a tract called *St. Augustine's Mannor* in Cecil Co. (1) Andrew Peterson of Newcastle Co., Del. that he took the deposition of John Heally of Blackbird Creek, Newcastle Co., Del., age ca. 69, on 17 Dec 1722, and that he stated Casparius Herman became the possessor of *Bohemia Manor* upon the death of his brother, Ephraim Herman. A neck of land belonged to Casparius Herman's brother, Thompson, in of his wife Judith, and there was also a neck of land belonging to his sister Franciana, which her husband Jas. [or Jos.] Wood sold. (2) William Davis, Sr. of Cecil Co., planter, age ca. 65, that about 30 years ago he went to Col. Pearce's house to his daughter's wedding who had married Thomas Church. (3) John Janart of Cecil Co., Gent., age ca. 53, that on 1 Nov 1716 he heard John Bavington, age ca. 54 say... and Guisbert Cox, age ca. 80 say... and Thomas Browning of Cecil Co., planter, age ca. 52, say... (Liber CL, p. 955).

26 Aug 1723. Depositions taken regarding Daniel of St. Thomas Jenifer of St. Mary's Co., Gent., being the son and heir of Daniel Jenifer, deceased. (1) Elizabeth Traverse, age ca. 76, that Daniel Jenifer of St. Mary's Co. married the widow Smith. After burying the said Smith, he went to Accomack, Virginia and married Mrs. Ann Toft. She always knew Daniel of St. Thomas Jenifer was called the son and heir of Daniel Jenifer and Ann his wife, and she never knew of any other son. (2) James Pattison, age ca. 65, that about 30 years ago he was with Daniel of St. Thomas Jenifer and Jacob Jenifer, his uncle who married this deponent's aunt. (3) Mary Hooper, age ca. 60. (4) John Keen, Sr., age ca. 66, that Jacob Jenifer was brother to Col. Jenifer. (5) John Robson, Sr., age ca. 53. (Liber CL, p. 972).

9 May 1723. The petition of Richard Cood, Justinian Jordan and Mary his wife, William Scot and Ann his wife, and Winifred Cood states that Richard, Mary, Ann and Winifred are children of Col. John Cood, late of St. Mary's Co., who has been deceased about 14 years. Cood left his wife, Elizabeth, sole extx.. Elizabeth then married William Hook. The deposition of Thomas Sykes of St. Mary's Co., age ca. 80. (Liber CL, p. 975).

29 Feb 1723. James Lindon and Margaret, his wife, daughter and heiress of Thomas Wilson of Somerset Co., deceased vs. John Scott and Jane, his wife, extx. of Peter Dent. The Bill of Complaint states that Thomas Wilson the elder, Margaret's grandfather, left a large personal estate to be divided among his wife, Thomas Wilson the younger, and Ephraim Wilson. Thomas Wilson the younger died before the Thomas Wilson the elder, after whose decease his widow married Peter Dent. She then died and Dent married Jane Pitman Gray. Peter Dent died, and Jane Pitman Gray Dent married the defendant Scott. The following depositions were taken: (1) Ephraim Wilson of Somerset Co., Gent., age ca. 56, that Thomas Wilson the elder was the father of himself, he being the eldest son. Thomas Wilson the younger was the father of Margaret, and she was

the only daughter and heiress who was a minor at her father's death. (2) Robert King, age ca. 34, that Jane Wilson, widow and relict of Thomas Wilson the elder, informed him that Peter Dent married with Elizabeth, the widow and relict of Thomas Wilson the younger, father of Margaret. (Liber CL, p. 979).

18 Apr 1722. William Frisby and John Dowdall vs. Gilbert Falconer, assignee of his Lordship. The Bill of Complaint states Morris Davis of Cecil Co. and Sarah, his wife, were indebted to Frisby. (Liber CL, p. 992).

Feb 1723. Docket. Anne Gordon requests that Nicholas Ridgeley be made a party to the suit against her since her marriage lately to him. (Liber CL, p. 1001).

Feb 1723. Docket. William Stone vs. James Holliday and Sarah, his wife. (Liber CL, p. 1002).

3 Jan 1723. Depositions taken regarding the bounds of a tract in St. Mary's Co. called *Guibel's Chance*. (1) Oswald Dash of St. Mary's Co., planter, age ca. 43, that his father, John Dash, told him of the bounds of said tract. (2) Thomas Chamberlain of St. Mary's Co., planter, age ca. 43. (3) John Anderson of St. Mary's Co., planter. (Liber CL, p. 1006).

3 Jan 1723. Depositions taken regarding the bounds of a tract in St. Mary's Co. called *Guibel's Chance*. (1) William Haydon of St. Mary's Co., planter, age ca. 49. (2) Richard Millard of St. Mary's Co., planter, age ca. 55. (3) Adam Boyd of St. Mary's Co., planter, age ca. 45. (Liber CL, p. 1007).

9 Apr 1723. Depositions taken regarding the bounds of a tract in Calvert Co. called *Hall's Craft*. (1) John Bowles, age ca. 57. (2) Thomas Hardesty, age ca. 50. (Liber CL, p. 1010).

30 Dec 1723. Depositions taken regarding the bounds of a tract near a branch called *French Woman's Branch* running out of Tuckahoe Creek in Queen Anne Co. called *Walnutt Ridge* containing about 600 ac. whereof George Robins of Talbot Co. is now seized. (1) Sarah Saxton, age ca. 32. (2) Richard Kemp, age ca. 36. (3) William Wrench, age ca. 45. (4) Matthew Williams, age ca. 38. (5) John Worley, age ca. 50. (Liber CL, p. 1012).

19 Nov 1722. Depositions taken regarding the bounds of a tract in Baltimore Co. called *Morley's Choice* whereas John Orrick of Baltimore Co. is seized. (1) John Mask, age ca. 64, that about 44 years ago he was a servant to John Cromwell and his master and his brother, William Cromwell, told him of the bounds. (2) Maurice Baker, age ca. 47, that he was with John Gadsby, grandfather in law to the heirs of George Norman, deceased, the late owner of the land called *Morley's Choice* and was shown the bounds. (3) Thomas Welch, age ca. 28. (Liber CL, p. 1015).

16 Jul 1722. Alexander Forbes vs. Bladen's heirs and representatives. The Bill of Complaint states that Thomas Bladen is son and heir at law of William Bladen. (Liber CL, p. 1033).

13 Sep 1725. Depositions taken on behalf of Alexander Contee of Prince George's Co. to prove himself heir at law to John Contee, Esq. deceased. (1) Andrew Hopkins, age ca. 34, that about 24 years ago John Contee gave to the deponent and his two nephews, John and Alexander Contee, sons of Peter, a

piece of money. John Contee was the son of Peter Contee, and the deponent went to school in the town of Barnstable in County Devon in Great Britain with John Contee and his brother, Alexander Contee, now of Prince George's Co. The deponent lived with them in the house of their father, Peter Contee. John Contee had attended to University of Oxford. About 1712, the deponent was informed by his brother-in-law, William Arnold of Biddeford Apothecary, that John Contee, son of Peter Contee, was dead. Two days later, the deponent went to the house of Peter Contee to see his mother, wife of Peter Contee. Peter Contee had married Francis Hopkins, mother of this deponent, relict of Capt. William Hopkins of Biddeford, Merchant, and they had several children together. William Arnold married the deponent's sister. The deponent knew of no other sons of Peter Contee, except a young Peter whose mother was Francis Hopkins. (2) John Frazer of Prince George's Co., Clerk, age ca. 50, that he knew John Contee, Esq. late of Charles Co. until the day of his death on 3 Aug 1708. John Contee married Mary, late the wife of Capt. William Rogers of Annapolis. Mary was reputed to be the cousin of John Seymour, Esq., Governor of Maryland, and that his brother Thomas and sister Lynes were fond of Mary also (20 Sep 1725). (3) Thomas Dent of Charles Co., age ca. 39. (4) Elizabeth Irelland, lately called Elizabeth Berry, age ca. 50, that John Contee was born in the town of ---avestock in the County of Devon, and that in 1703 he came last into this province from Plymouth in Great Britain. He married Mary Rogers about June 1704. (Liber CL, p. 1057-1063).

12 Jun 1723. St. Mary's Co. At the request of Richard Cooper of St. Mary's Co., acting as guardian for the daughter of Thomas Cooper, 20 ac. of land was surveyed. (Liber CL, p. 1064).

22 Jun 1724. Dorchester Co. Depositions were taken regarding the proof of a mortgage between William Dorrington and Col. Thomas Ennalls, deceased. (1) Joseph White, age ca. 27, that he heard Mary, relict and widow of William Dorrington, who afterwards married John Smith, say that William Dorrington made a mortgage to Col. Thomas Ennalls. (2) Ann Rich, age ca. 39. (Liber CL, p. 1066).

2 Jul 1723. Depositions taken regarding Peter Newall's title to 100 ac. part of a tract in Dorchester Co. called *Wollenbrough* containing 900 ac. (1) Ann Jones of Dorchester Co., age ca. 46, that Peter Glent, late of Dorchester Co., deceased, had possession of part of a tract called *Wollinsbrough*. She heard him say several times that Peter Newall was his sister's son and when he died he would leave all he had to Peter Newall. (2) Sarah Fowler of Talbot Co., age ca. 38. (3) James Merchant of Talbot Co., age ca. 39. (Liber CL, p. 1075).

19 Aug 1723. Deposition of Thomas Hays, age ca. 42, regarding the bounds of a tract in Charles Co. called *The Mistake* originally granted to Robert Middleton for 200 ac. whereas Bowling Speak of Charles Co. is now seized. (Liber CL, p. 1076).

1 Oct 1723. Deposition of Col. Edward Scott of Kent Co., regarding the bounds of a tract on the east side of the

northwest branch of Lankford's Bay called *The Plaines* formerly granted to Maj. James Ringold for 600 ac. whereas William Ringgold of Kent Co. is now seized. Scott states in his deposition that he was with Thomas Ringgold, now deceased, brother of William Ringgold several years ago and they showed him the bounds. (Liber CL, p. 1078).

4 Feb 1724. Depositions taken regarding whether Andrew Imbert, late of Queen Anne Co. Apothecary was married to Margaret Mirax. (1) John Hacker of Queen Anne Co., age ca. 70, that Margaret Mirax, widow, would never marry Dr. Imbert unless he gave her power of attorney to make a will. (2) Ann, wife of David Berry of Queen Anne Co., age ca. 37. (Liber CL, p. 1079).

12 Apr 1725. Depositions taken regarding the lineage of Gerrard Slye of St. Mary's Co. (1) John Greaves of St. Mary's Co., planter, age ca. 58, that he heard from Mrs. Elizabeth Blackistone, wife of Col. Nathaniel Blackistone, who was sister to Susanna, wife of Robert Slye and eldest daughter of Thomas Gerrard, Esq. formerly of New Hale in Great Britain; that Susanna was married to Col. John Coode after the death of Robert Slye. Capt. Gerrard Slye of Bushwood in St. Mary's Co. was acknowledged to be the eldest son of Robert Slye and Susannah his wife. Justinian and Thomas Gerrard died without issue and John Gerrard died leaving issue a son and daughter who both died without issue. (2) Thomas Sikes of St. Mary's Co., age ca. 80, believes it to be 52 years since Thomas Gerrard departed this life. It has been 55 years since Robert Slye died and Susanna married Col. John Coode, and about 44 years ago she died. Robert Slye left 2 sons, Gerrard and Robert Slye. At that time of his death, Thomas Gerrard left 3 sons-Justinian, Thomas, and John Gerrard. (3) Frances Mills of St. Mary's Co., age ca. 50, that Gerrard Slye of Bushwood, St. Mary's Co., now living is the eldest son and heir of Capt. Gerrard Slye of the same place who was the eldest son of Robert and Susannah Slye. (4) Daniel Henley of St. Mary's, planter, age ca. 74. (5) James French, age ca. 74. (6) Elizabeth Cole, age ca. 57, that Capt. Gerrard Slye, her brother was the eldest son of her father Robert Slye by Susannah her mother, and that Thomas Gerrard was her grandfather. (Liber CL, p. 1092-1095).

27 May 1723. Depositions taken regarding the bounds of land in dispute between Roger Woolford of Dorchester Co. and Capt. John Tunstale of Somerset Co. (1) John Windsor, Somerset Co., planter, age ca. 82, that his son in law Joseph Hurst lived on *South Marshes* or *Islands* now claimed by Capt. John Tunstale. (2) Elizabeth, the wife of John Windsor, age ca. 75. (Liber CL, p. 1095).

29 Nov 1723. Depositions taken regarding dispute over monies owed to Daniel Sherwood by John Oldham. (1) James Dawson of Talbot Co., Gent., age ca. 40. (MSA Vol. 4, p. 5).

30 Mar 1723. Deposition taken regarding dispute over monies

owed to Daniel Sherwood by John Oldham. (1) Sarah Dawson, wife of Robert Dawson of Talbot Co., age ca. 30. (MSA Vol. 4, p. 6)

20 Mar 1723. Deposition of William Hamilton, Jr. of Talbot Co., age ca. 23, regarding dispute over monies owed to Daniel Sherwood by John Oldham. Deponent stated that John Oldham asked this deponent if his sister, Sarah Dawson, had bought any calico from Daniel Sherwood (MSA Vol. 4, p. 7)

6 Dec 1723. Deposition of Benjamin Pemberton of Talbot Co., Gent., age ca. 25, regarding dispute over monies owed to Daniel Sherwood by John Oldham. Deponent stated that on 19 Aug 1719 at the house of Mary Plummer in Oxford, John Oldham paid Daniel Sherwood 17 shillings and 3 pence (MSA Vol. 4, p. 9).

29 Mar 1723. Deposition of William Skinner of Talbot Co., Gent., age ca. 54, regarding dispute over monies owed to Daniel Sherwood by John Oldham. (MSA Vol. 4, p. 10).

6 Dec 1723. Deposition of William Clayton of Talbot Co., Gent., age ca. 41, regarding dispute over monies owed to Daniel Sherwood by John Oldham. (MSA Vol. 4, p. 12)

6 Dec 1723. Depositions taken regarding dispute over monies owed to Daniel Sherwood by John Oldham. (1) Richard Nickson of Talbot Co., Schoolmaster, age ca. 30, that he was earlier employed to write for Mr. Foster Turbutt, then Clerk of Talbot Co. (2) Robert Ungle of Talbot Co., Esq., age ca. 65 (3) William Saunders of Talbot Co., planter, age ca. 52. (MSA Vol. 4, p. 13-16).

12 May 1724. John Caldwell vs. William Brewerton and Alexander Adams. Depositions taken at the house of Thomas Gillis in Somerset Co. 12 May 1724. (1) Jonathan Raymond, Sr. of Stepney Parish in Somerset Co., age ca. 58. (MSA Vol. 4, p. 23).

12 May 1724. Deposition of Thomas Dashiel of Somerset Parish in Somerset Co., age ca. 58; regarding Caldwell vs. Brewerton and Adams. (MSA Vol. 4, p. 24)

12 May 1724. Depositions taken regarding Caldwell vs. Brewerton and Adams. (1) Jonathan Raymond, Jr. of Stepney Parish. (2) Isaac Noble of Stepney Parish in Somerset Co., age ca. 43. (MSA Vol. 4, p. 25).

12 May 1724. Deposition of Dianna Brewerton of Stepney Parish in Somerset Co., age ca. 36; regarding Caldwell vs. Brewerton and Adams. (MSA Vol. 4, p. 26)

12 May 1724. Deposition of Joseph Manlester of Somerset Co., Esq., age ca. 39, regarding Caldwell vs. Brewerton and Adams. (MSA Vol. 4, p. 27).

12 May 1724. Depositions taken regarding Caldwell vs. Brewerton and Adams. (1) William Alexander of Stepney Parish in Somerset Co., planter, age ca. 50. (2) William Haymond of Somerset Co., planter, age ca. 56. (3) George Goddard of Somerset Co., cooper, age ca. 38. (MSA Vol. 4, p. 28).

29 Jun 1724. Depositions taken regarding Caldwell vs. Brewerton and Adams. (1) Alexander Hall, late Clerk of Somerset Co., age ca. 60. (2) Judith Raymond of Somerset Co. (MSA Vol. 4, p. 30)

12 May 1724. Deposition of Solomon Turpin of Stepney Parish in Somerset Co., age ca. 29; regarding Caldwell vs. Brewerton

and Adams. (MSA Vol. 4, p. 34).
12 May 1724. Depositions taken regarding Caldwell vs. Brewerton and Adams. (1) Robert Smith of Stepney Parish in Somerset Co., age ca. 28. (2) Peter Sherman of Stepney Parish in Somerset Co., age ca. 52. (MSA Vol. 4, p. 36).
15 Feb 1724. Kent Co. Deposition of Mrs. Hannah Waltham of said county, widow, age ca. 48, sister to William Brewerton. Alexander Adams purchased land from John Waltham, her husband, and also of William Brewerton. (MSA Vol. 4, p. 38).
15 Feb 1724. Deposition of Diana, wife of William Brewerton. (MSA Vol. 4, p. 39).
22 Feb 1723. Answer of John Docura of Prince George's Co. to complaint filed against him states his father was Thomas Docura. (MSA Vol. 4, p. 49).
4 Feb 1724. Docket. William Deacon and Mary, his wife vs. Brent Nuthall and James Angle. (MSA Vol. 4, p. 55).
6 Jan 1724. Docket. Daniel Sherwood vs. Anne Lloyde, John Hawkins, and Deborah his wife, surviving executors of Robert Grundy. (MSA Vol. 4, p. 56).
5 Feb 1724. Docket. Charles Bell vs. William Renshaw and Anne his wife, extx. of Thomas Fletchall. (MSA Vol. 4, p. 56).
27 Nov 1727. Deposition of Bryan Philpot of Newbury in County of Berks, Gent., age ca. 32 was taken at the dwelling house of John Bulley called the Virginia Coffee House in St. Michael's Alley in Cornhill in London in the cause between John Furley and John Ward. (MSA Vol., p. 65).
3rd Tues of Jul 1725. Docket. John Hydes vs. Alexander Adair and Christian, his wife. (MSA Vol. 4, p. 82).
1st Tues of Dec 1725. Docket. William Deacon and Mary his wife vs. Vitus Herbert. (MSA Vol. 4, p. 99).
7 Feb 1723. Henry Hill of Anne Arundel Co. vs. Thomas Wattkins, son of Thomas Watkins regarding a tract called *Smith's Neck* now known as *Lydia's Rest*. The Bill of Complaint states that Henry Hill was formerly of Dorchester Co. He moved to Anne Arundel Co. and purchased the tract called *Smith's Neck*. John Baldwin had devised the land to his grandson, Thomas Watkins, in his will dated 12 Jun 1683. If Watkins died without issue the land would descend to the next heir lawfully begotten of his daughter, Lydia Bittenson, mother of said grandchild. Mention is made of Edward Beetersoy [Bittenson] and Lydia, his wife. (MSA Vol. 4, p. 131)
7 Feb 1723. Depositions taken regarding a tract now called *Lydia's Rest*. (1) Anthony Ruley, age ca. 60. (2) Henry Bateman, a Quaker, age ca. 36, that his father, William Bateman, told him of the bounded tree of *Lydia's Rest*. (MSA Vol. 4, p. 138).
8 Feb 1723. Alexander Frazer of Calver Co., Gent. vs. William Deale of Calvert Co., Gent.. Frazer states in his Bill of Complaint that his wife eloped from him. In his answer, William Deale states that soon after the marriage of Alexander Frazer and Sarah, his wife, Frazer left this province for a considerable number of years, never making provision for the support of his wife and children. Deale advanced money to Sarah Frazer. Deale stated she never eloped but came to his house one night seeking refuge after

her husband kicked her out and locked the door. The next
morning, Frazer came to Deale's house and stripped his wife
naked and left with her clothes. Deale lent her some of his
servant's clothes. Depositions taken: (1) Francis
Hollandshead, that he knew Sarah Frazer when she was
Sterling's widow. (2) Alexander Deale, age ca. 17, that his
father is William Deale. (MSA Vol. 4, p. 150).

30 Aug 1725. Charles Calvert of Annapolis, Chirurgeon vs.
Charles Blake of Queen Anne Co., Gent.. The Bill of
Complaint states that Calvert made application to Blake for
permission to court Dorothy, his now wife, one of Blake's
daughters. Charles Calvert and Dorothy were married in 1723.
Calvert believed that Charles Blake's father was alive in
Great Britain. (MSA Vol. 4, p. 177-184).

30 Mar 1726. Depositions taken regarding Calvert vs. Blake.
(1) Philemon Lloyd, Esq., age ca. 54. (MSA Vol. 4, p. 184).

30 Mar 1726. Deposition of Mrs. Henrietta Maria Stringfellow,
age ca. 26, regarding Calvert vs. Blake. Deponent states
that she was the sister of Dorothy, daughter of Charles
Blake. Deposition of Madam Alice Lloyd, age ca. 45, that she
heard Mr. Blake say he would give his daughter a Negro girl
named Betty. (MSA Vol. 4, p. 187).

30 Mar 1726. Depositions taken regarding Calvert vs. Blake.
(1) Sarah Harris, age ca. 20. (2) Philemon Blake, age ca. 29,
that he was the brother of Dorothy. (3) John Blake, age ca.
30, that he was the son of Charles Blake. (MSA Vol. 4, p.
188).

24 Jun 1727. Depositions taken regarding the conveyance or
deed of sale for *Christian Temple Manor* lying in Charles Co.
from Charles Allison, son and heir at law of Thomas Allison
of Charles Co. (1) William Stone, age ca. 60, that Charles
Allison was the eldest son and heir at law of Thomas Allison.
That Charles' sister married Edward Ford. Charles Allison
fled to Virginia. (MSA Vol. 4, p. 198).

24 Jun 1727. Deposition of Richard Combes, age ca. 74, that
about 30 years ago he heard that Edward Ford purchased
Christian Temple Manor from Charles Allison while Charles was
a minor under the care of Ford. Thomas Whichaley married the
widow of Edward Ford. (MSA Vol. 4, p. 200).

24 Jun 1727. Deposition of John Speake, age ca. 62, that
Charles Allison had a son named Thomas Allison in the case
regarding *Christian Temple Manor*. (MSA Vol. 4, p. 201).

16 Oct 1729. Depositions taken regarding the release of rents
obtained by Kenelyn Cheseldyne. (1) Rev. Robert Scott,
Rector of All Faiths Parish, age ca. 62. (MSA Vol. 4, p.
205).

7 Mar 1728/9. Deposition of Samuel Williamson, age ca. 71,
regarding the release of rents obtained by Kenelyn
Cheseldyne. (MSA Vol. 4, p. 207).

16 Nov 1722. Deposition of Gerrard Slye, age ca. 43, regarding
the release of rents obtained by Kenelyn Cheseldyne. (MSA
Vol. 4, p. 208).

26 Dec 1722. Deposition of Justinian Jordan, age ca. 37
regarding the release of rents obtained by Kenelyn
Cheseldyne. (MSA Vol. 4, p. 209). 7 Mar 1728/9. Deposition
of Justinian Jordan, age ca. 43, regarding the release of

rents obtained by Kenelyn Cheseldyne. (MSA Vol. 4, p. 209).
7 Mar 1728. Deposition of Robert Elliott, age ca. 31, regarding the release of rents obtained by Kenelyn Cheseldyne. (MSA Vol. 4, p. 210).
1st Tues of Dec 1727. Docket. Edward Fetterel and Anne, his wife vs. James Dawson and Mary, his wife. It was ordered that John Hawkins and Deborah, his wife, be made complainants. (MSA Vol. 4, p. 217).
1st Tues of Dec 1727. Docket. Richard Bennett vs. George Buchanan and Margaret, his wife, and Edward Sprigg. (MSA Vol 4, p. 220).
19 May 1727. Margaret Macnemara of Annapolis, widow and admx. of Thomas Macnemara of the same place vs. Thomas Hatchman. The Bill of Complaint states that Hatchman, now an innholder in Baltimore Co., was a taylor by trade and was indentured to Macnemara for 4 years beginning ca. 1717. Depositions taken: (1) Daniel Carroll, age ca. 30. (MSA Vol. 4, p. 223-233).
19 May 1727. Depositions taken regarding Macnemara vs. Hatchman. (1) Michael Taylor, age ca. 33. (2) Mrs. Joyce Bradford, age ca. 40, that about 1717, the defendent was at work at her house. (3) Daniel Dulany, Esq. age ca. 38, that in the summer of 1718, Thomas Macnemara went to England. (4) John Wisely deposed that in the spring of 1717 or 1718, he heard of his brother's, the defendent, arrival and being a servant. (MSA Vol. 4, p. 234).
19 May 1727. Deposition of William Cummings, age ca. 30, regarding Macnemara vs. Hatchman. (MSA Vol. 4, p. 235).
16 Jul 1727. Samuel Chew vs. Alexander Adair and Christian, his wife. The Bill of Complaint states that Christian is the daughter and sole heir of Thomas Sterling, late of Calvert Co., who was seized of a tract called *Bennett*. The land was originally granted in 1658 to Richard Bennett, deceased, who assigned it to Mary Brasheer, widow now deceased. Her son, Robert Brasheer, sold the land to Thomas Starling of Calvert Co., grandfather to the defendant's wife. (MSA Vol. 4, p. 250).
3rd Tues of Jul 1729. Docket. John Brannock vs. John Eccleston, Susanna his wife, and Henry Tripp. (MSA Vol. 4, p. 275).
20 May 1729. Mary Codd, wife of St. Ledger Codd of Kent Co. vs. St. Ledger Codd. She states in her Bill of Complaint that on 8 Oct 1700 she married St. Ledger Codd in the Church of England, and that for 20 years she has suffered cruel treatment. Her husband left and built another house in which he lived and that he denied her support. He refuses to cohabit with her. St. Ledger Codd answered that he married under age and against the wishes of his father. (MSA Vol. 4, p. 275).
1 Feb 1723. William Stone of Charles Co., Gent. and James Holyday of Talbot Co., Gent. and Sarah, his wife, extx. of Edward Lloyd. The Bill of Complaint states that Sarah Lloyd, widow and extx. of Edward Lloyd, is now the wife of James Hollyday of Talbot Co. (MSA Vol. 4, p. 281).
2 Dec 1730. Depositions taken regarding the bounds of 2 tracts in Baltimore Co. called *Barely Hills* and *Howard's Chance* seized by Dr. Charles Carroll of Annapolis. (1) John

Glassington, age ca. 60, that he heard Jane Vandiver, widow and relict of John Gill late of Baltimore Co., talk of the bounded tree. (MSA Vol. 4, p. 301).

2 Dec 1730. Deposition of Charles Wells, age ca. 28; regarding the bounds of *Barely Hills* and *Howard's Chance*. (MSA Vol. 4, p. 302).

2 Dec 1730. Deposition of Patrick Murphy, age ca. 74, regarding the bounds of *Barely Hills* and *Howard's Chance* (MSA Vol. 4, p. 303).

2 Dec 1730. Deposition of Agnes Droughed, regarding the bounds of *Barely Hills* and *Howard's Chance*. Deponent states that about 24 years ago she lived with Turlow Mcleone and his widow until she was 16 years old, and that Turlow's widow married Matthew Organ. (MSA Vol. 4, p. 304).

29 Jun 1730. Depositions taken in Somerset Co. at the house of Robert Weer regarding a division line made by John Kirk, late of Somerset Co. deceased, of 2 tracts-*Kirk's Purchase* and *Overmarsh* in Somerset Co. (1) Anthony Bell of Somerset Co., planter, age ca. 72, that on 7 Aug 1714 he and his children, Thomas, Isaac, and George Bell were called to see the land called *Kirk's Purchase*. (MSA Vol. 4, p. 306).

29 Jun 1730. Deposition of Charles Cottingham of Somerset Co., planter, age ca. 55; regarding the bounds of *Kirk's Purchase* and *Overmarsh*. (MSA Vol. 4, p. 307)

29 Jun 1730. Deposition of John Kelham of Somerset Co., planter, age ca. 50; regarding the bounds of *Kirk's Purchase* and *Overmarsh*. (MSA Vol. 4, p. 308).

29 Jun 1730. Depositions taken regarding the bounds of *Kirk's Purchase* and *Overmarsh*. (1) Job Sherry of Somerset Co., taylor, age ca. 50. (2) Thomas Bell of Somerset Co., planter, age ca. 35. (3) Isaac Bell of Somerset Co., mariner, age ca. 34. (4) George Bell of Somerset Co., age ca. 32. (MSA Vol. 4, p. 309).

17 Jul 1730. Depositions taken regarding the purchase of a tract by Richard Kewellirin from William Brewer called *Batchelor's Rest* in St. Mary's Co. (1) William Hooke, age ca. 47. (2) Teresa Winsett, wife of Richard Winsett, late widow of Thomas Cooper late of St. Mary's Co., innkeeper, age ca. 25. (3) Richard Power, age ca. 36. (MSA Vol. 4, p. 310-311).

15 Mar 1730. Depositions taken regarding the age of Edward Pindor of Dorchester Co. (1) Bettingly Bronack, age ca. 43. She states Edward Pindar the younger was born in January or February of 1710. (MSA Vol. 4, p. 312).

15 Mar 1730. Deposition of Ellinor Pullen, age ca. 50, regarding the age of Edward Pindor. Deponent states that in Jan 1710 she was married to John Nowell and that Edward Pinder, son of Edward Pinder and Jane Pinder was born the same month as this deponent's marriage. Edward Pinder the younger died in January 1729. (MSA Vol. 4, p. 313).

12 Apr 1731. Deposition of Philemon Lecompt, age ca. 40, regarding the age of Edward Pindor. (MSA Vol. 4, p. 314).

31 Jul 1730. Depositions taken regarding the purchase and possession of a tract called *Ricarton* sold by Daniel Jones of Kent Co. upon Delaware, formerly of Talbot Co.; part of which is now in the possession of John Kirk of Dorchester Co. The

Bill of Complaint shows Mary Jones giving her husband her consent for his act and deed dated 3 Nov 1671. (1) Arthur Whitely, age ca. 78, that about 45 years ago John Kirk, father of John Kirk aforesaid, had possession of part of the land called *Ricarton*. (2) Margarett Smith, age ca. 53, that her father, John Kirk, had purchased the land in the Towne of Cambridge from Daniel Jones. 14 Aug 1730. (3) John Brannock, age ca. 63. 17 Nov 1730. (4) John Hodson of Dorchester Co., Gent., age ca. 55. 19 Nov 1730. (5) James Woolford of Dorchester Co., Gent., age ca 51. 26 Dec 1730. (MSA Vol. 4, p. 315).

15 Jul 1729. Docket. Thomas McWilliams vs. Thomas Guibert - abated by the death of the defendant. (MSA Vol. 5, p. 5).

15 Dec 1729. Docket. Alexander Parran vs. John Brannock - abated by the death of the complainant. (MSA Vol. 5, p. 7).

15 Dec 1729. Docket. Thomas Colemore vs. James Carrol - abated by the death of the defendant. (MSA Vol. 5, p. 7).

15 Dec 1729. Docket. Richard Bennett vs. George Buchanan and Margaret his wife and Edward Sprigg. (MSA Vol. 5, p. 8).

15 Dec 1729. Docket. John Midford vs. Nicholas Ridgeley and Ann his wife, extx. of James Gordon - abated by the death of the complainant. (MSA Vol. 5, p. 8).

15 Dec 1729. Docket. John Oldham vs. Excs. of Robert Grundy - abated by the death of the complainant. (MSA Vol. 5, p. 8).

10 Feb 1729. Mentions Ninian Mariarte, son of Daniel Mariarte, high sheriff of Anne Arundel Co. (MSA Vol. 5, p. 18).

14 Jul 1730. Docket. Eleanor Addison, widow and extx. of Thomas Addison, Esq. vs. Indian Tom. (MSA Vol. 5, p. 34).

14 Jul 1730. Docket. Griffin Thomas vs. George Tull - abated by the death of the complainant. (MSA Vol. 5, p. 34).

16 Jan 1729. Richard Bennett of Queen Anne Co., Esq. vs. George Buchanan, Margaret his wife, and Edward Sprigg. The Bill of Complaint states that Richard Bennett had corresponded in trade with Robert Levett of Prince George's Co., deceased. His widow and admx. was Elizabeth Levett. Elizabeth died and her accounts were administered by Margarett, the now wife of George Buchanan of Prince George's Co., Merchant, and Edward Sprigg of Prince George's Co., Gentleman. (MSA Vol. 5, p. 34).

12 Jun 1732. Depositions taken regarding the bounds of a tract called *Cole's Caves* in possession of Charles Carrol of Annapolis, Surgeon. (1) Richard Jones, age ca. 55. (2) John Cole, age ca. 63. (3) Richard Gist, age ca. 48. (MSA Vol. 5, p. 59-61).

14 Jul 1723. Henry Darnal, Esq., Assignee of the Right Honorable Lady Baltimore, extx. of the Right Honorable Charles, late Baron of Baltimore vs. Thomas Layfield, et al Representatives of Col. William Stevens, deceased. Mentions Lady Baltimore, Margaret, the widow of Charles, late Lord Baltimore. (MSA Vol. 5, p. 62).

30 Jun 1724. Answer of Thomas Layfield of Somerset Co. in reference to above case against him. The relict of said Col. William Stevens married George Layfield, deceased, uncle of this respondant. Elizabeth, widow of Stevens, died and George Layfield married Priscilla White, with whom he had issue 1 daughter. His widow is still living in Virginia and

his daughter is in Somerset Co., wife of Peter Collier. After the death of George Layfield, Samuel Layfield father of this respondant claimed real estate as the heir at law to his brother George. The respondent's father made a will leaving most of his estate to his widow, since deceased, and a sister of this respondant living in Great Britain near Bury St. Edmonds in the county of Suffolk married to John Barham. (MSA Vol. 5, p. 67).

3 Mar 1730. Docket. John Parran, son and heir at law of Alexander Parran and Mary Parran, admx. of Alexander vs. Charles Carrol and Daniel Carrol. (MSA Vol. 5, p. 82).

3 Mar 1730. Docket. Benjamin Brayne vs. John Howell, heir or devisee of Thomas Howell. (MSA Vol. 5, p. 83).

13 Mar 1730. William Loch, Esq. vs. George Chocke and Rachel, his wife for physician's services provided. Bill of Complaint states that William Loch was a physician of Anne Arundel Co. Services were provided to Rachel, former wife of John Giles of Anne Arundel Co., deceased. (MSA Vol. 5, p. 84-96).

13 Mar 1730. Deposition of David Weems, age ca. 25, regarding Loch vs. Chocke. (MSA Vol. 5, p. 97)

13 Mar 1730. Depositions taken regarding Loch vs. Chocke. (1) Robert Franklin, age ca. 56, a Quaker. (2) James Weems, age ca. 32. (MSA Vol. 5, p. 98).

13 Mar 1730. Deposition of Dr. John Hamilton, regarding Loch vs. Chocke. (MSA Vol. 5, p. 100).

13 Mar 1730. Deposition of William Ford, a Quaker, regarding Loch vs. Chocke. (MSA Vol. 5, p. 101).

9 Aug 1731. John Parran and Mary Parran vs. Charles Carrol and Daniel Carrol. The Bill of Complaint states that John Parran is the eldest son and heir at law of Alexander Parran, late of Calvert Co. Mary Parran is the admx. of Alexander Parran. Charles Carrol and Daniel Carrol are the excs. of Charles Carrol, Esq. Charles Carrol died in 1721. Alexander Parran died in May 1729. Negroes delivered to Charles Carrol by Mary Parran were Jack, Nell, Joe, Jamey, Peter, Abigall, Moll, Sam, Nanny, Farimbo, Bess, Robin, Rose, Bess, Flora, Turah, Munday, Ben, Pegg, Sango, Hannah, Seiche, Cesar, Tenny, Will, Dick, Lucy, Sue, Harry, London, Coyne, Sambo, and Hercules. (MSA Vol. 5, p. 140).

1 Jul 1727. John Hall vs. William Holland and Francis Holland. The Bill of Complaint states that Francis Holland is the son of William Holland of Anne Arundel Co. Edward Hall is the son of John Hall. (MSA Vol. 5, p. 160-177).

14 Oct 1730. Deposition of John Lawson of Anne Arundel Co., Gent., regarding Hall vs. Holland and Holland. (MSA Vol. 5, p. 178).

14 Oct 1730. Deposition of Vachell Denton, Esq., regarding Hall vs. Holland and Holland. Deponent states a letter dated 13 Aug 1724 from William Holland to John Hall states Francis' wife requested him to make over his plantation to his daughter, Mary. (MSA Vol. 5, p. 179).

24 Mar 1723. Jonathan Forward, merchant of London vs. Samuel Peele. The Bill of Complaint states that John Goodwyn, late of London, merchant, died in 1711 leaving numerous unpaid accounts payable to him in Maryland and Virginia. John

Tucker of Viriginia has a brother named Robert. Mary Matthew is the widow and relict of Jonathan Matthew, late of London, merchant. (MSA Vol. 5, p. 194).

1 Feb 1731. Prior Smallwood of Charles Co. vs. Daniel Bryon. Bill of Complaint states that John Lane, deceased, was seized of a tract called *St. Bridgett's* containing 250 ac. in Charles Co. assigned to John Godshall who sold and conveyed a deed to Pryor Smallwood. (MSA Vol. 5, p. 212).

29 Nov 1732. Samuel Magruder vs. Edward Sprigg and Ralph Crabb. The Bill of Complaint states that Samuel Magruder, Prince George's Co., merchant, together with John Midleton (who became insolvent and since ran away out of this Province) at the request of Josiah Wilson, late of Prince George's Co., Gentleman, exex. of Maj. Josiah Wilson, his father deceased, became bound with Josiah for payment of the filial portions of the orphans of said Josiah Willson, testator. (MSA Vol. 5, p. 278).

12 Dec 1732. Answer of William Vernon, Def. to Bill of Complaint of John Kanbury, Compl. The defendent states that his father, Christopher Vernon, bequeathed a considerable part of his personal estate of Ann Vernon, the defendent's father's aunt. The defendent went home to London in 1725. (MSA Vol. 5, p. 284).

8 Feb 1727. Charles Digges vs. William Digges. The Bill of Complaint states that ca. 1714 Edward Digges, late of Prince George's Co., merchant, brother of Charles Digges, departed this life. Charles Digges and William Digges were brothers of Edward Digges. Another brother was John Digges. The answer of William Digges dated 29 Jul 1728 mentions his brother John and sister Mary Diggs. (MSA Vol. 5, p. 294-318).

18 Aug 1730. Depositions of (1) William Chandler of Charles Co., Gent., regarding Digges vs. Digges. (2) Capt. Thomas Clagett of Prince George's Co., Gent. (MSA Vol. 5, p. 319).

18 Aug 1730. Depositions taken regarding Digges vs. Digges. (1) Col. James Haddock of Prince George's Co. (2) John Digges of Prince George's Co., Gent. (MSA Vol. 5, p. 320).

18 Aug 1730. Depositions taken regarding Digges vs. Digges. (1) Phillip Key of St. Mary's Co., Gent. states that Tobias Bowles was the father of James Bowles. (2) Clement Hill, Sr. of Prince George's Co. (MSA Vol. 5, p. 321).

18 Aug 1730. Deposition of Raphael Neale of Charles Co., son of Anthony Neale, regarding Digges vs. Digges. (MSA Vol. 5, p. 322).

18 Aug 1730. Depositions taken regarding Digges vs. Digges. (1) John Thompson of Charles Co., planter. (2) Alexander Hambleton of Charles Co. (MSA Vol. 5, p. 323).

18 Aug 1730. Deposition of Leonard Green of Charles Co., planter, regarding Digges vs. Digges. (MSA Vol. 5, p. 324).

Feb 1731. Docket. Robert Alexander vs. John Cox and Mark Penn - abated by death of the complainant. (MSA Vol. 5, p. 333).

Feb 1731. Docket. Thomas Claggett vs. Phillip Lee, Esq. - abated by death of the complainant. (MSA Vol. 5, p. 337).

Feb 1731. Docket. Charles and Daniel Carrol vs. Philemon Lloyd, Esq. - abated by the death of the defendant. (MSA Vol. 5, p. 337).

Mar 1731. Mary Wooten of Great Britain, widow vs. Michael Taylor. The Bill of Complaint states that Thomas Bale, late of Baltimore Co. deceased, his wife Sarah and daughter Urah, extxs. bequeathed to Mary Wooten, then known as Mary Bale, 5 lbs. of sterling. Anthony Bale, brother to Thomas died; and Ann Bale was made extx. of Anthony Bale. Ann became possessed of Thomas Bale's and Anthony Bale's lands. Ann then married Michael Taylor of Prince George's Co., Gentleman. Ann died and Michael Taylor was possessed of said land. (MSA Vol. 5, p. 340-346).

16 Feb 1731. Deposition of Roger Mathews of Baltimore Co., Gent., regarding Wooten vs. Taylor. Deponent states that Anthony Beale bequeathed his estate to his wife, Ann, who later married Michael Taylor. (MSA Vol. 5, p. 347).

16 Feb 1731. Deposition of Joanah Hall of Baltimore Co., regarding Wooten vs. Taylor. Deponent states that she knew Anthony Bale for about 16 years since he married her sister. (MSA Vol. 5, p. 349).

16 Feb 1731. Deposition of Christopher Randall, Sr. of Baltimore Co., regarding Wooten vs. Taylor. Deponent states that the complainant demanded 10 lbs. of sterling which was bequeathed by Anthony Bale to his mother, Urah Carnell. (MSA Vol. 5, p. 351).

30 Jan 1730. Thomas Sparrow of Anne Arundel Co., planter vs. Thomas Gassaway. The Bill of Complaint states that Thomas Sparrow had the misfortune to lose his parents when he was very young and chose Thomas Gassaway of Anne Arundel Co. to be his guardian, with whom he lived 5 or 6 years. He came of age in 1720, and shortly thereafter lost the use of one of his legs. The answer of Thomas Gassaway mentions William Richardson is the uncle to Thomas Sparrow. (MSA Vol. 5, p. 354-377).

20 Apr 1732. Deposition of William Sellman, age ca. 42, regarding Sparrow vs. Gassaway. (MSA Vol. 5, p. 377).

20 Apr 1732. Deposition of Turner Wootton, age ca. 36, regarding Sparrow vs. Gassaway. (MSA Vol. 5, p. 380).

20 Apr 1732. Deposition of Samuel Burton, age ca. 50, regarding Sparrow vs. Gassaway. (MSA Vol. 5, p. 382).

21 Apr 1732. Deposition of Samuel Smith, age ca. 36, regarding Sparrow vs. Gassaway. (MSA Vol. 5, p. 384).

21 Apr 1732. Deposition of John Cotter, age ca. 34, regarding Sparrow vs. Gassaway. Deponent states that one-third of the land conveyed from Thomas Sparrow to Thomas Gassaway, possessed by William Sellman, is in the right of his wife, widow of the complainant's father. (MSA Vol. 5, p. 385).

26 Apr 1732. Deposition of William Chapman, age ca. 40, regarding Sparrow vs. Gassaway. (MSA Vol. 5, p. 388).

1 May 1732. Deposition of John Wilmott, age ca. 36, regarding Sparrow vs. Gassaway. (MSA Vol. 5, p. 390).

21 Apr 1732. Deposition of William Richardson, age ca. 64, a Quaker, regarding Sparrow vs. Gassaway. (MSA Vol. 5, p. 392).

26 Apr 1732. Deposition of David Macklefish, age ca. 29, regarding Sparrow vs. Gassaway. Deponent states that he had lived with the defendant, and that William Sellman had married the complainant's mother-in-law. (MSA Vol. 5, p.

396).
14 Jun 1731. Enault Hawkins vs. Risdon Bozman, Thomas Bullen and John Knowles. The Bill of Complaint states that John Hawkins, deceased, is the father of Ernault Hawkins of Queen Anne Co., Gentleman. James Knowles, deceased, named his brothers-in-law, Risdon Bosman and Thomas Bullen his exrs. John Knowles is the brother and heir at law to James Knowles. The answer of Risdon Bosman dated 8 Dec 1731 states that Lawrence Knowles is the father of the said James Knowles and to Francis, this defendant's wife. (MSA Vol. 5, p. 408).

8 Oct 1731. Prince George's Co. Mrs. Margery Sprigg, admx. of Maj. Thomas Sprigg, states that Sprigg was her deceased husband. (MSA Vol. 5, p. 427).

3 Feb 1728. John Abington of Prince George's Co., Gentleman and Mary, his wife vs. John Stoddert. The Bill of Complaint states that Mary Abington is one of the daughters and legal representative of William Hutchinson of Prince George's Co., merchant. He died leaving a daughter Mary, a son William, and 2 other daughters-Ann, who since married Gabriel Parker of Calver Co., Gentleman; and Elizabeth, who since married William Piles of Prince George's Co., Gentleman. All 4 children were under age at their father's death. He named James Stoddert his exec. James Stoddert died about 1726 or 1727, and named in his will 2 sons, James and John, and his wife Elizabeth, his extx. James, the eldest, died within a few months of his father. James' wife renounced her executorship, so John Stoddert proved his father's will. (MSA Vol. 5, p. 436-449).

19 Oct 1730. Deposition of George Noble of Prince George's Co., age c. 40, regarding Abington vs. Stoddert. Deponent states that William Hutchinson died ca. 1711. John Sheppard of Whitehaven, merchant, was this deponent's father-in-law. (MSA Vol. 5, p. 449).

19 Oct 1730. Depositions taken regarding Abington vs. Stoddert. (1) Charles Beale of Prince George's Co., planter, age ca. 59. (2) Edward Brawnor of Charles Co., planter, age ca. 48. (MSA Vol. 5, p. 451).

19 Oct 1730. Depositions taken regarding Abington vs. Stoddert. (1) Thomas Stonestreet of Prince George's Co., planter, age 49. (2) John Allison of Prince George's Co., planter, age ca. 51. (3) Robert Taylor of Prince George's Co., planter, age ca. 65. (MSA Vol. 5, p. 452).

19 Oct 1730. Depositions taken regarding Abington vs. Stoddert. (1) John Hanson of Charles Co., Gentleman, age ca. 49. (2) William Midleton of Charles Co., Gentleman, age ca. 45. (MSA Vol. 5, p. 453).

19 Oct 1730. Deposition of Richard Wheeler of Charles Co., planter, age ca. 47, regarding Abington vs. Stoddert. (MSA Vol. 5, p. 454).

19 Oct 1730. Depositions taken regarding Abington vs. Stoddert. (1) Robert Midleton of Charles Co., planter, age ca. 48. (2) Henry Barnes of Charles Co., planter, age ca. 56. (MSA Vol. 5, p. 455).

19 Oct 1730. Deposition of Robert Clyde of Prince George's Co., carpenter, age ca. 56, regarding Abington vs. Stoddert. (MSA Vol. 5, p. 459).

19 Oct 1730. Deposition of John Queen of Prince George's Co., planter, age ca. 45, regarding Abington vs. Stoddert. Deponent states that he married the relict of Henry Robins. (MSA Vol. 5, p. 461).

19 Oct 1730. Deposition of Edward Edelin of Prince George's Co., planter, age ca. 54, regarding Abington vs. Stoddert. (MSA Vol. 5, p. 462).

19 Oct 1730. Deposition of William Atchison of Charles Co., planter, age ca. 44, regarding Abington vs. Stoddert. (MSA Vol. 5, p. 463).

19 Oct 1730. Deposition of Joseph Noble of Prince George's Co., Gent., age ca. 42, regarding Abington vs. Stoddert. (MSA Vol. 5, p. 464).

19 Oct 1730. Deposition of Stephen Jerman of Prince George's Co., planter, age ca. 60-70, regarding Abington vs. Stoddert. (MSA Vol. 5, p. 466).

19 Oct 1730. Deposition of George Dickson of Prince George's Co., planter, age ca. 48, regarding Abington vs. Stoddert. (MSA Vol. 5, p. 467).

19 Oct 1730. Deposition of Francis Wheeler, Sr. of Prince George's Co., planter, age ca. 50-60, regarding Abington vs. Stoddert. (MSA Vol. 5, p. 468).

19 Oct 1730. Depositions taken regarding Abington vs. Stoddert. (1) Giles Vermulen of Prince George's Co., planter, age ca. 45. (2) Christopher Thompson of Prince George's Co., age ca. 60. (3) Hickford Lemon of Prince George's Co., planter, age ca. [blank] yrs. (MSA Vol. 5, p. 470).

7 May 1728. George Neilson vs. William Digges and Charles Carrol. Bill of Complaint states that William Digges would speak to his cousin, Charles Carroll, on behalf of George Neilson. (MSA Vol. 5, p. 487).

1 Dec 1729. Edmund Jenings and Arriana, his wife, extx. of Thomas Bordley, Esq. vs. Elizabeth Hepburne, admx. of Patrick Hepburne. The Bill of Complaint states that Ariana, wife of Thomas Bordley during his life, then married Edmund Jenings. Elizabeth Hepburne was the relict of Patrick Hepburne. (MSA Vol. 5, p. 512).

7 Aug 1733. Depositions taken regarding a dispute over the incorrect recording by Alexander Adams against John Caldwell. (1) Benjamin Cottman of Somerset Co., planter, age ca. 60. (2) Peter Sirman of Somerset Co., planter, age ca. 62. (MSA Vol. 5, p. 557).

7 Aug 1733. Depositions taken regarding Adams vs. Caldwell. (1) John Christopher, Sr. of Somerset Co., planter, age ca. 63. (2) Christopher Dowdel of Somerset Co., schoolmaster, age ca. 37. (3) Lewes Dishroom of Somerset Co., planter, age ca. 55. (MSA Vol. 5, p. 558).

7 Aug 1733. Depositions taken regarding Adams vs. Caldwell. (1) Thomas Gillis of Somerset Co., joyner, age ca. 38. (2) Levin Gale of Somerset Co., planter, age ca. 28. (MSA Vol. 5, p. 559).

7 Aug 1733. Depositions taken regarding Adams vs. Caldwell. (1) James Mackmorrie of Stepney Parish, age ca. 61. (2) John Handy of Somerset Co., Gent., age ca. 38, that the following deposition was taken 14 Jan 1724/5: Deposition of Jonathan

Raymond of Stepney Parish in Somerset Co., planter, age ca. 51. (MSA Vol. 5, p. 560).
18 May 1731. Jonathan Forward vs. Michael Taylor. Deposition of Michael Taylor, age ca. 30. (MSA Vol. 5, p. 584).
10 May 1731. Mary Woodward and Elizabeth Ginn of Great Britain, widows, complained that William Hopkins devised land called *Hopkin's Forbearance* and *Piny Neck* in Anne Arundel Co. to John Jobson, son of John Jobson and Ann his wife. John Jobson died without issue and the land descended to Thomas Jobson as brother and heir at law to John Jobson, the son. (MSA Vol. 5, p. 588).
13 May 1731. Deposition of Mary Eagle of Anne Arundel Co., age ca. 71, regarding land called *Hopkin's Forbearance* and *Piny Neck*. Deponent states that her husband, James Orrick, purchased John Jobson and Ann Cook; and they were servants to this deponent. She heard later than Ann was to marry Charles Rivers. (MSA Vol. 5, p. 590).
28 Jun 1731. Depositions taken regarding a mortgage of part of a tract called *Painter's Rest* made by Thomas Cook, formerly of Annapolis to Nathaniel Hynson of Kent Co. (1) Benjamin Pearce of Cecil Co., Gent., age ca. 50. (MSA Vol. 5, p. 602).
28 Jun 1731. Deposition of James Heath of Cecil Co., Gent., regarding a tract called *Painter's Rest*. (MSA Vol. 5, p. 604).
2 Aug 1731. Deposition of James Smith of Cecil Co., Gent., age ca. 48, regarding a tract called *Painter's Rest*. (MSA Vol. 5, p. 606).
14 Aug 1731. Deposition of Peregrine Frisby of Cecil Co., Gent., age ca. 42, regarding a tract called *Painter's Rest*. (MSA Vol. 5, p. 607).
3rd Tues of Feb 1734. A commission set to examine evidences of damage if 20 ac. of land should be granted to Christopher Williams of Queen Anne Co. to build a water mill on. Mentions James Mumford, son of Thomas Mumford of Somerset Co. receiving 20 ac. on Chappell Branch of St. Martin's River in Somerset Co. to build a mill. (MSA Vol. 5, p. 617).
12 Nov 1734. Depositions taken regarding evidences relating to the affinity between Dennis O'Higgerty, late of Kent Co. on Del. deceased and Federa O'Dougherty of Kent Co. aforesaid. (1) Robert Carney, age ca. 79, that he knew both when they lived in Somerset Co. About 40 years ago, Haggerty asked this deponent to go with him to see his sister, who had lately come into the Province and was married to Hugh Lash. O'Higgerty and O'Dougherty considered themselves cousins. (MSA Vol. 5, p. 619).
12 Nov 1734. Deposition of Honnor Larramore, age ca. 73, regarding relationship between Dennis O'Higgerty and Federa O'Dougherty. Deponent states that 30 or 40 years ago her then husband, Richard Plunkett, informed her that O'Higgerty and O'Dougherty were kin to each other. (MSA Vol. 5, p. 620).
3rd Tues of Feb 1734. Docket. Thomas Bond vs. John Ward - abated by the death of the complainant. (MSA Vol. 5, p. 645).
3rd Tues of Feb 1734. Docket. Patrick Sympson vs. John Taillour, Gilbert Higginson, and John Moale - abated by the

death of the complainant. (MSA Vol. 5, p. 645).

3rd Tues of Feb 1734. Docket. William Alexander vs. Alexander Adams - abated by the death of the complainant. (MSA Vol. 5, p. 648).

25 May 1734. Aquila Paca and Rachel, his wife vs. John Howell. The Bill of Complaint states that Thomas Howell was granted a tract called *Dale Town* in Kent Co. His will devised that tract to his son, John Howell. He devised to Nathaniel Howell the tract lying between *Dale Town* and the land formerly *Godlington's* now in the possession of Col. John Owen. If both sons should die without issue, the lands should go to Cecil Co. Gasper Hood married Sarah, daughter and heiress at law of Sarah Vanack of Kent Co., deceased. *Dale Town* was sold to William Blay, late of Kent Co., Gent. deceased. He died leaving 3 daughters-Rachel, [blank], and Isabella, co-heiresses. Rachel married Aquila Paca, and was formerly known as Rachel Brown. John Tilden married the other [unnamed] daughter of William Blay. The answer of John Howell dated 16 Nov 1734: The grantee, Thomas Howell, was the great-grandfather of John Howell. Thomas Howell's eldest son was John Howell, and left issue Thomas Howell, this defendent's father. The defendent John Howell came into this province ca. 1728 from Philadelphia where he lived from infancy. (MSA Vol. 5, p. 661).

20 Sep 17--. [20th year of dominion] Thomas Stockett and Elizabeth, his wife, extx. of Thomas Larkin of Anne Arundel Co., Gent. vs. Charles Cole of Annapolis, Merchant. The Bill of Complaint states that Elizabeth Stockett was the widow of Thomas Larkin. (MSA Vol. 5, p. 673).

18 Feb 1733. Depositions taken in the cause between Aaron Rawlings and the exrs. of James Carrol, deceased. (1) Edmund Larner, age ca. 45. (2) Mrs. Elizabeth Larner, age ca. 40. (3) John Williams, age ca. 78. (MSA Vol. 5, p. 747).

13 Feb 1735. Samuel Hastings, Samuel Minskie and John Evitt brought their bill of complaint against Benjamin Tasker and George Plater, Esq. and Onorio Razolini, Gent., exrs. of Rebecca Calvert, deceased, relict and admx. of Charles Calvert, Esq. deceased. Samuel Hastings was a shipbuilder in the province of Pennsylvania. Samuel Minskie was a blacksmith in the city of Annapolis. Joseph Evitts was a joiner from Annapolis. (MSAVol. 5, p. 761).

15 Jun 1731. Deposition of Martin Depost, age ca. 66, regarding the bounds of a tract in dispute between Richard Deavour and James Lee, both of Baltimore Co. (MSAVol. 5, p. 777).

19 Mar 1730. Depositions taken regarding the bounds of several tracts-*Painter's Range, The Grove, Wiltshire,* and *Dorchester* now in the possession of Richard Bennett of Queen Anne Co., Esq. (1) Andrew Grey, age ca. 27, that about 15 years ago his father, Thomas Grey, showed him a bounded white oak of *The Grove*. (MSA Vol. 5, p. 779).

19 Mar 1730. Deposition of Cornelius Johnson of Dorchester Co., age ca. 50, regarding several tracts--*Painter's Range, The Grove, Wiltshire,* and *Dorchester*. (MSA Vol. 5, p. 780).

30 Sep 1732. Depositions taken regarding whether Mary Pattison was the wife of John Pattison of Dorchester Co. Mary

Pattison, formerly called Mary Atkow, daughter of Thomas Atkow late of Dorchester Co., deceased, was heiress at law to the lands of Garney Crow, late of the same co., deceased.
(1) Mathew Travers, age ca. 60, that about 40 years ago he was with Thomas Atkow and Gurney Crow, and he heard them call themselves cousins. (MSA Vol. 5, p. 781).

30 Sep 1732. Deposition of Mary Hooper, age ca. 65, regarding Pattison, heir to Crow. Deponent stated that about 45 years ago Thomas Atkow lived at her house. (2) Ann Lewis, age ca. 68, that her husband told her that Thomas Atthow and Gurney Crow were the children of brothers and sisters. (MSA Vol. 5, p. 782).

Oct 1732. A jury was summoned to examine if there would be damage to us or others if we grant Sarah Kirke of Dorchester Co., widow of John Kirke, 20 ac. of land to build a water mill. (MSA Vol. 5, p. 783).

4 May 1736. Anne Arundel Co. Petition of Benjamin Tasker of Annapolis, Esq. that he is the heir at law of Thomas Tasker, late of Calvert Co., deceased. He states that witnesses could prove his father's marriage with his mother, and also the death of his elder brother and his issue. (MSA Vol. 5, 797-799).

4 May 1736. Deposition of Clement Brooke of Prince George's Co., age ca. 59, regarding petition of Benjamin Tasker. Deponent states that he knew Thomas Tasker, Sr. of Calvert Co., Merchant, who died about 40 years ago. His wife's name was Brook. Thomas Tasker, Sr. had 3 sons-Thomas, John, and Benjamin. He heard that Thomas the son died about 40 years ago in England never having married. John, the second son, had a son named Thomas who died about 3 years ago leaving only one son whose name was John and is since dead about a year ago. (MSA Vol. 5, p. 800).

4 May 1736. Deposition of Col. John Smith of Calvert Co., age ca. 60, regarding the petition of Benjamin Tasker. Deponent states that Thomas the son died sometime before his father. (MSA Vol. 5, p. 801).

1 May 1736. Deposition of John Hall, Esq. of Baltimore Co., age ca. 79, regarding the petition of Benjamin Tasker. Deponent states that about 60 years ago Thomas Tasker, Sr. married Mrs. Brooke, widow, and that she died a few years before her husband. (MSA Vol. 5, p. 802).

22 Feb 1736. Annapolis. John Rousby, Collector of his Majesty's customs vs. Mitchell Phillips and Richard Mayning. The Bill of Complaint states that in Provincial Court in Annapolis 15 May 1696, a Henry Mitchell, late of Calvert Co., deceased, was convicted of a debt of 1000# sterling which had not been paid to his Majesty. On 22 Sep 1716 the Sheriff of Calvert Co. was commanded to seize all lands and goods and chattels of Henry Mitchell at the time of his death or those in possession of Daniel Philips or Grace Mitchell, widow and admx. Mitchell Philips, grandson and heir at law of Henry Mitchell, and Richard Manying of Dorchester Co., planter, were accused of illegally obtaining false title to the lands seized for debt. Answer of Mitchell Philips states that in 1664 Thomas Manning obtained a patent for the tract called *Bush Manning* and that John Manning by his deed dated 16 Oct

1684 sold 1000 ac. part to Nathaniel Manning who dyed 7 May 1731 and left Richard Manning, his son and heir. 12 Oct 1733. Answer of Richard Mayning states that he was the son of Nathaniel Manning. (MSA Vol. 6, p. 4).

27 May 1735. Deposition of John Mackall of Calvert Co., aged ca. 66 yrs, that Mitchell Philips is reputed to be the grandson of Henry Mitchell and that Henry Mitchell died about 33-34 years ago. That Col. Mitchell's reputed daughter is the mother of Mitchell Philips, and the father was Daniel Philips. (MSA Vol. 6, p. 8).

27 May 1735. Deposition of Thomas Manning of Calvert Co., planter, aged ca. 56 yrs, that his grandfather was the original patentee of a tract called *Shepbush Manning*. (MSA Vol. 6, p. 9).

25 Nov 1732. Thomas Gittings of Prince George's Co. vs. William Beckwith. Gittings states in his Bill of Complaint that he was seized of a parcel in Prince George's Co., called --- which was conveniently situated for William Beckwith of the same county who pretended to be seized as heir at law to his father, Charles Beckwith, deceased, of a parcel in St. Mary's Co. called *Halley's Mannour* which lay very convenient for Thomas Gittings, and the two men exchanged title. *Halley's Mannour* was actually mortgaged for the full value by Charles Beckwith, father of said William Beckwith. (MSA Vol. 6, p. 11).

29 Oct 1736. Deposition of Ann Miller, wife of John Miller, of Prince George's Co., aged ca 48, in above case. She states that she had by right of dower a tract on St. Jerome's Creek in St. Mary's Co. which she made over to Thomas Gittings. (MSA Vol. 6, p. 21).

8 Dec 1735. Deposition of Basil Beckwith of Prince George's Co., planter, aged ca. 25, in above case. (MSA Vol. 6, p. 24).

9 Dec 1735. Deposition of George Beckwith of Prince George's Co., planter, aged ca. 29, in above case. (MSA Vol. 6, p. 25).

22 Mar 1735. Deposition of John Magruder of Prince George's Co., Gent., aged ca. 42, in above case, that his brother is Samuel Magruder of Prince George's Co. (MSA Vol. 6, p. 27).

8 May 1736. Deposition of Charles Carroll of Annapolis, aged ca. 34 yrs, regarding above case. (MSA Vol. 6, p. 29).

9 Apr 1736. Deposition of John Magruder of Prince George's Co., aged ca. 42 yrs, regarding above case. (MSA Vol. 6, p. 30).

6 May 1736. Deposition of Ignatius Perry of Prince George's Co., planter, aged ca. 34 yrs., regarding above case. (MSA Vol. 6, p. 31).

6 May 1736. Deposition of James Perry of Prince George's Co., planter, aged ca. 36 yrs., regarding above case. (MSA Vol. 6, p. 32).

20 Aug 1733. George Plater vs. John Rousby. Bill of Complaint states that William Harrison and Frances, his wife, late of Calvert Co., deceased, were seized by right and as estate of Frances of several tracts: 215 ac. called *Mile End* in Calvert Co. and 132 ac. called *Mill Run* in Calvert Co. and a reversion of 60 1/2 ac. (another part of *Mile End*) which

William Harrison and Frances, his wife, agreed to sell to George Plater, late of Calvert Co., decd., father of complainant, with Ann Plater, the mother of the complainant. Ann Plater later intermarried with John Rousby of Calvert Co. Ann then died without bearing any children to John Rousby. George Plater is the only son and heir of George Plater the elder. (MSA Vol. 6, p. 33).

29 Jun 1736. John Rousby answers that he is aware of an indenture of Bargain and Sale dated 13 Jun 1708 by George Young, Jr. of Calvert Co. and Elizabeth, his wife, who was entitled to some right of dower in lands so conveyed by Harrison and his wife to Ann Plater, and at that time Frances Harrison was under 21 yrs. (MSA Vol. 6, p. 36).

29 Jun 1736. Deposition of Daniel Dulany aged ca. 48 yrs. regarding above case states that Harrison's wife was born in Calvert Co. (MSA Vol. 6, p. 39).

29 Jun 1736. A conveyance recorded among the Land Records of Calvert Co. shows an indenture made 12 Jul 1718 between William Harrison of Calvert Co. and Frances, his wife, one of the daughters and coheirs of Tobias Miles the Elder, decd. and a sister and coheir of John Miles and Tobias Miles the Younger, decd. who died intestate and without issue. Tobias Miles by his Last Will and Testament dated 16 Aug 1691 mentions his son John Miles, wife Elizabeth, son Tobias Miles, and daughter Mary Miles, now wife of George Young Jr., and daughter Frances. John and Tobias both died intestate and without issue. Elizabeth then married John Fisher, now decd. (MSA Vol. 6, p. 41).

29 Jun 1736. Regarding above case, a letter written to "Dear Nanny" dated 23 May 1718 and signed "Ann Rousby, your loving mother" mentions her sister Giver and her child Josey. (MSA Vol. 6, p. 48).

15 Jul 1729. Thomas Colmore of London, Merchant brought his Bill of Complaint against Sarah Perry, late of Prince George's Co., widow, relict and admx. of Samuel Perry, decd. Sarah Perry died during the suit and Sarah Haddock, widow, and Richard Marsham Waring obtained letters of administration. (MSA Vol. 6, p. 50).

1 Jul 1731. A commission was issued to examine evidences re: Thomas Colmore vs. Sarah Perry, now wife of Patrick Andrews. (MSA Vol. 6, p. 70).

22 Jan 1732. Depositions of (1) John Barber, Lord Mayor of the City of London. (2) John Moore of the Parish of St. Thomas Apostles in London. (MSA Vol. 6, p. 74).

21 Jun 1735. Answer of Sarah Haddock and Richard Marsham Waring states that Sarah Perrie dyed in Aug 1733. (MSA Vol. 6, p. 95).

14 Feb 1735. Daniel Dulany filed his Bill of Complaint against James Moccal, Thomas Worthington, John Galloway, Richard Dorsey and Elizabeth his wife, that William Nicholson late of Anne Arundel Co., decd. Merchant, had an estate in remainder in fee simple after the death of John Beale, late of Anne Arundel Co. William Nicholson left his last will and testament dated 28 Dec 1731 which mentions his son, Beale Nicholson (then still a minor), and his wife, Elizabeth, as extx. By Codicil dated 29 Dec 1731 he appointed John Beale

to the the guardian to said minor. Upon Beale's death, the codicil provided that Nicholson's friends, James Mocal, Thomas Worthington and John Galloway take guardianship of his son. Elizabeth Nicholson, widow of William and mother of Beale Nicholson, later intermarried with Richard Dorsey of Anne Arundel Co., Gent. (MSA Vol. 6, p. 97).

1 Mar 1736. Vachel Denton undertook the guardianship of Beale Nicholson. (MSA Vol. 6, p. 102).

23 Nov 1733. Susannah Stokes, Humphrey Wells Stokes, George Stokes and John Stokes of Baltimore Co, exrs. of John Stokes vs. John Hammond of Cecil Co., Gent. (MSA Vol. 6, p. 123).

15 Jul 1736. Deposition of Comfort Dorsey of Anne Arundel Co. aged ca. 50 yrs, in above case states that she had known Col. John Dorsey, late of Baltimore Co. as her husband for more than 30 yrs. and that he left this province about 10 yrs. ago at the end of October. (MSA Vol. 6, p. 128).

15 Jul 1736. Deposition of Joshua Dorsey, Jr. of Annapolis, planter aged ca. 24 yrs. in above case states that Col. John Dorsey was his father. (MSA Vol. 6, p. 129).

15 Jul 1736. Deposition of Catherine Randall, wife of Christopher Randall of Balto. Co. planter, aged ca. 29 yrs. that she heard Col. John Dorsey's wife say that her son, Greenbury Dorsey... (MSA Vol. 6, p. 130).

6 Dec 1737. Joseph Howard, a minor, appeared before the court desiring Ephraim Howard to be appointed his guardian. (MSA Vol. 6, p. 134).

15 Jun 1732. Daniel Carrol vs. David Crawford and Charles Beale regarding a land dispute. The Bill of Complaint states that Col. Ninian Beale named as his son and heir, Charles Beale. Henry Darnall left a son Henry Darnall, Jr. (MSA Vol. 6, p. 138).

17 Jan 1735. Deposition of Henry Darnall, Esq. of St. Mary's Co. aged ca. 53 yrs. that his father was Col. Henry Darnall and that he died in 1711. Daniel Carroll married this deponent's daughter about 13 or 14 yrs. ago. (MSA Vol. 6, p. 153).

25 Feb 1735. Deposition of Alexander Contee of Prince George's Co., Gent. aged ca. 44 yrs. (MSA Vol. 6, p. 155).

6 Mar 1735. Deposition of Capt. Richard Lee of Prince George's Co., Gent. aged ca. 30 yrs. (MSA Vol. 6, p. 156).

2 Apr 1736. Deposition of Clement Hill, Sr. of Prince George's Co., Gent. aged ca. 66 yrs. that he believes Col. Henry Darnall died in 1711 and that Col. Ninian Beale died about 18 yrs. ago. (MSA Vol. 6, p. 159).

22 Apr 1736. Deposition of Edward Reston of Prince George's Co., planter, aged ca. 42 yrs. (MSA Vol. 6, p. 161).

2 Apr 1736. Deposition of Abigail Tent of Prince George's Co., free mulatto, aged ca. 67 yrs. (MSA Vol. 6, p. 162).

24 Feb 1735/6. William Beale and James Beale of Prince George's Co., planters, and James Edmondson vs. Thomas Butler. The Bill of Complaint states that James Butler, late of Prince George's Co., decd., died intestate leaving his son and heir Thomas Butler in his minority. Sometime after John Bradford, late of said county, Gent. decd., intermarried with Joice, the widow and relict of James Butler. (MSA Vol. 6, p. 167).

28 Apr 1733. Thomas Pattison and Mary his wife of Dorchester Co. vs. James Stout and Ann his wife of Kent Co. The Bill of Complaint states that Mary Pattison is the sister of Berkley Codd of Sussex Co., PA, Gent. decd. His last will and testament mentioned his beloved wife Mary Codd, brother St. Ledger Codd, sister Mary Patterson wife of Thomas Patterson of Dorsett Co. [sic]. St. Ledger Codd died intestate before carrying out the terms of administration, which were passed to Ann Codd in Kent Co., his eldest daughter who is now intermarried with James Stout of Kent Co. (MSA Vol. 6, p. 175).

23 Oct 1736. Deposition of John Brannock of Dorchester Co., planter, aged ca. 60 yrs. (MSA Vol. 6, p. 182).

23 Oct 1736. Deposition of John Abbott of Dorchester Co., planter, aged ca. 63 yrs. (MSA Vol. 6, p. 183).

20 Oct 1737. Deposition of John Williams of Kent Co., aged ca. 31 yrs. (MSA Vol. 6, p. 186).

20 Oct 1737. Deposition of Nathaniel Kinward of Kent Co., aged ca. 42 yrs. (MSA Vol. 6, p. 187).

21 Oct 1737. Deposition of Frances Barnes of Queen Anne's Co., planter, aged ca. 61 yrs. (MSA Vol. 6, p. 188).

15 May 1734. Michael Fletcher of Talbot Co., Gent. vs. Matthew Kirby of Talbot Co. regarding a dispute over payment for services rendered. (MSA Vol. 6, p. 190).

27 Oct 1736. Deposition of Perry Benson of Talbot Co., Gent. aged ca. 40 yrs. (MSA Vol. 6, p. 198).

25 Oct 1736. Deposition of Michael Howard of Talbot Co. aged ca. 40 yrs. (MSA Vol. 6, p. 199).

27 Oct 1736. Deposition of Thomas Bozman of Talbot Co., Gent., aged ca. 43 yrs. (MSA Vol. 6, p. 200).

21 Oct 1736. Deposition of Francis Armstrong of Talbot Co., planter, aged ca. 45 yrs. (MSA Vol. 6, p. 202).

21 Oct 1736. Deposition of John Parr of Talbot Co. aged ca. 39 yrs. (MSA Vol. 6, p. 204).

20 Apr 1736. Jane Pattison vs. Jeremiah Pattison. Her Bill of Complaint states that Jane Pattison was the wife of Jeremiah Pattison of Calvert Co. for about 12 yrs, and that he became possessed of a large estate belonging to her and her children by a former husband. He beat her cruelly and threw her out of his house. (MSA Vol. 6, p. 207).

28 Nov 1737. Deposition of Susannah Currant, wife of James Currant of Calvert Co. planter, aged ca. 26 yrs. that about 8 or 9 years ago she was hired in the house of the defendant as a servant. (MSA Vol. 6, p. 212).

28 Nov 1737. Deposition of Ann Smith, wife of John Smith of Calvert Co. planter, aged ca. 50 yrs. that she knew the complainant during the time of her former husband's, Samuel Abbott, life. (MSA Vol. 6, p. 213).

28 Nov 1737. Deposition of Hannah, wife of John Clare of Calvert Co. planter, aged ca. 28 yrs. (MSA Vol. 6, p. 215).

28 Nov 1737. Deposition of Ann Evans of Calvert Co., spinster, aged ca. 18 yrs. (MSA Vol. 6, p. 216).

29 Nov 1737. Deposition of Rutter Lawrence of Calvert Co. planter aged ca. 38 yrs. (MSA Vol. 6, p. 218).

29 Nov 1737. Deposition of Dr. James Somerville of Calvert Co. aged ca. 44 yrs. (MSA Vol. 6, p. 219).

29 Nov 1737. Deposition of Edmund Hungerford of Calvert Co. planter aged ca. 22 yrs. (MSA Vol. 6, p. 220).
29 Nov 1737. Deposition of William Gray of Calvert Co. planter aged ca. 56 yrs. (MSA Vol. 6, p. 221).
29 Nov 1737. Deposition of John Darrumple of Calvert Co. Gent. aged ca. 42 yrs. (MSA Vol. 6, p. 222).
29 Nov 1737. Deposition of Charles Clagett of Calvert Co. Gent. aged ca. 46 yrs. (MSA Vol. 6, p. 223).
29 Nov 1737. Deposition of John Rigby of Calvert Co. planter aged ca. 38 yrs. (MSA Vol. 6, p. 225).
29 Nov 1737. Deposition of Barbara, wife of Benjamin Mackall of Calvert Co. Gent., aged ca. 44 yrs. (MSA Vol. 6, p. 226).
1 Dec 1737. Deposition of John Games of Calvert Co. planter aged ca. 46 yrs. that he lived in the defendant's house for about 4 mos. (MSA Vol. 6, p. 229).
1 Dec 1737. Deposition of Abraham Spikernall of Calvert Co. planter aged ca. 37 yrs. (MSA Vol. 6, p. 230).
30 Nov 1737. Deposition of James Hellen of Calvert Co. aged ca. 49 yrs. (MSA Vol. 6, p. 231).
30 Nov 1737. Deposition of Rosamond Wilkinson, wife of Thomas Wilkinson of Calvert Co. planter, aged ca. 53 yrs. (MSA Vol. 6, p. 233).
30 Nov 1737. Deposition of Elenor, wife of John Darrumple of Calvert Co., aged ca. 45 yrs. (MSA Vol. 6, p. 234).
30 Nov 1737. Deposition of Obed Dickson of Calvert Co. aged ca. 29 yrs. (MSA Vol. 6, p. 235).
30 Nov 1737. Deposition of Martin Driver of Calvert Co. aged ca. 31 yrs. (MSA Vol. 6, p. 237).
13 Oct 1734. Daniel Dulany vs. Edmond Jenings Esq. in right of Ariana his wife, late wife of devisee of Thomas Bordley; Stephen Bordley, heir at law or devisee of Thomas Bordley; Charles Calvert Esq.; Charles Hammond Esq.; Robert Gordon Esq.; William Cuming Esq.; William Alexander, heir or devisee of Robert Alexander; John Bullen; James Donaldson; Simon Duff; John Simmes; John Lomax in right of Margaret his wife. This case was in reference to a resurvey of lands from original patents and/or warrants. That Thomas Hall died in 1655 leaving issue Christopher Hall, his only son and heir, who devised 20 ac. to his mother, Elizabeth Hall, by his last will and testament. (MSA Vol. 6, p. 240).
Robert Busby devised 90 ac. part of *Todd's Harbour* by his last will and testament dated 19 Jun 1674 to his loving wife with the child in her belly. Robert dyed without issue and no heirs. (MSA Vol. 6, p. 243).
Lancelott Todd pretended to be the heir of Thomas Todd, both of Anne Arundel Co. (MSA Vol. 6, p. 244).
Richard Hill purchased 3 ac. of land from the relict of James Rawbone and 90 ac. of land part of *Todd's Harbour* devised by Robert Busby to his wife, Elizabeth, later called Elizabeth Rawbone, who sold it to Richard Hill. (MSA Vol. 6, p. 274).
Thomas Hall died leaving Christopher Hall as his only son and heir and that Christopher devised 20 ac. of land to his mother, Elizabeth, and that said Elizabeth died intestate and without issue. (MSA Vol. 6, p. 280).
After his death, Elizabeth, widow of Robert Busby, intermarried with James Rawbone who dyed without issue. After her second

husband died, Elizabeth Rawbone sold 90 ac. part of 120 ac.
of land called *Todd's Harbour* to Richard Hill, deceased,
father of Henry Hill of Anne Arundel Co. around 1684. (MSA
Vol. 6, p. 281).
Thomas Bordley devised unto his sons, John and Thomas, 4 lotts
and his son, Matthias, 5 ac. and his daughter, Elizabeth, the
remainder of 2 houses and lotts. The testator [Thomas
Bordley] died on 11 Oct 1726. (MSA Vol. 6, p. 343).
All other children of Thomas Bordley which are devisees of
several parts of the land in question are William, Elizabeth,
John, Thomas, Matthias, and Beale with whom his wife was with
child at the time of the making of his will. (MSA Vol. 6, p.
352).
Testimony of Robert MacLeod states that Elizabeth MacLeod, wife
of Robert, was formerly married to James Walker, carpenter.
(MSA Vol. 6, p. 346).
12 Oct 1736. Deposition of Abraham Child of Anne Arundel Co.
planter aged ca. 90 yrs, that he knew Thomas Todd, his son
Thomas and great-grandson Lance Todd of Anne Arundel Co.,
decd. (MSA Vol. 6, p. 376).
16 Feb 1736. Depositions of (1) John Maccubbin of Anne Arundel
Co. Gent. aged ca. 70 yrs. that he knew John, the son of
Henry Acton. (2) Richard Hampton of Anne Arundel Co. planter
aged ca. 77 yrs. that he was not acquainted with Thomas Todd,
decd., uncle of the late Thomas Todd. (MSA Vol. 6, p. 378).
17 May 1736. Deposition of Vachel Denton of Annapolis Gent.
aged ca. 40 yrs. that he knows Stephen Bordley and his late
father, Thomas Bordley. (MSA Vol. 6, p. 379).
17 Feb 1736. Deposition of Henry Hill of Anne Arundel Co.
Gent. aged ca. 65 yrs. that Thomas Bordley was Clerk or
Register in the Land Office in 1702. This affirmant's father
was Richard Hill of Anne Arundel Co. Esq., decd., and his
brother was Joseph Hill, decd. (MSA Vol. 6, p. 382).
18 Feb 1736. Deposition of John Young of Anne Arundel Co.
planter aged ca. 77 yrs. (MSA Vol. 6, p. 386).
21 Feb 1736. Deposition of Benjamin Tasker of Annapolis Esq.
aged ca. 45 yrs. (MSA Vol. 6, p. 387).
22 Feb 1736. Deposition of Griffith Beddoe of Annapolis Gent.
aged ca. 36 yrs. (MSA Vol. 6, p. 388).
22 Nov 1736. Deposition of Thomas Tobson of Annapolis Gent.
aged ca. 37 yrs. (MSA Vol. 6, p. 394).
19 Feb 1736. Deposition of Henry Ridgeley of Anne Arundel Co.
Gent. aged ca. 46 yrs. that he has been employed as Deputy
Surveyor of Anne Arundel Co. about 8 yrs. (MSA Vol. 6, p.
397).
Copy of an indenture made 1 May 1672 between Thomas Todd of
Anne Arundel River in Anne Arundel Co. planter and Robert
Busby of said county and river, Gent. (MSA Vol. 6, p. 403).
p.408
Copy of will of Dr. Robert Busby of Anne Arundel Co. bequeathed
to his friend, Francis Jones, daughter of John Jones. Also
mentions his daughter-in-law, Frances Vedgby; his brother,
Thomas Busby; and his wife, Margaret Busby with the child in
her belly. (MSA Vol. 6, p. 408).
[This case was unusual in that it was an attempt to reconstruct
and fill in missing land records lost in a fire in Annapolis.

The "trial" was lengthy and had little genealogical value.- MSA Vol. 6, p. 240-408].

28 Feb 1737. Docket. William Alexander, exec. of Robert Alexander vs. Samuel James and Enoch Jenkins. (MSA Vol. 6, p. 419).

31 Oct 1738. John Outchterlony vs. Gilbert Higginson and John Taillor. The Bill of Complaint states that John Outchterlony of Prince George's Co., Merchant, in 1715 employed Gilbert Higginson of London, Merchant, as a factor. In 1722, Higginson became bankrupt. He then married Margarett, the daughter of John Taillor of London, Merchant. (MSA Vol. 6, p. 425).

7 Dec 1734. Attorney General on behalf of Lord Baltimore vs. John Rider, Esq. and Richard Willis regarding unpaid debt. (MSA Vol. 6, p. 440).

7 Dec 1734. Deposition of John Carter of Somerset Co., planter, aged ca. 74 yrs. in above case stated that about 40 yrs. ago he was employed as a carpenter by Col. Charles Hutchens, late of Dorchester Co. (MSA Vol. 6, p. 442).

7 Dec 1734. Deposition of Peter Samuel of Somerset Co., planter, aged ca. 61 yrs. in above case stated that about 40 yrs. ago he heard his father, Richard Samuel, say that... (MSA Vol. 6, p. 443).

7 Dec 1734. Depositions of (1) John Wilson of Somerset Co., planter, aged ca. 49 yrs. that about 25 or 30 yrs. ago he heard his father, Thomas Wilson, say that he and David Cuffin, his Master... (2) Charles Thompson of Dorchester Co., planter, aged ca. 56 yrs. (3) Thomas Hicks of Dorchester Co., Gent., aged ca. 47 yrs, that about 20 yrs. ago his father, Thomas Hicks,... (MSA Vol. 6, p. 444).

7 Dec 1734. Deposition of William Rawleigh of Dorchester Co., planter, aged ca. 47 yrs. that Richard Hacker of Somerset Co. was father-in-law to Richard Willis. (MSA Vol. 6, p. 445).

7 Dec 1734. Depositions of (1) Nehemiah Messick of Somerset Co., planter, aged ca. 60 yrs. that Col. Charles Hutchins had ordered his servants, Anguish Murroe and Peter Bodie... (2) Leonard Jones of Dorchester Co., planter, aged ca. 66 yrs. (3) John Hudson of Dorchester Co., Gent., aged ca. 50 yrs. (MSA Vol. 6, p. 446).

7 Dec 1734. Depositions of (1) John Hudson, Jr. of Dorchester Co., planter, aged ca. 43 yrs. that about 32 yrs. ago he was with John Taylor, Surveyor of Dorchester Co., and Roger Woolford, Sheriff of Dorchester Co. That Francis Fisher was reputed to be the father of John Wilson. (2) Peter Taylor of Dorchester Co., Gent., aged ca. 54 yrs. that his father was Thomas Taylor. (MSA Vol. 6, p. 447).

last Tues of Oct 1738. Docket. Leonard Wayman vs. Thomas Athorpe and Catherine his wife. (MSA Vol. 6, p. 454).

5 Dec 1738. Stokes Executors vs. Smith and Chapman. The Bill of Complaint states that Humphrey Wells Stokes and George Stokes, sons and 2 of the exrs. of John Stokes late of Baltimore Co. decd., brought their Bill of Complaint against Philip Smith and William Chapman, admin. of Philip Smith of London, Merchant, decd. In 1735 Philip Smith [decd.] sent his son, Philip Smith, to Maryland with a power of attorney to settle all his affairs. Susannah was the widow and relict

of John Stokes, decd. (MSA Vol. 6, p. 456).
27 Feb 1738. Gabriel Parker of Calvert Co. vs. John Mackall. The Bill of Complaint states that George Parker, late of Calvert Co. decd. and father of Gabriel Parker, made his last will and testament in 1710 making Susannah, his wife and mother of Gabriel Parker, his extx. George died ca. 4 Mar 1710, at which time Gabriel Parker was ca. 12 yrs. About 1713 Susannah intermarried with John Mackall, Esq. Gabriel Parrott, late of Anne Arundel Co. Merchant, was grandfather to Gabriel Parker. Gabriel Parker married at about age 16. (Liber JK, No. 4, p. 2).
3 Mar 1738. Answer of John Mackall states that he married Susannah Parker on 6 Sep 1713. The will of Gabriel Parrott devised 500 ac. to Elizabeth, daughter of George and Susannah Parker, and the residue to be divided among the 5 children of George and Susannah. (Liber JK, No. 4, p. 9).
20 Apr 1737. Deposition of Thomas Sanner of St. Mary's Co., planter, aged ca. 49 yrs. in above case. (Liber JK, No. 4, p. 20).
21 Apr 1737. Deposition of John Biscoe [Briscoe] of St. Mary's Co., planter, aged ca. 44 yrs. in above case. (Liber JK, No. 4, p. 21).
21 Apr 1737. Deposition of James White of St. Mary's Co., planter, aged ca. 56 yrs. referred to William Jones, son of Solomon Jones in above case. (Liber JK, No. 4, p. 23).
17 Sep 1737. Deposition of James Duke of Calvert Co., Gent., aged ca. 46 yrs. in above case. (Liber JK, No. 4, p. 25).
17 Sep 1737. Deposition of Frances Games of Calvert Co., planter, aged ca. 37 yrs. in above case. (Liber JK, No. 4, p. 26).
29 Sep 1737. Deposition of Walter Phelps of Anne Arundel Co., planter, aged ca. 57 yrs. in above case. (Liber JK, No. 4, p. 27).
29 Oct 1737. Deposition of Jonathan Taylor of Anne Arundel Co., planter, aged ca. 64 yrs. that he was overseer to George Parker for about 15 yrs. in above case. (Liber JK, No. 4, p. 29).
17 Sep 1737. Deposition of John Games of Calvert Co., planter, aged ca. 47 yrs. in above case. (Liber JK, No. 4, p. 30).
17 Sep 1737. Deposition of Josias Sunderland of Calvert Co., planter, aged ca. 46 yrs. in above case. (Liber JK, No. 4, p. 32).
17 Sep 1737. Deposition of Samuel Griffin of Calvert Co., planter, aged ca. 47 yrs. in above case. (Liber JK, No. 4, p. 33).
17 Apr 1737. Deposition of Gabriel Parker of Calvert Co., Gent. in above case. (Liber JK, No. 4, p. 34).
22 Oct 1737. Deposition of Adderton Skinner of Calvert Co., Gent., aged ca. 60 yrs. in above case. Deponent states that for a small time after his marriage, Gabriel Parker lived with Col. Greenfield. (MSA Vol. 6, p. 37).
22 Oct 1737. Deposition of William Skinner of Calvert Co., Gent., aged ca. 61 yrs. in above case. (Liber JK, No. 4, p. 39).
Explanation of the division of the estate of Gabriel Parrott is as follows: 500 ac. to G. Elizabeth Parker, daughter of

George and Susannah Parker. Part to Trueman Greenfield in right of his wife. Part to Gideon Dare in right of his wife. Part to Michael Jenifer in right of his wife, Susannah. Part to James Stoddart, Jr. in right of Sarah, his wife. (Liber JK, No. 4, p. 44).

29 Jan 1738. Deposition Samuel Taylor of Prince George's Co., planter, aged ca. 38 yrs. in above case. (Liber JK, No. 4, p. 45).

29 Jan 1738. Deposition of Thomas Ireland aged ca. 59 yrs. in above case states that he was overseer to John Mackall at the plantation where Gabriel Parker now lives. (Liber JK, No. 4, p. 48).

25 Nov 1738. Deposition of Adderton Skinner of Calvert Co., Gent., aged ca. 60 yrs. in above case states that there were 2 white women servants in the estate of George Parker, Mary Monk and Mary Ruff. (Liber JK, No. 4, p. 50).

25 Nov 1738. Deposition of George Freeman of Calvert Co., planter, in above case. (Liber JK, No. 4, p. 51).

27 Feb 1738. A petition by William Beall, Jr. of Prince George's Co. that a patent was granted to his father, Thomas Beall, in 1701 for a tract of land. (Liber JK, No. 4, p. 63).

27 Feb 1738. A petition by George Ogg of Baltimore Co. that a patent was granted to his father, George Ogg, in 1710. (Liber JK, No. 4, p. 63).

14 Mar 1738. Jane Lynthicumb vs. George Lynthicumb. It was decided that the estate of John Ford, late husband of complainant, be left under the care and maintenance of the defendant. (Liber JK, No. 4, p. 65).

1 Mar 1738. Lord Proprietary vs. Charles Carrol, Esq. that a warrant was issued 28 Nov 1732 to lay out a survey for Daniel Carroll, Gent., decd., the defendant's brother, and Mary Carroll, the defendant's sister for 10,000 ac. of land. Daniel Carroll died and devised by his last will and testament part of the said lands to his 2 daughters, Mary and Elenor. (Liber JK, No. 4, p. 69).

29 May 1739. A petition by Edward Day and Avarilla, his wife, of Baltimore Co. that a tract of land was granted by patent dated 20 Mar 1724 to Thomas Taylor, father to the petitioner Avarilla. (Liber JK, No. 4, p. 81).

30 Oct 1739. Randolph Johnson of Prince George's Co. vs. John Wallingford of Prince George's Co. The Bill of Complaint states that Wallingford, planter, trespassed and shot and killed a horse belonging to Randolph Johnson. Benjamin Wallingsford, brother of the defendant, is mentioned. (Liber JK, No. 4, p. 84).

6 Dec 1738. John Orchard of Prince George's Co., planter; Robert Pearle of Prince George's Co., planter; ---; William Cumming of Annapolis, Gent; Jonathan Davis of Calvert Co., Merchant vs. John Smith and Mary his wife, extx. of Gunder Erickson, decd. and Peter Hoggins of Prince George's Co. The Bill of Complaint states that Gunder Erickson died and made his wife, Mary Erickson, his extx. Mary Erickson [also referred to as Elizabeth Erickson] intermarried with John Smith of Prince George's Co., planter. (Liber JK, No. 4, p. 89).

30 Apr 1739. John Merrykin petitioned to have Hugh Merrykin, his brother, declared insane. (Liber JK, No. 4, p. 95).
10 Oct 1739. Depositions taken in above case (1) Philip Jones of Anne Arundel Co. aged ca. 66 yrs. (2) Robert Boon of Anne Arundel Co. aged ca. 59 yrs. (3) Richard Moss of Anne Arundel Co., planter, aged c. 40 yrs. (Liber JK, No. 4, p. 96).
10 Oct 1739. Deposition of William Lewis of Anne Arundel Co. aged ca. 34 yrs. in above case. (Liber JK, No. 4, p. 97).
13 Oct 1736. Charles Carroll, Esq. of Annapolis vs. John Warren of St. Mary's Co., Gent. The Bill of Complaint brought by Charles Carroll, son and heir at law of Charles Carroll, late of said place, states that Michael Curtiss of St. Mary's Co., Gent. decd. and Sarah his wife, in right of Sarah, were possessed of diverse lands. Sarah was formerly the wife of Justinian Gerard of the same co. Thomas Gerrard was father to Justinian Gerrard. John Warren is heir at law to Sarah, wife of Michael Curtiss. (Liber JK, No. 4, p. 100).
15 Dec 1736. Answer of John Warren in above case states that he is the nephew of Sarah, she being a sister of whole blood of this defendant's mother, and that said Sarah was the widow and extx. of Justinian Gerard of St. Mary's Co. (Liber JK, No. 4, p. 105).
29 Jul 1738. Deposition of Justinian Jordan aged ca. 52 yrs. in above case. (Liber JK, No. 4, p. 111).
29 Jul 1738. Depositions of (1) Mary Jordan, aged ca. 46 yrs. that before her marriage to Justinian Gerard, Sarah was married to a Manders. (2) Henry Wharton aged ca. 64 yrs. (Liber JK, No. 4, p. 113).
22 Aug 1738. Depositions of (1) Jane Wharton aged ca. 50. (2) Elizabeth Jordan aged ca. 78 yrs. in above case. (Liber JK, No. 4, p. 114).
22 Aug 1738. Deposition of Peter Mills aged ca. 62 yrs. in above case. (Liber JK, No. 4, p. 115).
22 Aug 1738. Deposition of Justinian Jordan aged ca. 52 yrs. in above case states that Sarah Curtis died before Michael Curtis and that Samuel Williamson, Philip Briscoe, and Elizabeth Jordan were exrs. This deponent's mother, Elizabeth Jordan, received one-third part of Curtis' estate exclusive of legacies. (Liber JK, No. 4, p. 116).
22 Aug 1738. Depositions taken in above case (1) Mary Jordan aged ca. 46 yrs. that Sarah Curtis had a sister who lived with her some time. (2) Henry Wharton aged ca. 64 yrs. (3) Jane Wharton aged ca. 50 yrs. (Liber JK, No. 4, p. 117).
22 Aug 1738. Deposition of Elizabeth Jordan aged ca. 78 yrs. in above case states that she did not know Thomas Warren, father of the defendant, but she knew the defendant's mother, Rebecca Warren. Rebecca Warren was sister-in-law to Sarah Curtis, that Rebecca and Sarah had one mother and 2 fathers. (Liber JK, No. 4, p. 118).
22 Aug 1738. Depositions taken in above case (1) Peter Mills aged ca. 62 yrs. that he believes that John Warren, the defendant, is the eldest son and heir of Thomas Warren and Rebecca, whis wife, and that Rebecca Warren and Sarah Curtis were sisters of whole blood. (2) Ubgal Reeves aged ca. 69

yrs. [male]. (Liber JK, No. 4, p. 119).
22 Aug 1738. Depositions taken in above case (1) Mary
Bloomfield aged ca. 60 yrs. (2) James Bloomfield aged ca. 63
yrs. (Liber JK, No. 4, p. 120).
22 Aug 1738. Depositions taken in above case (1) Ann Phipard
aged ca. 53 yrs. (2) John Stanfill aged ca. 28 yrs. (3)
George Forbes aged ca. 52 yrs. (Liber JK, No. 4, p. 121).
Copy of indenture made 6 Sep 1705 between John Cole and Hannah,
his wife, of Baltimore Co. planter, and Charles Carroll, Esq.
of Anne Arundel Co. to make over 2 tracts of land. (Liber
JK, No. 4, p. 123).
15 Oct 1736. Nicholas Hammond of Annapolis, Gent. and Mary,
his wife vs. Elizabeth Feaudry. The Bill of Complaint states
that Mary Hammond was extx. of Alexander Steward of
Annapolis, Tanner, decd. and that a Moses Feaudry of Anne
Arundel Co., decd., became indebted to Alexander Steward.
Elizabeth, his widow, refused to pay the debt. (Liber JK,
No. 4, p. 132).
29 Oct 1736. Answer of Elizabeth Feaudry states that Moses
Feaudry died the end of Oct 1728, and that Samuel Guichard
died in Aug 1733 leaving his wife, Ann Guilschard as his
extx. (Liber JK, No. 4, p. 135).
31 Jan 1738. Deposition of John Hamilton of Calvert Co.,
Doctor of Physick in above case. (Liber JK, No. 4, p. 140).
26 Jan 1738. Deposition of David Weems of Anne Arundel Co. in
above case. (Liber JK, No. 4, p. 141).
Dec 1739. A petition by Bayne Smallwood of Charles Co. that a
tract of land was granted by patent to his father, Prior
Smallwood, dated 19 May 1725. (Liber JK, No. 4, p. 168).
Dec 1739. A petition by John Bickerton and Mary his wife; John
Hubbard and Elizabeth his wife, daughter of Ann Day; and Day
Scott all of Somerset Co. set forth that Edward Day, late of
said co. decd. had on 13 Aug 1684 a tract of land called
Providence lying in Queen Anne's Co. granted by patent.
(Liber JK, No. 4, p. 169).
Dec 1739. A petition by Henry Thomas and William Thomas of
Kent Co. that their father had a tract of land granted by
patent on 18 Feb 1659. (Liber JK, No. 4, p. 169).
24 Feb 1740. A petition by John Baldwyn of Cecil Co., that a
tract in Anne Arundel Co. was granted by patent in 1664 to
John Baldwyn, the petitioner's grandfather. (Liber JK, No.
4, p. 185).
24 Feb 1740. William Gardiner of Anne Arundel Co. vs. Thomas
Cockey regarding an unpaid debt. Deposition of William
Turner of Anne Arundel Co., planter, aged ca. 31 yrs (12 Dec
1735). (Liber JK, No. 4, p. 193).
13 Dec 1735. Deposition of Philip Howard of Anne Arundel Co.,
planter, aged ca. 31 yrs. in above case. (Liber JK, No. 4,
p. 194).
12 Jan 1735. Deposition of Capt. Thomas Homewood of Anne
Arundel Co. aged ca. 31 yrs. in above case mentions Lance
Todd, son of Richard. (Liber JK, No. 4, p. 197).
Feb 1737. Case abated by the death of the defendant. 1738. A
motion that the Court might issue against John Cockey, exr.
of Thomas Cockey to show cause, in above case. (Liber JK,
No. 4, p. 202).

13 Aug 1736. Philip Thomas of Anne Arundel Co., Gent. vs. William Whitehead and Ann, his wife of Anne Arundel Co. The Bill of Complaint states that John Deaver made his last will and testament and devised his estate to Hannah, his wife, now wife of William Whitehead. (Liber JK, No. 4, p. 216).

3 Sep 1736. Peregrine Frisby of Cecil Co. vs. Mary Carroll of Cecil Co., widow. Frisby states in his Bill of Complaint that his brother, William Frisby, late of Cecil Co. died leaving his wife, Mary Frisby and son, Nicholas Frisby. Nicholas survived his father, but died in 1728 at age 8. Mary Frisby later intermarried with Dominick Carroll, late of Cecil Co. decd. (Liber JK, No. 4, p. 222).

12 Apr 1737. Answer of Mary Carroll states that within 18 mos. of making his last will and testament, William and Mary Frisby had another child, Mary Frisby, who died a short time after her brother, Nicholas. Mary had by her late husband, Dominick Carroll, 5 daughters-Mary, Julian, Elinor, and Susannah before Dominick's decease, and Annastasia after his decease. All are now alive. (Liber JK, No. 4, p. 229).

May Court 1738. Above case abated by the death of the complainant. May Court 1739. Elizabeth Frisby, widow of Peregrine Frisby brought her Bill of Complaint against Mary Carroll. (Liber JK, No. 4, p. 232).

May Court 1740. Deposition on behalf of Mary Baldwin, formerly called Mary Carroll, the defendant in above case. (1) Susannah Douglas, wife, aged ca. 52 yrs. that she has known the complainant and defendant all her life as they are her sisters. William Frisby died in 1724 and Peregrine Frisby died in 1738. Mary Frisby, infant, died in 1736; and at that time had 4 sisters of half blood living. (Liber JK, No. 4, p. 236).

May Court 1740. Deposition of Hugh Mathews of Cecil Co., Doctor in Physick, aged ca. 50 yrs. in above case. (Liber JK, No. 4, p. 238).

May Court 1740. Deposition of William Mills, Mariner, Commander of a ship belonging to the Port of Topsham in England, aged ca. 40 yrs. in above case. (Liber JK, No. 4, p. 239).

May Court 1740. Deposition of John Roberts, Sr. of Cecil Co., Planter, aged ca. 56 yrs. in above case states that he had lived with both Frisby families for several years. (Liber JK, No. 4, p. 240).

28 Feb 1738. William Smith vs. John Worthington regarding unpaid debt. Deposition of Thomas Worthington of Anne Arundel Co., Gent., aged ca. 47 yrs. (Liber JK, No. 4, p. 258).

26 May 1739. Deposition of William Chapman of Anne Arundel Co., aged ca. 47 yrs. in above case. (Liber JK, No. 4, p. 259).

1 Oct 1739. Charles Carroll vs. William Black regarding a disagreement of partnership between Darnall and Black. Deposition of Alexander Black of Anne Arundel Co., Merchant, aged ca. 25 yrs. that the defendant is his brother (24 May 1740). (Liber JK, No. 4, p. 328).

24 May 1740. Deposition of Henry Darnall, Esq. of Prince George's Co. aged ca. 37 yrs. in above case states that Henry

Darnall of Prince George's Co., Esq. decd. was his father. (Liber JK, No. 4, p. 331).

22 Fab 1742. Charles Carrol vs. John Townsend and William Macclaine of Baltimore Co. The Bill of Complaint states that Hector Macclane, late of Baltimore Co., planter decd., made his last will and testament in 1722 making his wife, Amy, extx. Amy later intermarried with John Townsend, Surgeon. William Macclane, son of Hector, lived with John Townsend. (Liber JK, No. 4, p. 356).

5 May 1739. Death of John Townsend abated the case against him. (Liber JK, No. 4, p. 359).

25 Feb 1741. Deposition of George Buchanan of Baltimore Co., Doctor of Physick, aged ca. 43 yrs. in above case. (Liber JK, No. 4, p. 364).

25 Feb 1741. Depositions taken in above case (1) Benjamin Tasker of Annapolis aged ca. 51 yrs. (2) John Carroll of Baltimore Co., Gent., aged ca. 50 that he is brother to the complainant. (Liber JK, No. 4, p. 365).

25 Feb 1741. Depositions taken in above case (1) Daniel Dulany of Annapolis aged ca. 50 yrs. (2) Joshua Hopkinson of Annapolis, Gent., aged ca. 30 yrs. (Liber JK, No. 4, p. 366).

Copy of the will of Hector McClane of Baltimore Co. mentions his daughter, Sarah Bailly (land where George Bailly is now settled); son, John McClane; son, William McClane; daughter, Sarah McClane; former wife, Ann McClane (her children); and loving wife, Amy McClane. (Liber JK, No. 4, p. 368).

8 Sep 1740. Deposition of William Hammond of Baltimore Co., Gent., aged ca. 38 yrs. in above case states that at the time of his death Hector McClane left a widow and 3 children, William McClane and two daughters Sarah and Catherine. (Liber JK, No. 4, p. 372).

20 Mar 1739. Deposition of George Bailey of Baltimore Co., planter, aged ca. 63 yrs. in above case states that at the time of his death Hector McClane left a daughter named Catharine, a son named William, and a daughter named Sarah, all by his widow; and one son, John, and a daughter, Sarah, by a former wife. (Liber JK, No. 4, p. 373).

20 Mar 1739. Deposition of Richard Marsh of Baltimore Co., planter, aged ca. 27 yrs. in above case. (Liber JK, No. 4, p. 374).

30 May 1743. William Woodward; Mary Holmes; Cornelius Cahoon and Sarah, his wife; Benjamin Baron and Elizabeth, his wife vs. Levin Gale and William Chapman. Bill of Complaint states that William Woodward was of London, a goldsmith. Mary Holmes was of Newington Buffs in County of Surrey, a widow. Cornelius Cahoon was of the Burrough of Southwark, a barber. Benjamin Baron is presently on this province, an upholsterer. Amos Garret, late of Annapolis decd., died without wife or children leaving only 2 sisters, Elizabeth Ginn and Mary Woodward. Amos Woodward was a nephew to Amos Garret. Amos Woodward died leaving his widow, Acksah, who later intermarried with Edward Fottrell. Acksah died intestate. Mary Garret was the mother of Amos Garret. (Liber JK, No. 4, p. 390).

11 Jan 1739. William Middleton of Charles Co., Gent. vs. Edward Cole and Edward Jenkins regarding a lease of land.

Bill of Complaint mentions 3 sons of William Middleton-Samuel, Robert, and Hugh Middleton. (Liber JK, No. 4, p. 399).

2 Mar 1740. Answer of Edward Cole of St. Mary's Co. states that after the death of Randall Garland, his widow intermarried with William Murphey. (Liber JK, No. 4, p. 404).

6 Jan 1741. Deposition of Richard Roby of Charles Co., planter, aged ca. 46 yrs. in above case states that Randall Garland had a lease on *Lachia Mannor* from Col. Truman Greenfield, decd of St. Mary's Co., for the term of 3 lives-Garland's own life, that of Mary, his wife, and for the life of Mary Garland, their daughter. Garland's second wife, Ann, survived him; she later went by the name of Ann Murphey. Thomas Jenkins is the son of Edward Jenkins, one of the defendants. Deponent's father was John Roby, who died in 1724 aged ca. 76 yrs. and his mother is Sarah Roby, now living. (Liber JK, No. 4, p. 411).

26 Jan 1741. Deposition of Timothy Carrington of Charles Co., planter, aged ca. 59 yrs. in above case states that Garland's lease was for the term of his own life, that of his then wife Mary, and his daughter Elizabeth, who is now married to Leadston Smallwood of Charles Co. Mary was the second daughter of Randal Garland. (Liber JK, No. 4, p. 414).

15 Feb 1741. Deposition of Thomas Steward of Charles Co., planter,. aged ca. 31 yrs. in above case. (Liber JK, No. 4, p. 415).

15 Feb 1741. Deposition of John Marten of Charles Co., planter, aged ca. 48 yrs. in above case states that his father was Michael Marten. (Liber JK, No. 4. p. 418).

16 Feb 1741. Deposition of Henry Brook of Prince George's Co. aged ca. 37 yrs. in above case. (Liber JK, No. 4, p. 419).

16 Feb 1741. Deposition of Daniel Steward of Charles Co. aged ca. 62 yrs. in above case. (Liber JK, No. 4, p. 423).

18 Feb 1741. Deposition of Thomas Steward of Charles Co., planter, aged ca. 31 yrs. in above case states that Ann Garland intermarried with William Murphey, School Master, about 3 weeks after her husband died. (Liber JK, No. 4, p. 427).

19 Feb 1741. Deposition of Edward Cole, Jr. of Prince George's Co., aged ca. 23 yrs. in above case. (Liber JK, No., 4, p. 428).

20 Feb 1741. Deposition of Francis Goodrick of Charles Co., Gent. aged ca. 69 yrs. in above case states that he heard his father, Francis Goodrick, now decd... (Liber JK, No. 4, p. 431).

22 Feb 1741. Deposition of Thomas Roby of Charles Co., planter, aged ca. 49 yrs. that his brother was John Roby, decd. (Liber JK, No. 4, p. 433).

28 Feb 1743. A petition by Thomas Reynolds of Calvert Co. on behalf of Thomas Holland, a minor, that Thomas Holland, late of Calvert Co. decd., father of said minor appointed Sarah, his wife extx. Sarah since intermarried with Robert Freeland of said co. (Liber JK, No. 4, p. 441).

26 Feb 1744. Roger Boyce, exr. of Roger Boyce, late of Calvert Co. vs. John Bradford, admr. of Thomas Ingram, late of Prince

George's Co., decd. Bill of Complaint states that Roger Boyce was the son of Roger Boyce, decd. John Bradford, son of John Bradford who died in 1734. (Liber JK, No. 4, p. 456).

6 Oct 1743. Deposition of James Sawell aged ca. 46 yrs. in above case states that about 20 yrs. ago he was bookkeeper to Roger Boyce, decd. (Liber JK, No. 4, p. 468).

27 Aug 1743. Deposition of Henry Chew, Sr. of Calvert Co., aged ca. 50 yrs. in above case. (Liber JK, No. 4, p. 469).

26 Feb 1744. A petition by Rachel Croker of Cecil Co. for a patent for 525 ac. granted to her decd. husband called *None so Good in Finland* to be vacated. (Liber JK, No. 4, p. 474).

26 Feb 1744. A petition by James Philips of Baltimore Co. set forth that his grandfather, James Philips, had on 1 Aug 1673 granted by patent a tract of land in Baltimore Co. called *Pocoson* containing 100 ac. He requested the patent be vacated. (Liber JK, No. 4, p. 475).

26 Feb 1744. A petition by James Boarman of Charles Co., grandson of William Boarman late of Charles Co. decd., that on 10 Nov 1703 elder Boarman received 200 ac. by patent called *Timberwell*. Petition by William Boarman of Charles Co., great-grandson and heir at law of Major William Boarman, decd. (Liber JK, No. 4, p. 475).

3 Dec 1745. Patrick Allison of Somerset Co. vs. John Fleming. Bill of Complaint states that in 1735 a treaty of marriage was to be solemnized between Patrick Allison and Elizabeth, his late wife and daughter of John Flemming of Somerset Co., planter. The answer of John Flemming states that Patrick Allison came into Somerset Co. and set up a school of dance. A younger daughter of Fleming's, Sarah, and a son, William, attended that school. Before her marriage, Patrick Allison got Elizabeth [Fleming] with child. Robert Allison is brother to Patrick Allison. For 15 months after their marriage, the complainant and his wife lived with the defendant, and during that time his wife bore 2 children. Two or 3 years after the marriage, the complainant's wife died. (Liber JK, No. 4, p. 490).

4 Feb 1742. Deposition of Robert Allison of Lancaster Co., PA, farmer, aged ca. 34 yrs. in above case states that Patrick Allison is his brother. He has known the complainant [sic] since Sep 1735, a few days before the marriage of Patrick Allison and the defendant's daughter. (Liber JK, No. 4, p. 498).

4 Feb 1742. Deposition of Mary McCuddy, wife of John McCuddy of Somerset Co. joyner, aged ca. 30 yrs. in above case. (Liber JK, No. 4, p. 500).

4 Feb 1742. Depositions of (1) William Flemming of Somerset Co., planter, aged ca. 30 yrs. in above case states that he has been acquainted with the defendant since his infancy. (2) George Brown, Jr. of Somerset Co., planter, aged ca. 25 yrs. (Liber JK, No. 4, p. 501).

4 Feb 1742. Deposition of Dr. Patrick Stewart of Somerset Co. aged ca. 41 yrs. in above case. (Liber JK, No. 4, p. 502).

4 Feb 1742. Deposition of Francis Allen, Jr. of Worcester Co. aged ca. 27 yrs. in above case mentions William Flemming, son of the defendant. (Liber JK, No. 4, p. 503).

4 Feb 1742. Deposition of Peter Taylor of Worcester Co. aged ca. 27 yrs. in above case. (Liber JK, No. 4, p. 504).
4 Feb 1742. Deposition of Levin Gale, Esq. of Somerset Co. aged ca. 39 yrs. in above case states that the defendant's daughter left a child after her death. (Liber JK, No. 4, p. 505).
4 Feb 1742. Deposition of Mary McCuddy aged ca. 30 yrs. in above case states that during her pregnancy Elizabeth lived with the defendant's sister in New Castle Co. and that the marriage took place in Somerset Co. at the home of Robert Hodges. The first child was born dead in Sep about a fortnight after their marriage. (Liber JK, No. 4, p. 506).
4 Feb 1742. Deposition of John McCuddy of Worcester Co. aged ca. 37 yrs. in above case. (Liber JK, No. 4, p. 508).
4 Feb 1742. Deposition of William Flemming of Somerset Co. aged ca. 30 yrs. in above case states that Elizabeth lived at the house of David Wallace in Cecil Co., who married a sister of the defendant's while she was pregnant. She was then moved to the house of Henry Molliston, cousin to the defendant's wife, in Kent Co. upon Delaware. (Liber JK, No. 4, p. 509).
4 Feb 1742. Deposition of John Lane of Worcester Co. aged ca. 47 yrs. in above case. (Liber JK, No. 4, p. 511).
4 Feb 1742. Deposition of George Benston of Worcester Co. aged ca. 25 yrs. in above case. (Liber JK, No. 4, p. 512).
25 Feb 1745. Jacob Wendell and Edmund Quincey of New England, Merchant vs. John Harris and Sarah, his wife of Dorsett [sic] Co. The Bill of Complaint states that Sarah is the widow and relict of Mindert Wimple, late factor to the complainants, and she intermarried with John Harris. (Liber JK, No. 4, p. 513).
25 Feb 1745. Catherine Pritchard, relict and widow of John Prichard late of Prince George's Co. vs. Rebecca Tilley. The Bill of Complaint states that Catherine was married to Prichard in England and he left her there while going to other places, but finally brought her to America. Prichard died making Rebeccah Tilley of Prince George's Co., widow, his extx. and gave legacies to the children of Rebeccah Tilley. (Liber JK, No. 4, p. 530).
25 Feb 1745. Ann Mason, guardian of George Mason vs. Bayne Smallwood regarding a dispute of land boundaries. The Bill of Complaint states that Bayne Smallwood became possessed of a parcel called *Smallwood's Park* in Charles Co. by the death of his father, Prior Smallwood. Part of the same land was possessed by George Mason, son and heir of George Mason, a minor. Ann Mason, widow of George Mason, was mother of George Mason, minor. (Liber JK, No. 4, p. 545).
27 May 1746. Joyce Bradford, John Bradford, and Thomas Gant, exrs. of Jon Bradford, decd. vs. Turner Wootton of Prince George's Co., Gent. (Liber JK, No. 4, p. 557).
20 Feb 1744. Deposition of William Murdock of Prince George's Co. aged ca. 34 yrs. in above case. (Liber JK, No. 4, p. 564).
20 Feb 1744. Depositions taken in above case (1) Thomas Lancaster of Prince George's Co., Gent., aged ca. 48 yrs. (2) Henry Wright of Prince George's Co., Gent., aged ca. 63 yrs.

(Liber JK, No. 4, p. 565).

27 May 1746. Richard Pile and William Pile, infants by George Parker, their guardian vs. Edward Sprigg of Prince George's Co., Gent. The Bill of Complaint dated 18 Oct 1743 states that Richard and William Pile were the only sons of William Pile, late of Prince George's Co. decd, Doctor in Physick. Richard Pile died 24 May 1738 leaving his wife, Mary; one son, William; and a daughter, Elizabeth, who was then married to Edward Sprigg. Mary Pile, widow, died ca. Jan 1732. William Pile died 5 Nov 1732 leaving a wife and 2 sons. The widow then intermarried with George Parker. Jane Griffith, now a wife of Ninian Mariatee, is a daughter of the intestate of a former marriage. Elizabeth Pile, the complainants' mother, is now the wife of George Parker. (Liber JK, No. 4, p. 571).

29 May 1745. Deposition of John Magruder of Prince George's Co., Gent., aged ca. 51 yrs. in above case. (Liber JK, No. 4, p. 590).

29 May 1745. Depositions taken in above case (1) Ninian Tannyhill of Prince George's Co., planter, aged ca. 52 yrs. that Elizabeth, wife of George Parker is decd. (2) Osborn Sprigg of Prince George's Co., Gent., aged ca. 38 yrs. (Liber JK, No. 4, p. 591).

29 May 1745. Deposition of Jacob Henderson of Prince George's Co., Clerk, aged ca. 60 yrs. in above case. (Liber JK, No. 4, p. 592).

29 May 1745. Deposition of Nathanial Offutt of Prince George's Co., planter, aged ca. 29 yrs. in above case. (Liber JK, No. 4, p. 593).

14 Jun 1745. Deposition of Elizabeth Parker of Prince George's Co. aged ca. 27 yrs. in above case mentions Richard Sprigg, son of Edward Sprigg and grandson of Dr. Richard Pile. (Liber JK, No. 4, p. 594).

14 Jun 1745. Deposition of Thomas Harris of Prince George's Co., planter, aged ca. 46 yrs. in above case. (Liber JK, No. 4, p. 595).

14 Jun 1745. Deposition of Ninian Mariartee of Prince George's Co., planter, aged ca. 44 yrs. in above case. (Liber JK, No. 4, p. 596).

21 Oct 1746. William Dawson of Talbot Co., planter vs. Robert Newcomb of Talbot Co. The Bill of Complaint states that in 1659 Anthony Griffith was granted 110 ac. called *Harbour Rouse*, who then assigned the land in 1666 to a Jones who sold the land to James MacGregory. His heir, Hugh MacGregory, sold the land to Abraham Morgan in 1695. He then sold it to John Dawson, late of Talbot Co. decd., father of William Dawson, the complainant. John Dawson died leaving the land to his son, John Dawson, who died without issue in 1726, and the land reverted to William Dawson. The patent fell into the hands of Ann, wife of John Dawson, who later intermarried with Robert Newcomb of Talbot Co., planter. (Liber JK, No. 4, p. 602).

28 Jan 1741. Deposition of Woolman Gibson of Talbot Co., planter, aged ca. 46 yrs. in above case states that Ann, late wife of the defendant, was the complainant's sister and the widow of John Price before marrying Robert Newcomb. (Liber

JK, No. 4, p. 610).
17 Apr 1742. Deposition of Ephraim Start of Talbot Co., planter, aged ca. 34 yrs. in above case. (Liber JK, No. 4, p. 613).
17 Apr 1742. Deposition of Richard Gibson of Talbot Co., planter, aged ca. 37 yrs. (Liber JK, No. 4, p. 614).
8 Apr 1742. Deposition of John Carslake of Talbot Co., planter, aged ca. 48 yrs. in above case. (Liber JK, No. 4, p. 616).
26 Jan 1741. Deposition of Risden Bozman of Talbot Co., Gent., aged ca. 41 yrs. in above case. (Liber JK, No. 4, p. 617).
12 Jan 1741. Deposition of Thomas Hopkins of Talbot Co., planter, aged ca. 74 yrs. in above case states that he heard that John Dawson, the father, came into possession of the land by his intermarriage with the daughter of Bryan Omeha. (Liber JK, No. 4, p. 618).
3 Nov 1742. Deposition of John Carslake of Talbot Co., planter, aged ca. 48 yrs. in above case states that Woolman Gibson was married to the complainant's sister. (Liber JK, No. 4, p. 620)
3 Nov 1742. Deposition of Nicholas Benson of Talbot Co., Gent., aged ca. 42 yrs. in above case. (Liber JK, No. 4, p. 621).
[jumps to page 736]
3 Nov 1742. Deposition of Pery Benson of Talbot Co., Gent., aged ca. 48 yrs. in above case states that Woolman Gibson decd. was first married to one of the granddaughters of Bryant Omely and was last married to Elizabeth, sister of the complainant. (Liber JK, No. 4, p. 736).
3 Nov 1742. Deposition of Richard Gibson of Talbot Co., planter, aged ca. 37 yrs. in above case states that he is brother of Woolman Gibson, decd. (Liber JK, No. 4, p. 738).
28 Oct 1746. Docket. Joseph Jenings and Mary, his wife vs. Richard Chase, admr. of Chase. (MSA Vol. 8, p. 3).
28 Oct 1746. Docket. Richard Snowden vs. William Beall, son of Ninian. (MSA Vol. 8, p. 4).
2 Dec 1746. Docket. Thomas Clark, admr. of Jane his wife vs. John Williamson, admr. of Rippon. (MSA Vol. 8, p. 8).
28 Oct 1747. Lyonel Loyde and Edward Cooper vs. Henry Darnall and George Attwood and exrs. of William Digges regarding a dispute over quit rents. (MSA Vol. 8, p. 45).
17 Jan 1743. Deposition of John Davison of Prince George's Co., Schoolmaster, aged ca. 54 yrs. in above case states that he knew William Digges, father of Ignatius and Nicholas Digges. (MSA Vol. 8, p. 45).
17 Jan 1743. Deposition of Richard Lee of Prince George's Co. aged ca. 37 yrs. in above case. (MSA Vol. 8, p. 46).
17 Jan 1743. Deposition of Philip Lee of Prince George's Co., Esq. aged ca. 60 yrs. in above case. (MSA Vol. 8, p. 48).
17 Jan 1743. Deposition of William Hopkins aged ca. 25 yrs. in above case. (MSA Vol. 8, p. 49).
17 Jan 1743. Deposition of Luke Marbury of Prince George's Co., planter, aged ca. 33 yrs. in above case. (MSA Vol. 8, p. 50).
28 Oct 1745. Deposition of George Plater of St. Mary's Co., Esq. aged ca. 40 yrs. in above case. (MSA Vol. 8, p. 60).

29 Oct 1745. Depositions taken in above case (1) George Gordon of Prince George's Co. aged ca. 45 yrs. (2) Capt. Henry Morgan of Baltimore Co. aged ca. 46 yrs. (MSA Vol. 8, p. 61).
-- Feb 1745. Deposition of Richard Keene of Prince George's Co., Gent., aged ca. 55 yrs. in above case. (MSA Vol. 8, p. 63).
20 Sep 1743. George Rock and Mary, his wife, admx. of Robert Storey vs. Thomas Colwell of Cecil Co., admr. of John Copson, Merchant. The Bill of Complaint states that Mary Rock was the relict and widow of Robert Storey, late of Cecil Co., Merchant, who died intestate in 1737. (MSA Vol. 8, p. 83).
17 Aug 1746. Deposition of Rachel Smith heretofore Rachel Kelley in above case. (MSA Vol. 8, p. 95).
25 May 1747. Philip Walker of Talbot Co., Merchant and Elizabeth, his wife, late Elizabeth Richardson, widow and relict of Anthony Richardson; Anthony Richardson and Thomas Richardson, children of Anthony Richardson decd. and Elizabeth vs. Anthony Bacon of Talbot Co. The Bill of Complaint states that the will of Anthony Richardson mentions a newphew, Anthony Bacon, as exec. and guardian of son Anthony and the child which Elizabeth was carrying. Elizabeth later intermarried with Philip Walker. Anthony Bacon was from England. (MSA Vol. 8, p. 132).
19 May 1747. The Answer of Anthony Bacon in above case stated that Elizabeth Richardson was a Quaker. (MSA Vol. 8, p. 145).
12 Feb 1742. Henry, by Edward Dorsey his guardian; Mary, Elizabeth, and Eleanor Woodwards, by Richard Dorsey their next friend, infants vs. Levin Gale and William Chapman, adms. of Edward Fottrell, Achsah Fottrell and Amos Woodward. The Bill of Complaint states that the complainants were the children of Amos Woodward, late of Annapolis, who died 16 Mar 1734 intestate leaving a wife, Achsah and 4 very young children. Achsah intermarried with Edward Fottrell of Anne Arundel Co., Gent. Achsah died about the beginning of February last intestate, and Edward Fottrell died the end of February and appointed Basill Dorsey of Anne Arundel Co. and Alexander Lawson of Baltimore Co. his exrs. They refused to execute letters of admin. so the will of Edward Fottrell was annexed to Levin Gale of Somerset Co., Esq. and William Chapman of Anne Arundel Co., Gent. Mary and Elizabeth are 14 and 12; and Elinor is 8. (MSA Vol. 8, p. 157).
16 Nov 1745. Deposition of Edward Dorsey of Anne Arundel Co., Gent., aged ca. 27 yrs. in above case states that Amos Woodward died about mid-March 1734 and Edward Fottrell and Achsah his wife both died in Feb 1741. This deponent lived at the house of Amos Woodward about 3 yrs. and was employed in the store of Amos Woodward. Achsah was his sister. (MSA Vol. 8, p. 183).
16 Nov 1745. Deposition of John Lomas of Anne Arundel Co., Gent., aged ca. 51 yrs. in above case states that he lived with Amos Woodward for 5 yrs. before his death and was employed as his bookkeeper. (MSA Vol. 8, p. 187).
30 Apr 1746. Aaron Lusby of Prince George's Co., planter vs. Eleanor Wells and Mary Watkins. The Bill of Complaint states that John Lusby of Anne Arundel Co. decd., father of Aaron Lusby, died ca. 1732 leaving behind his wife Eleanor Lusby

and 8 children-Jacob Lusby, John Lusby, Aaron Lusby, Thomas
Lusby, Samuel Lusby, Rachel Lusby, Mary Lusby, and Eleanor
Lusby. Eleanor Lusby, widow, later intermarried with Thomas
Wells of Anne Arundel Co., planter, now decd. Sisters
Rachel, Mary, and Eleanor are since decd., unmarried and
intestate. (MSA Vol. 8, p. 221).
20 Aug 1746. Mary Scott of Prince George's Co., wife of Andrew
Scott of same co. vs. Andrew Scott, Doctor in Physick. The
Bill of Complaint states that Mary Scott is the late widow
and extx. of John Abbington, late of same co., Merchant,
decd. She later married Andrew Scott, who has treated her
cruelly and turned her out of doors. (MSA Vol. 8, p. 237).
21 Jan 1745. Mary Sim, widow and admx. of Patrick Sim, late of
Prince George's Co., Surgeon decd. vs. Lucy Brooke, extx. of
Thomas Brooke, late of said co., Gent. decd.; and Thomas
Brooke, son and heir of said Thomas Brooke. The Bill of
Complaint cited a dispute over repayment of a mortgage.
Patrick Sim died 24 Oct 1740. (MSA Vol. 8, p. 257).
29 Jan 1744. Allen Davis of Charles Co. vs. Charles Craycroft
of same co., planter in dispute over land boundaries. The
Bill of Complaint states that Jonathan Davis, father of the
complainant, bought a parcel of land from Charles Craycroft.
(MSA Vol. 8, p. 268).
21 May 1745. The answer of Charles Craycroft in above case
states that Ignatius Craycroft was father of the defendant.
Ignatius died when the defendant was 3 yrs. (MSA Vol. 8, p. 275).
6 May 1747. Deposition of Robert Hanson of Charles Co., Gent.
aged ca. 67 yrs. in above case. (MSA Vol. 8, p. 288).
6 May 1747. Deposition of William Hanson of Charles Co.,
Gent., aged ca. 37 yrs. in above case. (MSA Vol. 8, p. 290).
7 May 1747. Deposition of John Davis of Prince George's Co.,
planter, aged ca. 59 yrs. in above case states that he is
brother to Allen Davis, complainant. (MSA Vol. 8, p. 295).
7 May 1747. Deposition of Peter Hoggins of Prince George's Co.
aged ca. 55 yrs. in above case states that he knew Jonathan
Davis, the complainant's father, about 40 yrs. ago in
England. (MSA Vol. 8, p. 296).
8 May 1747. Deposition of Jonathan Davis of Charles Co., Gent.
aged ca. 73 yrs. in above case states that he is the father
of Allen Davis, the complainant. (MSA Vol. 8, p. 298).
8 May 1747. Deposition of William Carter of Charles Co.,
planter, aged ca. 44 yrs. in above case states that his
father was William Carter. (MSA Vol. 8, p. 301).
9 May 1747. Deposition of Thomas Matthews, Jr. of Charles Co.,
Clerk to Mr. Edmund Porteus, Clerk of said co. aged ca. 15
yrs. in above case. (MSA Vol. 8, p. 303).
9 May 1747. Deposition of John Farthing of St. Mary's Co.,
carpenter, aged ca. 60 yrs. in above case states that his
father-in-law was George Walls and that James Davis, now
decd. was the brother of Allen Davis. (MSA Vol. 8, p. 305).
9 May 1747. Deposition of Alice Walls of Charles Co., widow,
aged ca. 54 yrs. in above case states that her husband was
George Walls. (MSA Vol. 8, p. 306).
19 May 1747. Deposition of James Hagon of Charles Co.,
planter, aged ca. 76 yrs. in above case. (MSA Vol. 8, p.

308).
19 May 1747.   Deposition of William Carter aged ca. 81 yrs. in above case. (MSA Vol. 8, p. 309).
19 May 1747.   Deposition of John Hawkins, Jr. of Prince George's Co. aged ca. 33 yrs. in above case. (MSA Vol. 310).
19 May 1747.   Depositions taken in above case (1) John Johnson of Charles Co., carpenter, aged ca. 24 yrs. (2) Rachel Hurdle of Charles Co. aged ca. 47 yrs. that her father was William Carter. (MSA Vol. 8, p. 311).
30 Jun 1747.   Deposition of Ann Edelin, wife of Mr. Richard Edelin, aged ca. 58 yrs. in above case. (MSA Vol. 8, p. 314).
14 Dec 1740.   Kenelinn Cheseldine of St. Mary's Co., son and heir of Kenelinn Cheseldine vs. George Gordon and Kenelinn Greenfield Jowles, exrs. of George Forbes, and Ann Greenfield, extx. of Thomas Trueman Greenfield, Dryden Jowles now called Dryden Forbes, extx. of Henry Peregrine Jowles. The Bill of Complaint states that Kenelinn Cheseldine, father, made his wife Mary, mother of the complainant, his extx. and appointed his brothers-in-law Thomas Trueman Greenfield and Henry Peregrine Jowles guardians of the complainant after his mother's marriage. At his father's death, the complainant was about 4 yrs. After his father's death, George Forbes late of St. Mary's Co., Merchant, intermarried with Mary, eldest sister of Kenelinn Cheseldine, father. Thomas Trueman Greenfield's first wife was Susanna, another of the complainant's father's sisters. Henry Peregrine Jowles intermarried with Dryden, another sister of the complainant's father. Dryden Jowles later intermarried with John Forbes, now decd. (MSA Vol. 8, p. 339).
23 May 1743.   The answer of George Gordon states that Kenelinn Cheseldine, father of complainant's father, died in 1708 and mentioned in his will a son, Kenelinn Cheseldine and 3 daughters-Mary Hayes, Susanna Greenfield, and Dryden. Kenelinn Cheseldine, complainant's father, died in 1717. George Gordon believes that Mary Phippard, mother of complainant, and Kenelinn Cheseldine, father of complainant, were never married. (MSA Vol. 8, p. 344).
23 May 1743.   Present were George Hamilton who intermarried with a daughter of George Gordon; Kenelinn Trueman Greenfield, oldest son and heir of Col. Thomas Trueman Greenfield; and James Forbes, only son of Mrs. Dryden Forbes; in above case. (MSA Vol. 8, p. 369).
14 Dec 1747.   Simon Wilmer vs. Thomas Marsh of Kent Co. regarding the purchase of a slave who was sick. Deposition of John Williamson of Kent Co., Gent. aged ca. 30 yrs. (MSA Vol. 8, p. 420).
14 Dec 1747.   Deposition of Thomas Warscope of Kent Co. aged ca. 50 yrs. in above case. (MSA Vol. 8, p. 423).
14 Dec 1747.   Deposition of Ann Dougherty, wife of Walter Dougherty, aged ca. 40 yrs. in above case. (MSA Vol. 8, p. 425).
14 Dec 1747.   Deposition of John Jackson of Cecil Co., Practitioner in Physick, aged ca. 40 yrs. in above case. (MSA Vol. 8, p. 426).
14 Dec 1747.   Deposition of Lambert Wilmer, Jr. of Kent Co.,

joiner, aged ca. 20 yrs. in above case states that the complainant is his brother. (MSA Vol. 8, p. 427).
14 Dec 1747. Deposition of Samuel Massey of Kent Co., hatter, aged ca. 30 yrs. in above case. (MSA Vol. 8, p. 428).
14 Dec 1747. Deposition of Sarah Massey, wife of Samuel Massey, aged ca. 30 yrs. in above case. (MSA Vol. 8, p. 429).
14 Dec 1747. Deposition of James MacLean of Kent Co., cordwainer, aged ca. 50 yrs. in above case. (MSA Vol. 8, p. 431).
14 Dec 1747. Deposition of Rebecca Ringgold of Kent Co., aged ca. 18 yrs. in above case. (MSA Vol. 8, p. 432).
14 Dec 1747. Deposition of John Hynson of Kent Co., planter, aged ca. 26 yrs. in above case. (MSA Vol. 8, p. 433).
14 Dec 1747. Deposition of Mary Grainger, wife of William Grainger of Kent Co., aged ca. 30 yrs. in above case. (MSA Vol. 8, p. 435).
14 Dec 1747. Deposition of Thomas Warcope of Kent Co., barber, aged ca. 50 yrs. in above case. (MSA Vol. 8, p. 436).
15 Jul 1746. Ann Vinton of Charles Co. vs. John Martin, Peter Mitchell, and John Singleton of the same co. The Bill of Complaint states that William Ansell, late of Charles Co., was the complainant's former husband. William Ansell around 2 Apr last intermarried with Ann Moore, otherwise Church widow. She later married Solomon Vinton, who left this province for about 2 yrs. (MSA Vol. 8, p. 440).
15 Aug 1748. James Calder vs. James Cann regarding a property dispute. Deposition of Mary Pattison, widow of Dorchester Co., aged ca. 77 yrs. (MSA Vol. 8, p. 456).
1st Tues of Dec 1748. Docket. Attorney General at the Relation of John Howard, son of Gideon vs. William Cumming. (MSA Vol. 8, p. 463).
15 Mar 1742. William Bradford of Baltimore Co., planter vs. John Chamberlaine of the same co. The Bill of Complaint states that Thomas Chamberlain, late of Baltimore Co., died about 25 yrs. ago very much in debt. About 10 yrs. after his death, Henry Wetherall of Baltimore Co. intermarried with Mary, the widow of Thomas Chamberlaine. John Chamberlaine is the son of Thomas Chamberlaine, and he lived with Henry Wetherall until he reached his full age in 1734. Henry Wetherall died 24 Mar 1737. (MSA Vol. 8, p. 466).
20 Feb 1746. Francis Finn of Prince George's Co., exr. of Mary Ogden, late of Charles Co. vs. Nehemiah Ogden; Samuel Beall, Jr; and David Trail of Prince George's Co.; and Cornelius Sandford; Ralph Faulkner; and George Riddle of Charles Co. The Bill of Complaint states that Mary Ogden, decd., and Nehemiah Ogden, blacksmith, cohabited and were reputed man and wife. Mary kept an ordinary with Nehemiah's consent. He was so cruel to Mary that they agreed to live separately. She left in Feb 1737. Mary died in Jul 1743. Her will mentioned Mary Goatley, an orphan girl who lived with her; Penelope Musshett, wife of John Musshett; and beloved friend, Francis Finn. (MSA Vol. 8, p. 480).
10 Oct 1747. The answer of Nehemiah Ogden states that he and Mary were lawfully married according to the Church of England. (MSA Vol. 8, p. 497).
17 Oct 1748. The petition of John Merrikin of Anne Arundel Co.

that he has cared for his brother, Hugh Merrikin, a lunatic for 12 or 13 yrs. Hugh's two sons, Hugh and Jacob, are of full age now and are capable to manage their father's affairs. (MSA Vol. 8, p. 557).

29 May 1750. Docket. Cornelius and Edward Comegys vs. Thomas Barclay and Isabella, his wife extx. of Wethered. (MSA Vol. 8, p. 560).

1 Mar 1748. John Carville of Kent Co. and Jane, his wife; Hercules Coutts of Kent Co. and Mary, his wife; and Stephen Bordley of Kent Co. and Sarah, his wife vs. Ariana Margaritta Harris of Kent Co. The Bill of Complaint states that William Harris, late of Kent Co. decd. was the only whole blood brother of Jane Carvile, Mary Coutts, and Sarah Bordley. He died intestate ca. 2 Jun 1748, leaving a daughter since dead and a son, James Harris, about 7 yrs. The wife of John Conner is the aunt of James Harris and is co-heiress. Ariana Margaritta Harris is the widow and relict of William Harris. (MSA Vol. 8, p. 562).

28 Feb 1750. Lord Proprietary vs. Philip Thomas, Esq., surviving exr. of Samuel Chew. The Bill of Complaint dated 5 May 1747 states that Samuel Chew, decd. named his son, Samuel Chew and Philip Thomas exrs. Samuel Chew had entered into an agreement with John Hyde, Merchant of London. John Hyde died in 1732 and named his sons, John Hyde, Samuel Hyde and Herbert Hyde as exrs. They continued their dealings with Samuel Chew until John and Herbert Hyde no longer did business in this province. Samuel Chew, the son, is since decd. (MSA Vol. 8, p. 587).

28 Oct 1747. The answer of Philip Thomas states that he had married Ann, daughter of Samuel Chew. Samuel Chew, the son died in Jan 1736 and appointed Henrietta Maria, his wife, now wife of Daniel Dulany, Esq. and Philip Thomas as exrs. Samuel Chew, the son; Richard Chew; Mary Chew; and Ann, wife of this defendant are heirs of Samuel Chew, the elder. (MSA Vol. 8, p. 598).

30 Oct 1750. Thomas Butler, Thomas Owen and Richard Snowden, exrs. of John Thomas, decd. all of Frederick Co. and John Cook of Prince George's Co. vs. Rachel Sprigg, extx. of Osborn Sprigg. The Bill of Complaint states that John Thomas had been Sheriff of Frederick Co. Osborn Sprigg died about 8 Jan 1749. (MSA Vol. 8, p. 644).

6 Jun 1751. The petition of William Lane of Worcester Co., Gent. that William Probart of Worcester Co., Mariner, married this petitioner's daughter, who is still alive and bore him 5 children which are still alive. William Probart is now and has been for some time deprived of his reason and is unfit to manage his affairs. He thinks he is the Queen of England. (MSA Vol. 8, p. 652).

2 Dec 1751. Michael Macnemara of Annapolis vs. Charles Carroll, Surgeon regarding a dispute over the will of Margaret Macnemara. The Bill of Complaint dated 30 Apr 1747 states that Michael Macnemara is the son and only child of Margaret Macnemara. Joyce Bradford was the sister of Margaret Macnemara. Margaret Macnemara was the relict of Thomas Macnemara of Annapolis. Mary Clare Carroll is the daughter of Charles Carroll, and Mary Carroll is the mother

of Charles Carroll. Joyce Bradford died 22 Dec 1742. (MSA Vol. 8, p. 662).

Copy of the will of Margaret Macnemara mentions Joyce Bradford, widow and relict of Col. John Bradford of Prince George's Co. and "my good friend and relation, Dr. Charles Carroll." (MSA Vol. 8, p. 725).

31 Oct 1748. Deposition of Richard Keene of Prince George's Co., Gent. aged ca. 59 yrs. in above case. (MSA Vol. 8, p. 727).

31 Oct 1748. Deposition of Edward Rumney of Annapolis, Gent. aged ca. 38 yrs. in above case. (MSA Vol. 8, p. 728).

31 Oct 1748. Deposition of William Wilkins of Annapolis, Gent. aged ca. 40 yrs. in above case. (MSA Vol. 8, p. 729).

31 Oct 1748. Deposition of Jonas Green of Annapolis, Printer, aged ca. 35 yrs. in above case. (MSA Vol. 8, p. 730).

31 Oct 1748. Depositions taken in above case (1) John Lomas of Annapolis, Gent. aged ca. 55 yrs. (2) Sarah Bullen, wife of John Bullen of Annapolis, aged ca. 40 yrs. (MSA Vol. 8, p. 731).

31 Oct 1748. Deposition of Mary Burdus, wife of Richard Burdus of Annapolis, aged ca. 40 yrs. in above case. (MSA Vol. 8, p. 735).

31 Oct 1748. Depositions taken in above case (1) Charles Carroll of Annapolis aged ca. 46 yrs. (2) Frances Creagh, wife of Patrick Creagh of Annapolis, Merchant, aged ca. 48 yrs. (MSA Vol. 8, p. 736).

31 Oct 1748. Deposition of Patrick Creagh of Annapolis, Merchant, aged ca. 55 yrs. in above case. (MSA Vol. 8, p. 737).

31 Oct 1748. Deposition of Daniel Dulany of Annapolis aged ca. 60 yrs. in above case. (MSA Vol. 8, p. 738).

31 Oct 1748. Depositions taken in above case (1) Charles Croxall of Baltimore Co., Gent. aged ca. 25 yrs. (2) William Cumming of Annapolis, Esq. aged ca. 55 yrs. (MSA Vol. 8, p. 740).

31 Oct 1748. Deposition of Thomas Butler of Prince George's Co., Gent. aged ca. 41 yrs. in above case. (MSA Vol. 8, p. 741).

31 Oct 1748. Deposition of Joseph Douglas of Kent Co., planter, aged ca. 42 yrs. in above case. (MSA Vol. 8, p. 742).

31 Oct 1748. Deposition of Margaret Taylor of Prince George's Co., Gentlewoman, aged ca. 42 yrs. in above case states that she was informed by Mrs. Sarah Guyther, now wife of John Bullen, that she was with Margaret Macnemara at the time of her death. (MSA Vol. 8, p. 744).

31 Oct 1748. Deposition of Mrs. Ann Young, wife of Hon. Benjamin Young of Prince George's Co., aged ca. 38 yrs. in above case states that she believes Margaret Macnemara had a daughter who died several years earlier. (MSA Vol. 8, p. 747).

31 Oct 1748. Deposition of Elizabeth Beale of Anne Arundel Co., widow, aged ca. 60 yrs. in above case. (MSA Vol. 8, p. 748).

24 Jul 1750. Deposition of Elizabeth McLeod of Annapolis, widow, aged ca. 48 yrs. in above case. (MSA Vol. 8, p. 750).

24 Jul 1750. Deposition of Mary Burdus, wife of Richard Burdus of Annapolis, Gent., aged ca. 41 yrs. in above case states that the defendant's daughter, Mary Clare Carroll now Mary Maccubbin was cousin to Margaret Macnemara. (MSA Vol. 8, p. 751).
24 Jul 1750. Deposition of Richard Dorsey of Annapolis, Gent. aged ca. 36 yrs. in above case. (MSA Vol. 8, p. 752).
6 Jul 1749. Deposition of Thomas Williamson of Annapolis, Gent. aged ca. 26 yrs. in above case. (MSA Vol. 8, p. 775).
6 Jul 1749. Deposition of John Brice of Annapolis, Esq. aged ca. 43 yrs. in above case. (MSA Vol. 8, p. 783).
6 Jul 1749. Deposition of Richard Dorsey of Annapolis, Gent. aged ca. 35 yrs. in above case. (MSA Vol. 8, p. 784).
3 Jul 1750. Deposition of William Reynolds of Annapolis, Merchant, aged ca. 39 yrs. in above case. (MSA Vol. 8, p. 802).
28 Jul 1752. Ann Govane, wife of William Govane of Anne Arundel Co., Merchant vs. William Govane. The Bill of Complaint dated 30 Oct 1750 states that Ann Govane is the daughter of Charles Hammond of Anne Arundel Co., and her former husband was Thomas Homewood of Anne Arundel Co. She is possessed of a large estate by her father and former husband. Her present husband treats her in such a cruel manner that she desires to gain sole possession of her property. (MSA Vol. 8, p. 820).
1 Mar 1750. Deposition of John Jones of Anne Arundel Co., Mariner, aged ca. 28 yrs. in above case states that he knew the overseer on the Govane plantation from April to Sep 1749, John Merriken. The overseer's father is John Merriken, Sr. This deponents thinks that Merriken [Sr.] has a wife, no daughters, but a granddaughter that lives with him named Wealthy Hammond. (MSA Vol. 8, p. 833).
15 Mar 1750. Deposition of Ann Gray, wife of John Gray of Anne Arundel Co., planter, aged ca. 29 yrs. in above case states that she is a collateral cousin to the defendant. Nathan Hammond is uncle to the complainant. (MSA Vol. 8, p. 835).
16 Mar 1750. Deposition of Elizabeth Lewis of Anne Arundel Co., widow, aged ca. 33 yrs. in above case. (MSA Vol. 8, p. 837).
16 Mar 1750. Deposition of Rachel Hawkins, wife of Matthew Hawkins of Anne Arundel Co., planter, aged ca. 37 yrs. in above case. (MSA Vol. 8, p. 838).
21 Mar 1750. Deposition of Joshua Merriken of Anne Arundel Co., Mariner, aged ca. 28 yrs. in above case. (MSA Vol. 8, p. 841).
22 Mar 1750. Deposition of Jacob Watters of Queen Anne's Co., Mariner, aged ca. 30 yrs. in above case. (MSA Vol. 8, p. 843).
26 Mar 1751. Deposition of Frances Hammond of Anne Arundel Co., a Quaker, aged ca. 18 yrs. in above case states that she lived with the complainant and defendant about 7 yrs. and left them about 3 yrs. ago. The defendant is her father's brother by their mother's side, and the complainant's father and the deponent's father are first cousins. (MSA Vol. 8, p. 845).
29 Mar 1751. Deposition of John Davis of Anne Arundel Co.,

planter, aged ca. 24 yrs. in above case. (MSA Vol. 8, p. 848).
2 Apr 1751. Deposition of Wealthy Ann Hammond, daughter of William Hammond of Anne Arundel Co., Gent., aged ca. 18 yrs. in above case states that the defendant is her uncle by her father's side, and the complainant is her second cousin. There was a little girl named Rebecca Hammond who was niece to the defendant. The defendant's brother was Lawrence Hammond. This deponent is a granddaughter of John Merriken, Sr. (MSA Vol. 8, p. 851).
4 Apr 1751. Deposition of Susannah Evans, daughter of Joseph Evans, late of Queen Anne's Co., aged ca. 18 yrs. in above case states that the defendent is her great uncle and that Rebecca Hammond is the daughter of Lawrence Hammond. (MSA Vol. 8, p. 855).
5 Apr 1751. Deposition of Humphrey Boon of Anne Arundel Co., Gent., aged ca. 37 yrs. in above case. (MSA Vol. 8, p. 859).
11 Apr 1751. Deposition of Lawrence Hammond of Anne Arundel Co., Gent., aged ca. 41 yrs. in above case states that he is brother by mother's side of the defendant, and the complainant's father is cousin to this deponent. (MSA Vol. 8, p. 860).
7 May 1751. Depositions taken in above case (1) Mary Long, wife of Sewell Long of Anne Arundel Co., Shipwright, aged ca. 30 yrs. (2) Samuel White of Queen Anne's Co., Mariner, aged ca. 30 yrs (16 May 1751). (MSA Vol. 8, p. 863).
23 Jul 1751. Deposition of Jane Webb of Anne Arundel Co., Spinster, aged ca. 27 yrs. in above case. (MSA Vol. 8, p. 865).
9 Apr 1751. Deposition of John Merriken, Jr. of Anne Arundel Co., Gent., aged ca. 32 yrs. in above case. (MSA Vol. 8, p. 866).
23 Jul 1751. Deposition of Elizabeth Fowler of Anne Arundel Co., Spinster, aged ca. 22 yrs. in above case. (MSA Vol. 8, p. 876).
4 May 1750. Deposition of John Jones of Anne Arundel Co., Mariner, aged ca. 28 yrs. in above case. (MSA Vol. 8, p. 888).
23 Apr 1751. Deposition of Walter Chalmers of Westminster Parish in Anne Arundel Co., Clerk, aged ca. 34 yrs. in above case states that he is a Clergyman of the Church of England. Ann Hammond is the daughter of Nicholas Hammond, now decd. (MSA Vol. 8, p. 906).
24 Apr 1751. Deposition of Sarah Lamb, wife of John Lamb of Anne Arundel Co., ship carpenter, aged ca. 28 yrs. in the above case states that her sister is Molly. (MSA Vol. 8, p. 910).
7 May 1751. Deposition of Sarah Pratt, wife of Thomas Pratt of Anne Arundel Co., sawyer, aged ca. 43 yrs. in above case states that she had served Thomas Homewood about 8 yrs. both during the lifetime of his first wife and his second wife, the complainant. (MSA Vol. 8, p. 915).
29 Jun 1751. Deposition of George Stewart of Annapolis, Chyrurgeon, aged ca. 43 yrs. in above case states that he believes the complainant and the defendant have been married 10 yrs. He heard the defendant talk of relocating to Rhode

Island. (MSA Vol. 8, p. 926).

10 Jun 1751. Deposition of William Steuart of Anne Arundel Co., Gent., aged ca. 26 yrs. in above case states that his brother is Dr. George Stewart. (MSA Vol. 8, p. 928).

1 Jul 1751. Deposition of Charles Todd of Anne Arundel Co., planter, aged ca. 22 yrs. in the above case states that the complainant had 2 daughters. (MSA Vol. 8, p. 930).

2 Jul 1751. Deposition of Michal Owings, daughter of Mr. Henry Owings of Baltimore Co., planter, aged ca. 28 yrs. in the above case states that the complainant had a son. (MSA Vol. 8, p. 932).

5 Jul 1751. Deposition of John Lamb of Anne Arundel Co., planter, aged ca. 38 yrs. in the above case states that George Allen, a blacksmith, convict, servant belonged to the defendant. (MSA Vol. 8, p. 933).

9 Jul 1751. Deposition of Anne Greenbury Jones, wife of Capt. John Jones of Queen Anne's Co., Mariner, aged ca. 20 yrs. in the above case. (MSA Vol. 8, p. 936).

11 Jul 1751. Deposition of Margaret Todd, daughter of Mr. Lancelot Todd of Anne Arundel Co., planter, aged ca. 17 yrs. in the above case. (MSA Vol. 8, p. 937).

10 Aug 1751. Deposition of Susannah Evans, daughter of Joseph Evans late of Queen Anne's Co. Gent., aged ca. 18 yrs. in the above case. (MSA Vol. 8, p. 938).

21 Oct 1752. A petition by Nicholas Sewell of St. Mary's Co., Gent., that Henry Sewell of St. Mary's Co. on 17 May 1664 had a patent granted for a tract on the Pocomoke River containing 1000 ac. called *Wiccomico* and another 1000 ac. on the same river on the same day patented. Both tracts have become the right of Nicholas Sewell as great-grandson of Henry Sewell. (MSA Vol. 8, p. 955).

12 Dec 1752. William Hedges of Cecil Co., Gent. and Rebecca his wife, acting extx. of James Paul Heath, late of Cecil Co. Merchant decd. vs. John Lusby of Cecil Co. and Margaret his wife. The Bill of Complaint dated 8 May 1750 states that a tract in Cecil Co. of 109 ac. called *Larrimore's Addition* was granted on 10 Sep 1716 to Roger Larrimore, father of Margaret Lusby. (MSA Vol. 8, p. 959).

29 May 1753. Charles Homewood, Ann Homewood, and Rebecca Homewood by Charles Hammond, their grandfather and guardian vs. William Govane and Ann his wife, exrs. of Thomas Homewood. The Bill of Complaint dated 14 Dec 1750 states that Charles, Ann, and Rebecca are infants under the age of 21; and that they are the children of Thomas Homewood, decd. May 1739. Ann Govane was his widow and relict and was the mother of said 3 children. Sometime in 1740 Ann intermarried with William Govane of Anne Arundel Co. (MSA Vol. 8, p. 986).

14 May 1751. The answer of Ann Govane states that she paid his share to Peasly Ingram, Thomas Homewood's brother of half blood. (MSA Vol. 8, p. 992).

17 Sep 1751. Deposition of Sarah Pratt, wife of Thomas Pratt of Anne Arundel Co., sawyer, aged ca. 43 yrs. in above case states that the children's grandmother was Mrs. Rachel Hammond. (MSA Vol. 8, p. 1006).

12 Sep 1752. Deposition of William Fodergill of Anne Arundel

Co., labourer, aged ca. 50 yrs. in above case. (MSA Vol. 8, p. 1007).
25 Sep 1751. Deposition of Margaret Page, wife of George Page of Anne Arundel Co., innholder, aged ca. 41 yrs. in above case states that she had lived in the Hammond family for 18-19 yrs. (MSA Vol. 8, p. 1008).
24 Sep 1751. Deposition of George Page of Anne Arundel Co., innholder, aged ca. 37 yrs. in above case. (MSA Vol. 8, p. 1009).
15 Nov 1751. Deposition of John Andrews of Fairfax Co., VA, Clerk, aged ca. 34 yrs. in above case that he lived with Charles Hammond from 1741-1746, during which time Charles and Ann Homewood also lived with Charles Hammond. Rebecca Homewood also lived with him from 1744-1746. This deponent taught the 3 children while living there. (MSA Vol. 8, p. 1010).
16 Dec 1751. Deposition of John Jones of Anne Arundel Co., Mariner, aged ca. 30 yrs. in above case. (MSA Vol. 8, p. 1011).
26 Feb 1752. Deposition of Ann Jones of Anne Arundel Co., widow, aged ca. 47 yrs. in above case. (MSA Vol. 8, p. 1012).
2 Mar 1752. Deposition of Michal Owing, daughter of Henry Owing of Baltimore Co. planter, aged ca. 27 yrs. in above case. (MSA Vol. 8, p. 1013).
4 May 1752. Deposition of Rebecca Gaither, daughter of John Gaither of Anne Arundel Co., decd, aged ca. 40 yrs. in above case. (MSA Vol. 8, p. 1014).
14 Mar 1753. Deposition of Humphrey Boone of Anne Arundel Co., Gent. aged ca. 38 yrs. in above case. (MSA Vol. 8, p. 1015).
20 Mar 1752. Deposition of Elizabeth Merriot of Annapolis, widow, aged ca. 57 yrs. in above case. (MSA Vol. 8, p. 1016).
19 Feb 1752. Deposition of Philip Pettibone of Anne Arundel Co., planter, aged ca. 32 yrs. in above case. (MSA Vol. 8, p. 1023).
19 Feb 1752. Deposition of Joshua Jones of Anne Arundel Co., planter, aged ca. 50 yrs. in above case. (MSA Vol. 8, p. 1024).
19 Feb 1752. Deposition of Margaret Page, wife of George Page of Anne Arundel Co., aged ca. 42 yrs. in above case. (MSA Vol. 8, p. 1025).
20 Feb 1752. Deposition of Frances Campbell, wife of John Campbell of Annapolis, taylor, a Quaker, in above case. (MSA Vol. 8, p. 1026).
30 Oct 1753. John Coursey, admr. of James Coursey late of Queen Anne's Co. vs. Edward Tilghman and Thomas Hynson, admr. de bonis non admin. of James Coursey. The Bill of Complaint dated 30 Jul 1745 states that James Coursey was uncle to John Coursey. James Coursey died in May 1714 intestate, and William Coursey and William Tinbull took out letter of admin. William Coursey died intestate leaving his widow, Elizabeth. After her death, Thomas Hynson Wright of Queen Anne's Co. obtained letter of admin. on her. William Turbutt [sic] died intestate and Edward Tilghman obtained letters of admin. on him. Portions of James Coursey's estate went to William

Cummings in right of his wife, Elizabeth; John Brown in right of his wife, Jane; James Earle in his own right as admr. of his brother, Carpenter Earle; Juliana Coursey and Mordecai Hammond in right of his wife, Frances. William Turbutton [sic] compounded with and paid to Thomas Wilkinson in right of his wife, Elizabeth, one of the repr. of James Coursey, and that he also compounded with Henry Coursey, one of the repr. of James Coursey. (MSA Vol. 8, p. 1038).

30 Oct 1753. Jeremiah Gardner and Daniel Legg, assignees of Daniel Dodson who was the assignee of John Peele, decd. vs. William Peele's exrs. The Bill of Complaint dated 5 Oct 1750 states that Jeremiah Gardner is of London, Daniel Legg is of Cornhill London, and Daniel Dodson was late of Lincoln Inn in Middlesex. John Peele was late of London, bankrupt. William Peele was the admr. of Samuel Peel and Robert Peele. Samuel Peele and Robert Peele were brothers of John Peele and William Peele. (MSA Vol. 8, p. 1057).

4 Dec 1753. A petition by Robert Ridgeley of Baltimore Co. for a tract in said co. granted on 10 Jul 1725 to John Hammond, son of Charles, to be vacated. (MSA Vol. 8, p. 1085).

20 Feb 1754. Thomas Sprigg of Anne Arundel Co., Gent. vs. Benjamin Lawrence of the same co. The Bill of Complaint dated 29 May 1750 states that Sprigg in right of his present wife was entitled to an undivided part of a tract called *Barren Island* in Dorchester Co. together with Benjamin Lawrence. (MSA Vol. 8, p. 1090).

20 Sep 1750. The answer of Benjamin Lawrence states that this grandmother, Elizabeth Lawrence widow and relict of his grandfather, Benjamin Lawrence, intermarried with Richard Galloway of Anne Arundel Co. decd. and had issue by him, Richard Galloway, also decd. Richard Galloway, the father, died 12 or 14 yrs. ago leaving Richard Galloway his son and heir. The defendant states he is the eldest son and heir at law of Benjamin Lawrence of Anne Arundel Co. who was the eldest son and heir of Benjamin Lawrence by Elizabeth Lawrence. The defendant lived in the house of Richard Galloway for 2 yrs. This defendant's grandmother's first husband was James Preston. The complainant intermarried with Elizabeth, his present wife, the only daughter and heir at law of Richard Galloway the younger and also heir at law of Richard Galloway the elder. Richard Richardson of Baltimore was an uncle of the complainant's wife. (MSA Vol. 8, p. 1095).

29 Nov 1751. Deposition of Thomas Sparrow of Anne Arundel Co., Gent. aged ca. 40 yrs. in above case. (MSA Vol. 8, p. 1108).

29 Nov 1751. Deposition of Levin Lawrence of Anne Arundel Co., Gent. aged ca. 38 yrs. in above case. (MSA Vol. 8, p. 1109).

29 Nov 1751. Deposition of Edward Talbot of Anne Arundel Co., Gent. aged ca. 40 yrs. in above case. (MSA Vol. 8, p. 1110).

29 Nov 1751. Deposition of Richard Shipley of Anne Arundel Co., Gent. aged ca. 42 yrs. (MSA Vol. 8, p. 1111).

12 Dec 1751. Deposition of Sophia Galloway of Anne Arundel Co., widow; a Quaker, in above case. (MSA Vol. 8, p. 1112).

12 Dec 1751. Deposition of Thomas Brooke of Prince George's Co., Gent. aged ca. 34 yrs. in above case. (MSA Vol. 8, p. 1114).

12 Dec 1751. Deposition of Richard Burdus of Annapolis, Gent. aged ca. 37 yrs. in above case. (MSA Vol. 8, p. 1115).
12 Dec 1751. Deposition of Joseph Hill of Anne Arundel Co., Gent. aged ca. 48 yrs, a Quaker, in above case. (MSA Vol. 8, p. 1116).
24 Feb 1752. Deposition of Richard Richardson of Frederick Co., farmer, a Quaker, aged ca. 45 yrs. in above case. (MSA Vol. 8, p. 1121).
21 Feb 1754. John Colville of Fairfax Co. VA vs. Rebeccah Tilley of Prince George's Co., widow and extx. of John Pritchard late of Prince George's Co., Merchant regarding unpaid debt. (MSA Vol. 8, p. 1125).
20 Feb 1754. A petition by Basil Dorsey of Anne Arundel Co., Gent. that John Howard, son of Gideon, had on 31 Sep 1749 [sic] a tract laid out for him in Frederick Co. called *Howard's Range* which Dorsey purchased the right to it but now wants the patent vacated. (MSA Vol. 8, p. 1137).
25 Feb 1755. Samuel Howard of Anne Arundel Co., planter vs. Charles Carroll of Anne Arundel Co., Esq. regarding the bounds of a tract called *Howard's Range* in Baltimore Co. The Bill of Complaint dated 24 Oct 1751 states that Samuel Howard is grandson and heir at law of Phillip Howard late of Anne Arundel Co. decd; and that his father was the eldest son and heir at law of his father, and he is the eldest son and heir at law of his father. (MSA Vol. 8, p. 1161).
25 Feb 1755. Lucy Brooke of Prince George's Co., widow and extx. of Thomas Brooke of Prince George's Co. decd., who was the exr. of Thomas Brooke of Prince George's Co. decd. his father vs. Charles Carroll Esq. and Charles Carroll the younger. The Bill of Complaint dated 26 Oct 1753 states that Thomas Brooke was the eldest son and heir at law of Thomas Brooke. Michael Macnemara, son of Thomas Macnemara, is decd. (MSA Vol. 8, p. 1190).
28 Oct 1755. Richard Snowden of Anne Arundel Co., Gent. vs. Rebecca Tilley of Prince George's Co., widow and extx. of John Pritchard. The Bill of Complaint dated 16 Dec 1747 states that Richard Snowden was 11/16th owner of Patuxent Iron Works and John Pritchard was 1/16th owner. (MSA Vol. 8, p. 1203).
22 Feb 1750. Deposition of Thomas Hodgson of Parish of St. Magnus London, Merchant, aged ca. 43 yrs. in above case. (MSA Vol. 8, p. 1218).
2 Apr 1751. Deposition of Samuel Richardson aged ca. 44 yrs. in above case. (MSA Vol. 8, p. 1227).
29 Dec 1754. George Atkinson, exr. of Christopher Grindall vs. John Hall. Deposition of Henry Hall aged ca. 51 yrs. that he is John Hall's brother. (MSA Vol. 8, p. 1247).
24 Feb 1756. Vestry of William and Mary Parish in St. Mary's Co. vs. Thomas Palmer Waughop, guardian of John Waughop. The Bill of Complaint dated 17 Apr 1750 states that in 1679 Daniel Jenifer obtained a grant for a tract called *Jenifer's Gift* in St. Mary's Co. and in 1672 sold it to Thomas Dent. Thomas Dent died leaving William Dent, his eldest son and heir at law to whom the land descended. The land was then sold to Keneline Chiseldine and other Brethren Vestrymen of William and Mary Parish. (MSA Vol. 8, p. 1265).

24 May 1756. Edward Darnall of Charles Co., planter vs. Thomas Darnall. The Bill of Complaint dated 25 Oct 1754 states that Edward Darnall, being a single man, in 1749 made his addresses to Priscilla Moore of Charles Co., Spinster daughter of John Moore of Charles Co., planter with the approval of his father, Edward Darnall Sr. of Charles Co., planter and John Moore. To enable the 2 children of the respective fathers to live together in marriage comfortably, Edward Darnall promised to give Edward the son 60 ac. of land where Edward Darnall the father lived in Charles Co. along with other chattels. John Moore agreed to give his daughter 70 ac. in Charles Co. and other chattels. In Dec of that year, they married. In 1751 Thomas Darnall, brother of Edward, went to visit Elizabeth Thomas, wife of William Thomas and daughter of said Edward Darnall Sr. Thomas persuaded Edward Darnall Sr. to change his will to benefit Thomas. (MSA Vol. 8, p. 1280).

18 Feb 1756. Deposition of Richard Vincent in above case states that the Sat before last Christmas he met Edward Darnall, brother to Thomas, his wife and 2 children with John Moore Jr., son to John Moore, and John Moore son to Matthew Moore. Edward Darnell said he was going 700 mi. and this deponent has never heard from him since. (MSA Vol. 8, p. 1285).

31 May 1757. Docket. Mary Lawson admx. of Catherine Bouchell vs. George Catto and Araminta his wife. (MSA Vol. 9, p. 7).

31 May 1757. Docket. Philip Thomas Esq. vs. John Hepburne and Mary his wife, Richard Chew and Francis Chew. (MSA Vol. 9, p. 8).

6 Dec 1757. Docket. Ann Beall by John Bracco her guardian vs. William Carmichael. (MSA Vol. 9, p. 21).

28 Feb 1758. Docket. Jacob Giles and Joannah his wife, Anthony Drew, Mary Ann Drew, Amos Garrett and Frances his wife, and John Chandley and Drewcilla his wife vs. James Smith and Marmaduke Tilden, exrs. of Susannah Lusby. (MSA Vol. 9, p. 34).

28 Feb 1758. Docket. Nicholas Waters and Mary his wife, and Sarah Andrews vs. John Scott. (MSA Vol. 9, p. 34).

5 Dec 1758. Rachel Caldwell of Somerset Co. vs. James Caldwell, Christopher Piper, Matthew Kemp, and Samuel Ackworth. The Bill of Complaint dated 11 Apr 1749 states that Rachel Caldwell is the widow and relict of Christopher Piper late of Somerset Co. decd. She later intermarried with James Caldwell of Somerset Co. and sometime later agreed to a separation. (MSA Vol. 9, p. 51).

31 May 1749. Answer of Christopher Piper states that Rachel Caldwell is his mother and she was married to his father, Christopher Piper. (MSA Vol. 9, p. 56).

27 Jun 1751. Deposition of Elijah Hitch of Somerset Co., Gent. aged ca. 38 yrs. in above case. (MSA Vol. 9, p. 73).

27 Jun 1751. Deposition of Day Scott of Somerset Co., aged ca. 44 yrs. in above case. (MSA Vol. 9, p. 74).

27 Jun 1751. Deposition of David Polk of Somerset Co., Gent. aged ca. 46 yrs. in above case. (MSA Vol. 9, p. 77).

27 Jun 1751. Deposition of Job Piper of Somerset Co., Gent. aged ca. 22 yrs. in above case. (MSA Vol. 9, p. 78).

27 Jun 1751. Deposition of William Giles of Somerset Co., Gent. aged ca. 39 yrs. in above case. (MSA Vol. 9, p. 80).
1 Oct 1751. Deposition of Michael Dashiell of Somerset Co., Gent. aged ca. 50 yrs. in above case. (MSA Vol. 9, p. 82).
1 Oct 1751. Deposition of Christopher Piper of Somerset Co., Gent. aged ca. 24 yrs. in above case. (MSA Vol. 9, p. 84).
1 Oct 1751. Depositions taken in above case (1) Robert Turley of Somerset Co., Gent. aged ca. 41 yrs. that Rachel Caldwell married James Caldwell in 1746. James Caldwell has a daughter named Martha Caldwell. (2) Martha Caldwell of Somerset Co., Gentlewoman aged ca. 19 yrs. (MSA Vol. 9, p. 86).
1 Oct 1751. Deposition of Samuel Hackworth of Somerset Co., planter aged ca. 41 yrs. in above case. (MSA Vol. 9, p. 88).
1 Oct 1751. Deposition of John White of Somerset Co., Merchant aged ca. 40 yrs. in above case. (MSA Vol. 9, p. 90).
11 Feb 1756. Arthur McAllen of Worcester Co. vs. William Taylor of Worcester Co. regarding a property dispute. Deposition of Angus McFedding of Worcester Co., taylor aged ca. 40 yrs. (MSA Vol. 9, p. 105).
11 Feb 1756. Deposition of George Douglass, Gent. aged ca. 52 yrs. in above case. (MSA Vol. 9, p. 106).
11 Feb 1756. Deposition of John Scarborough of Worcester Co., Gent. aged ca. 62 yrs. in above case. (MSA Vol. 9, p. 110).
11 Feb 1756. Deposition of John Pope of Worcester Co., planter aged ca. 72 yrs. in above case. (MSA Vol. 9, p. 112).
11 Feb 1756. Deposition of Benton Harris of Worcester Co., Gent. aged ca. 40 yrs. in above case. (MSA Vol. 9, p. 115).
11 Feb 1756. Deposition of Joseph Houlston of Worcester Co., planter aged ca. 71 yrs. in above case. (MSA Vol. 9, p. 116).
11 Feb 1756. Depositions taken in above case (1) Richard Ward of Worcester Co., planter aged ca. 40 yrs. (2) William Sturgis of Worcester Co., planter aged ca. 28 yrs. (MSA Vol. 9, p. 117).
26 Mar 1756. Deposition of John Kellam of Worcester Co., aged ca. 42 yrs. in above case. (MSA Vol. 9, p. 120).
26 Mar 1756. Deposition of Whittington Johnson of Worcester Co., planter aged ca. 30 yrs. in above case. (MSA Vol. 9, p. 121).
26 Mar 1756. Deposition of Robert Milligan of Dorchester Co., planter aged ca. 30 yrs. in above case. (MSA Vol. 9, p. 122).
Copy of an indenture dated 1752 between William Taylor and Arthur McAllen, Alexander Buncle and Angus McFadden mentions John Killam late of Somerset Co. decd., grandfather of William Taylor. Also mentioned is Thomas Kellom, son of John Killam and Catherine, mother to said William whose heir is William. (MSA Vol. 9, p. 130).
5 Dec 1758. Docket. Henry Steele and Ann his wife vs. William Allen. (MSA Vol. 9, p. 142).
27 Feb 1759. Docket. Joseph Hill and Elizabeth his wife, Morgan Jones and wife vs. Sarah Connant. (MSA Vol. 9, p. 149).
28 Oct 1760. Docket. Thomas Gilpin vs. John Eccleston and Sarah his wife, extx. of John Porter decd. (MSA Vol. 9, p. 214).

28 Oct 1760. Docket. John Wilmot and Avarilla his wife vs. Joseph Taylor and Benjamin Brown. (MSA Vol. 9, p. 214).

24 Feb 1760. Mary Hammond of Anne Arundel Co., widow vs. John Gassaway, admr. of William Tower. The Bill of Complaint dated 12 Nov 1756 states that Mary Hammond is the widow of Nicholas Hammond late of Anne Arundel Co. decd. who died in Apr 1743 intestate. William Tower died intestate in 1754. (MSA Vol. 9, p. 224).

8 Sep 1761. Thomas Gilpin of Kent Co. vs. John Eccleston and Sarah his wife, extx. of John Porter decd. regarding a land dispute. The Bill of Complaint dated 13 Sep 1760 states that James Porter of Kent Co. in right of his wife Jane, and John Porter late of Kent Co. decd. in right of his wife Sarah were seized of a tract called *Hall's Harbour* containing 500 ac. in Queen Anne's Co. In 1755 Sarah Porter was an infant under 21 yrs. Before Sarah reached her full age, John Porter died making her his extx. After Sarah reached 21 yrs., she intermarried with John Eccleston of Kent Co., Merchant. (MSA Vol. 10, p. 7).

19 Aug 1761. Answer of John Eccleston and Sarah his wife states that she arrived at age 21 on 7 Nov 1758. (MSA Vol. 10, p. 14).

8 Dec 1761. Joseph Hill and Elizabeth his wife and Morgan Jones and Priscilla his wife of Anne Arundel Co., planters vs. Sarah Connant. The Bill of Complaint dated 25 Jan 1759 states that Elizabeth Hill is one of the daughters of Solomon Wooden late of Anne Arundel Co., planter decd. and a daughter of Sarah Wooden late of same co. decd. Priscilla Jones is one other of the daughters of the said Solomon Wooden and Sarah Wooden. Solomon Wooden died in Feb 1759. The will of Solomon Wooden mentions daughters Sarah, Elizabeth, and Priscilla Wooden. Sarah Wooden, the extx. died in Feb 1750 and appointed Charles Connant, husband of her daughter Sarah, the exr. Charles Connant died after 1750. (MSA Vol. 10, p. 25).

9 Feb 1762. Docket. Ignatius Fenwick and Sarah his wife, infants by Ignatius Fenwick their next friend vs. Edward Wheeler and Sarah his wife, extx. of Basil Brooke. (MSA Vol. 10, p. 50).

9 Feb 1762. Ann Bissett of Baltimore Co., widow vs. James Bissett. The Bill of Complaint dated 3 Jan 1761 states that her former husband was John Atkinson late of Baltimore Co. decd. She later intermarried with David Bissett of Baltimore Co. decd. David Bissett died without issue and intestate. His eldest brother was James Bissett, attorney at law, who was his heir. (MSA Vol. 10, p. 60).

8 Feb 1763. Docket. John Wilmot and Avarilla his wife vs. Joseph Taylor and Benjamin Bowen. (MSA Vol. 10, p. 112).

8 Feb 1763. John Mathews and Levin Mathews, exrs. of James Mathews of Baltimore Co. Gent. vs. James Osborne of Baltimore Co., Gent. The Bill of Complaint dated 15 Jul 1757 states

that James Mathews and James Osborn entered into an agreement to exchange land. James Osborn was to get a sufficient writing from his mother-in-law Catherine Bradford to stand her thirds and that James Mathews is to have the burying ground where his father and mother are buried (not exceeding a 1/4 ac.) dated 26 Feb 1754. (MSA Vol. 10, p. 116).

13 Jun 1759. Deposition of William Dallam of Baltimore Co., Gent. aged ca. 46 yrs. in above case. (MSA Vol. 10, p. 126).

13 Jun 1759. Depositions taken in above case (1) Luke Griffith of Baltimore Co, planter aged ca. 30 yrs. (2) William Smith of Baltimore Co., planter aged ca. 36 yrs. (MSA Vol. 10, p. 127).

13 Jun 1759. Deposition of John Bond of Baltimore Co., planter aged ca. 46 yrs., a Quaker, in above case. (MSA Vol. 10, p. 128).

13 Jun 1759. Deposition of Isaac Webster, Jr. of Baltimore Co., Gent. aged ca. 28 yrs, a Quaker, in above case. (MSA Vol. 10, p. 129).

13 Jun 1759. Depositions taken in above case (1) John Deaver of Baltimore Co., bricklayer, aged ca. 28 yrs, a Quaker. (2) Daniel Preston of Baltimore Co., planter, aged ca. 43 yrs. (MSA Vol. 10, p. 130).

13 Jun 1759. Depositions taken in above case (1) Thomas Lancaster of Baltimore Co., planter aged ca. 26 yrs. that in 1754 he was overseer to the complainant. (2) John Lockyear of Baltimore Co., yeoman aged ca. 24 yrs. (MSA Vol. 10, p. 132).

13 Jun 1759. Depositions taken in above case (1) Thomas Ross of Baltimore Co., planter aged ca. 30 yrs. (2) James Bradon of Baltimore Co., yeoman aged ca. 21 yrs. (MSA Vol. 10, p. 133).

13 Jun 1759. Deposition of John Paca of Baltimore Co., Gent. aged ca. 47 yrs. in above case. (MSA Vol. 10, p. 134).

13 Jun 1759. Depositions taken in above case (1) James Sewart of Baltimore Co., planter aged ca. 50 yrs. (2) John Mathews of Baltimore Co., Gent. aged ca. 45 yrs. (MSA Vol. 10, p. 135).

20 Jun 1759. Depositions taken in above case (1) Catherine Bradford of Baltimore Co., widow aged ca. 51 yrs. (2) John Everit of Baltimore Co., planter aged ca. 32 yrs. (3) Henry Wetheral of Baltimore Co., millwright aged ca. 30 yrs. (MSA Vol. 10, p. 139).

20 Jun 1759. Deposition of Daniel Preston of Baltimore Co., planter aged ca. 43 yrs. in above case. (MSA Vol. 10, p. 140).

20 Jun 1759. Depositions taken in above case (1) John Mathews of Baltimore Co., Gent. aged ca. 45 yrs. (2) Thomas Archer of Baltimore Co., planter aged ca. 40 yrs. (3) Moses Ruth of Baltimore Co., farmer aged ca. 62 yrs. (MSA Vol. 10, p. 141).

20 Jun 1759. Deposition of James Scott of Baltimore Co., planter aged ca. 39 yrs. that Roger Mathews was the father of the complainant. (MSA Vol. 10, p. 142).

5 Apr 1763. Attorney General vs. Sarah Rasin, extx. of William Rasin. The Bill of Complaint dated 26 Aug 1762 states that William Rasin late of Kent Co. Gent. decd. was Sheriff of

Kent Co. during 1756. Sarah Rasin is the relict and widow of William Rasin. (MSA Vol. 10, p. 177).

6 Sep 1763. Bequest of Richard Bennett names "Henry Darnall of *Portland Mannor* in Anne Arundel Co. and my cousin Elizabeth his wife, and to Francis Hall of Prince George's Co. and my cousin Dorothy his wife." Also mentioned are Elinor Darnall and Elizabeth Darnall, daughters of Henry Darnall. (MSA Vol. 10, p. 218).

6 Sep 1763. Blackstone Wilmer, William Ringgold and Sarah his wife of Kent Co. vs. John Garrett. The Bill of Complaint dated 8 Jan 1757 states that Sarah Blackstone on 26 Jan 1747 was sole and unmarried and made a Deed of Gift to Blackstone Wilmer and Sarah Wilmer (now Ringgold), her grandchildren, the children of Rose Wilmer-daughter of Sarah Blackstone. After said gift, Sarah Blackstone intermarried with John Garrett of Kent Co., Mariner. Sarah Blackstone was the extx. of Ebenezer Blackiston, her former husband decd. (MSA Vol. 10, p. 229).

6 Jan 1762. Deposition of Rose Wilmer, mother of plaintiffs in above case, aged ca. 40 yrs. that Sarah Garrett died 20 May 1761 and no issue were born after her intermarriage with John Garrett. Rose Wilmer's husband was William Wilmer. (MSA Vol. 10, p. 237).

6 Jan 1762. Depositions taken in above case (1) Sarah Reardon of Kent Co., spinster, aged ca. 46 yrs. (2) Richard Jolly of Kent Co., planter aged ca. 35 yrs. (MSA Vol. 10, p. 239).

6 Jan 1762. Deposition of John Burk of Kent Co., blacksmith aged ca. 50 yrs. in above case. (MSA Vol. 10, p. 240).

6 Jan 1762. Depositions taken in above case (1) William Hynson, Esq. of Kent Co. aged ca. 52 yrs. (2) Thomas Thomas of Kent Co., planter aged ca. 47 yrs. (MSA Vol. 10, p. 241).

6 Jan 1762. Depositions taken in above case (1) Pasco Ioce of Kent Co., farmer aged ca. 30 yrs. (2) Paul Whichote of Kent Co., planter aged ca. 45 yrs. that his mother was Mary Whichcote. (MSA Vol. 10, p. 242).

6 Jan 1762. Deposition of William Apsly of Kent Co., planter aged ca. 43 yrs. in above case. (MSA Vol. 10, p. 243).

A copy of the will of Sarah Blackiston mentions 3 grandchildren-Blackiston Wilmer, Sarah Wilmer and Dorcas Wilmer. (MSA Vol. 10, p. 246).

14 Feb 1764. Caleb Dorsey of Anne Arundel Co., Trade Master vs. Henrietta Maria Dulany regarding a dispute over payment. The Bill of Complaint dated 11 Dec 1762 states that Edward Dorsey late of Anne Arundel Co., Attorney at Law, was the brother of Caleb Dorsey. Henrietta Maria Dorsey was admx. to Edward Dorsey and since her death, Henrietta Maria Dulany is admx. Henrietta Maria Dorsey was the daughter of Edward Dorsey. (MSA Vol. 10, p. 315).

14 Apr 1763. The Answer of Henrietta Maria Dulany, admx. during the minority of Henrietta Maria Dorsey, an infant. (MSA Vol. 10, p. 320).

14 Feb 1764. John Stewart and Duncan Campbell of London, Merchants vs. Thomas Dorsey, exr. of Basil Dorsey. The Bill of Complaint dated 1 Feb 1764 states that Caleb Dorsey late of Anne Arundel Co., Gent. decd. was the son of Basil Dorsey late of same co. decd. (MSA Vol. 10, p. 342).

1 Feb 1764. The answer of Thomas Dorsey states that he was the brother of Caleb Dorsey. (MSA Vol. 10, p. 346).

3 Apr 1764. William Hitchman vs. Anthony Smith and Thomas Palmer regarding a dispute over the payment of a bond. Deposition of Robert Williams of Cecil Co., farmer aged ca. 57 yrs. (MSA Vol. 10, p. 370).

3 Apr 1764. Deposition of Samuel Taggart of Cecil Co., farmer aged ca. 57 yrs. in above case. (MSA Vol. 10, p. 371).

3 Apr 1764. Deposition of James Evans of Cecil Co., Gent. aged ca. 47 yrs. in above case. (MSA Vol. 10, p. 372).

3 Apr 1764. Deposition of John Smith of Cecil Co., farmer aged ca. 60 yrs. in above case. (MSA Vol. 10, p. 373).

3 Apr 1764. Deposition of James Stevenson of Cecil Co., farmer aged ca. 55 yrs. in above case. (MSA Vol. 10, p. 374).

3 Apr 1764. Deposition of Henry Baker of Cecil Co., Gent. aged ca. 53 yrs. in above case. (MSA Vol. 10, p. 375).

3 Apr 1764. Deposition of John Ewing of Cecil Co., farmer aged ca. 37 yrs. in above case. (MSA Vol. 10, p. 376).

3 Apr 1764. Deposition of Lewis Lee of Cecil Co., farmer aged ca. 48 yrs. in above case. (MSA Vol. 10, p. 377).

3 Apr 1764. Deposition of Robert Williams of Cecil Co., farmer aged ca. 57 yrs. in above case. (MSA Vol. 10, p. 380).

3 Apr 1764. Depositions taken in above case (1) Andrew Porter of Cecil Co., farmer aged ca. 57 yrs. (2) William Gillespie of Cecil Co., aged ca. 47 yrs. (MSA Vol. 10, p. 382).

3 Apr 1764. Deposition of James Harrison of Cecil Co., innkeeper aged ca. 49 yrs. in above case. (MSA Vol. 10, p. 386).

4 Sep 1764. Thomas Deale of Anne Arundel Co. vs. Susanna Johns and Richard Johns. The Bill of Complaint dated 4 Mar 1764 states that Susanna Johns is the widow of Kinsey Johns. Richard Johns is the eldest son of Kinsey Johns and is 13 yrs. old. (MSA Vol. 10, p. 415).

[Chancery Records from 1764 through 1767 were missing from the microfilmed records.]

2nd Tues in Dec 1767. John Sewellin of St. Mary's Co. vs. Benjamin Fendall of Charles Co. The Bill of Complaint dated 15 Jun 1765 states that the complainant's father died seized of a tract called *Westwood Mannor* in Wicomico Co. The land should have descended to the complainant being the only son and heir of his father --- Sewellin. Benjamin Fendall trespassed and took possession of the property. (MSA Vol. 11, p. 10).

2nd Tues in Dec 1767. Docket. Mrs. William Kitely and Elizabeth Carroll vs. James Carroll, David Carlisle and Mary his wife. (MSA Vol. 11, p. 16).

9 Feb 1768. Docket. William and David McIlvane vs. John Stump. (MSA Vol. 11, p. 20).

9 Feb 1768. Docket. Elizabeth and William Watson vs. Archibald Fisher. (MSA Vol. 11, p. 20).

9 Feb 1768. Charles Carroll Esq. of Anne Arundel Co. vs. Thomas Rutland. The Bill of Complaint dated 13 Apr 1761 states that Charles Carroll is the eldest son and heir of Charles Carroll, late of Annapolis decd. (MSA Vol. 11, p. 21).

9 Feb 1768. Docket. John Howard, son of Benjamin, and

Benjamin Howard vs. Charles Grahame and William Fitzhugh. (MSA Vol. 11, p. 35).

9 Feb 1768. John Beale Bordley and wife and William Paca and wife vs. Ann Thomas, extx. of Philip Thomas and Edward Lloyd, exrs. of Richard Bennett. The Bill of Complaint dated 17 Apr 1765 states that Margaret, wife of John Beale Bordley and Mary, wife of William Paca are daughters of Henrietta Maria Dulany and cousins of Richard Bennett late of Talbot Co. decd. and daughters of Samuel Chew decd. by Henrietta Maria who since his death intermarried with Daniel Dulany Esq. Samuel Chew Jr. died shortly after Samuel Chew Sr. Henrietta Maria had no other daughters by the surname of Chew other than Margaret and Mary. Philip Thomas died 29 Nov 1760. (MSA Vol. 11, p. 38).

A copy of the will of Samuel Chew Jr. lists daughters Mary and Margaret, and sons Richard, Francis and Samuel Chew. Philip Thomas is the brother-in-law of Samuel Chew, the son. (MSA Vol. 11, p. 44).

9 Feb 1768. William Paca vs. John Ridgely, Elijah Dorsey, Thomas Beale Dorsey and Caleb Dorsey. The Bill of Complaint dated 15 Jan 1767 states that Edward Dorsey Esq. late of Annapolis decd. had 2 daughters and his wife was with child when his last will and testament was made. Richard Dorsey died during the lifetime of Edward Dorsey. Upon Edward's death, his wife Henrietta Maria took out letters of admin. and had custody and guardianship of Henrietta Maria Dorsey, the only surviving child of Edward and Henrietta Maria Dorsey. Henrietta Maria Dorsey, widow, made her last will and testament leaving the guardianship of Henrietta Maria the child to her mother Henrietta Maria Dulany, and upon her death to her sister Mary Chew, who intermarried with William Paca. Henrietta Maria Dulany died 10 Dec 1765. The child died 4 Oct 1766. (MSA Vol. 11, p. 60).

9 Feb 1768. The answer of John Ridgely, Thomas Beale Dorsey, Elij. Dorsey and Caleb Dorsey, son of Richard. (MSA Vol. 11, p. 62).

9 Feb 1768. Mary Harris by Samuel Keen her next friend vs. George Garnett, Jr. The Bill of Complaint dated 31 Mar 1768 states that Mary Harris is the youngest daughter of Thomas Harris late of Queen Anne's Co. decd., an infant under 21. Rev. Samuel Keen married Sarah Harris, another daughter of Thomas Harris. The will of Thomas Harris mentions sons William, Thomas and Edward under the care of his son-in-law George Garnett Jr. The will also mentions daughters, including Elizabeth. George Garnett's wife is Elizabeth. (MSA Vol. 11, p. 66).

17 May 1768. Joseph Smith of Baltimore Co. vs. Edward Norwood. The Bill of Complaint dated 17 Aug 1763 states that Joseph Smith in right of his wife Deborah became seized of the iron works called Onions Iron Works in Baltimore Co. during the minority of Zacheus Onion. (MSA Vol. 11, p. 72).

14 Feb 1769. Thomas Harrison vs. William Perkins regarding a dispute over the shipment of goods. (MSA Vol. 11, p. 177).

1 Apr 1767. Depositions taken in above case (1) John Stinchcomb of Baltimore Co. aged ca. 67 yrs. (2) Robert Gilchrest of Baltimore Co. aged ca. 56 yrs. (3) Edward Orsler

of Baltimore Co. aged ca. 59 yrs. (MSA Vol. 11, p. 178).
1 Apr 1767. Depositions taken in above case (1) Michael Gladman of Baltimore Co. aged ca. 65 yrs. (2) Thomas Gist of Baltimore Co. aged ca. 54 yrs. (3) William Gist of Baltimore Co. aged ca. 56 yrs. (MSA Vol. 11, p. 179).
2 Apr 1767. Depositions taken in above case (1) John Bailey of Baltimore Co. aged ca. 54 yrs. (2) William Harvey of Baltimore Co. aged ca. 33 yrs. (3) Dr. William Lyon of Baltimore Co. aged ca. 50 yrs. (MSA Vol. 11, p. 180).
10 Apr 1767. Depositions taken in above case (1) Daubigny Buckler Partridge of Baltimore Co. aged ca. 45 yrs. (2) Samuel Meredith of Baltimore Co. aged ca. 55 yrs. (MSA Vol. 11, p. 181).
10 Apr 1767. Depositions taken in above case (1) Samuel Tipton of Baltimore Co. aged ca. 46 yrs. (2) George Ashman of Baltimore Co. aged ca. 52 yrs. (MSA Vol. 11, p. 182).
11 Apr 1767. Depositions taken in above case (1) Richard Hopkins of Baltimore Co. aged ca. 50 yrs. (2) John Merriman of Baltimore Co. aged ca. 62 yrs. (3) John Wilmott of Baltimore Co. aged ca. 50 yrs. (MSA Vol. 11, p. 183).
5 May 1767. Deposition of Nicholas Ruxton Gay of Baltimore Co. aged ca. 51 yrs. in above case. (MSA Vol. 11, p. 184).
5 May 1767. Depositions taken in above case (1) Andrew Buchanan of Baltimore Co. aged ca. 33 yrs. (2) Henry Carroll of St. Mary's Co. aged ca. 40 yrs. (MSA Vol. 11, p. 185).
5 May 1767. Deposition of John Stevenson of Baltimore Co. aged ca. 42 yrs. in above case. (MSA Vol. 11, p. 186).
6 May 1767. Deposition of Charles Carroll of Annapolis aged ca. 65 yrs. in above case. (MSA Vol. 11, p. 187).
14 Feb 1769. Joseph Watkins and Ann his wife vs. Robert Swanns exrs., Robert Conden of Anne Arundel Co. and Thomas Richardson. The Bill of Complaint dated 25 Oct 1765 states that Rev. Archibald Spencer died making Robert Swann his exr. and leaving the proceeds of his estate to his nearest relation, Ann Brown now living with Mrs. Jenings widow of Thomas Jennings decd. Ann Brown would reach age 21 on 1 May 1766. In 1763 Ann Brown intermarried with Joseph Watkins. (MSA Vol. 11, p. 232).
3rd Tues of Oct 1769. Charles Carroll of Annapolis, Benjamin Tasker, Charles Carroll Barrister at Law, Charles Carroll of Prince George's Co, Daniel Dulany and Walter Dulany Esq. vs. Edward Norwood. The Bill of Complaint dated 28 Jun 1764 states that a tract in Baltimore Co. called *Combe's Adventure* was granted to George Combes in 1671. Combes died intestate without heirs and the land was granted by escheat to Robert Parker who deeded the land in 1715 to a Mary Scutt. She later intermarried with William Douglas who had a son named James Douglas. James became heir to the property upon the death of Mary and William Douglas. In 1750 James Douglas granted and conveyed the land to Daniel Dulany Sr., father of Daniel Dulany the complainant; Walter Dulany; Charles Carroll; Benjamin Tasker and Charles Carroll of Prince George's Co.; and Charles Carroll late of Annapolis decd., Surgeon, who was the father of Charles Carroll Barrister at Law, the complainant. John Smith, a tenant on the property, died in 1760 and his son John Smith became the tenant.

Afterwhich Edward Norwood forcibly took possession of the property. (MSA Vol. 11, p. 269).

7 Feb 1765. The answer of Edward Norwood states that he believes that Mary and William Douglas had 4 sons other than James. Mary and William Douglas sold the land on 7 Jul 1720 to Tobias Emison. After his death, his widow Elizabeth Emison had possession of the land; and after her death John Hurd of Baltimore Co. was possessed of the land, and he rented it to James Smith. (MSA Vol. 11, p. 274).

3rd Tues of Oct 1769. Thomas Sprigg of Anne Arundel Co., Gent. vs. John Traverse. The Bill of Complaint dated 16 Mar 1767 states that Sprigg, in right of his wife Elizabeth, was possessed of the island tract lying in the Chesapeake Bay in Dorchester Co. containing 700 ac. called *Barren Island*. Matthew Traverse entered the premises and ousted Sprigg. John Traverse is the son of Matthew Traverse. (MSA Vol. 11, p. 278).

3rd Tues of Oct 1769. Docket. Arthur Emory and Ann his wife vs. Sewell Long and Ann his wife, and Emory Sudler. (MSA Vol. 11, p. 297).

2nd Tues of Dec 1769. Lancelot Jacques and Thomas Johnson Jr. vs. Evan Shelby. (MSA Vol. 11, p. 311).

12 Aug 1768. Deposition of John Denton of the County of Cumberland in the Parish of Sabraham in Great Britain aged ca. 53 yrs. in above case. (MSA Vol. 11, p. 311).

11 Dec 1770. Rev. Thomas Chase, Rector of St. Paul's Parish in Baltimore Co. vs. Dr. John Stevenson. The Bill of Complaint dated 4 Oct 1762 states that Richard Chase by his last will and testament devised to his son Jeremiah Chase all this real estate. Children mentioned in the will were Jeremiah Chase and Frances Halton Chase. Samuel Chase is the son of Rev. Thomas Chase. (MSA Vol. 11, p. 437).

11 Dec 1770. John Paca of Baltimore Co., Gent., admr. of Edward Hankin late of London vs. Philip Thomas Sr. admr. of Samuel Chew, and Ann his wife; Henrietta Maria Dulany, extx. of Samuel Chew the younger; John Hepburn and Mary his wife; Richard Chew and Francis Chew. The Bill of Complaint dated 16 Mar 1762 states that Samuel Chew was greatly indebted to Edward Hankin during his lifetime. Mary Chew, daughter of Samuel Chew, intermarried with John Hepburne of Prince George's Co., Esq. (MSA Vol. 11, p. 472).

Feb 1771. Docket. Thomas Richardson and Anthony Stewart, exrs. of Andrew Thompson vs. Robert Johnson and Anne his wife, admx. of John Golder. (MSA Vol. 12, p. 6).

Feb 1771. Docket. Thomas Given and Mary his wife vs. John Broughton and Mary his wife. (MSA Vol. 12, p. 26).

Feb 1771. Docket. Thomas Love and Dorothy his wife, and Peregrine Chunn vs. Andrew Chunn. (MSA Vol. 12, p. 26).

21 May 1771. Thomas Bruce of Cecil Co. Merchant and Bernard Gratz of Philadelphia Merchant vs. Mark, Daniel, Theophilus, Amos, and Nathaniel Alexander. The Bill of Complaint dated 30 Oct 1769 states that Moses Alexander and Dan Alexander, both of Cecil Co., were indebted to Thomas Bruce and Bernard Gratz. Dan Alexander was the youngest son of Moses Alexander. Nathaniel Alexander is the grandson and heir at law of Moses Alexander. (MSA Vol. 12, p. 38).

15 Oct 1771. Docket. John Vansant vs. Thomas Little, William Merrit and James Hynson, son of Thomas. (MSA Vol. 12, p. 36).
10 Dec 1771. Docket. Thomas Browning vs. John Wilmer and William Geddes and Mary his wife. (MSA Vol. 12, p. 66).
10 Dec 1771. Docket. Elizabeth Orrick by Caroline Orrick her mother and next friend vs. Susannah and Charles Orrick. (MSA Vol. 12, p. 67).
11 Feb 1772. Docket. John Moore and Cassandra his wife vs. Aquila Hall. (MSA Vol. 12, p. 78).
19 May 1772. Philemon Young of Calvert Co. vs. Rebecca Arnold. The Bill of Complaint dated 5 Jan 1770 states that Rebecca Arnold is the admx. of David Arnold. (MSA Vol. 12, p. 85).
19 May 1772. Docket. William Thompson, Cornelius Thompson, John Thompson, and Angus McDonald and Ann his wife vs. Josiah Clapham and Sarah his wife, and Ann Carey and Mary his wife [sic]. (MSA Vol. 12, p. 93).
19 May 1772. Docket. John Darnall, son and heir of John Darnall vs. Orlando Griffith. (MSA Vol. 12, p. 93).
19 May 1772. Docket. Charles Carroll and Bennett Chew vs. John Lee Webster, Daniel Charles Heath, Daniel Dulany son of Walter, and Benjamin and Ann Dulany. (MSA Vol. 12, p. 94).
20 Oct 1772. Docket. Charles Robinson and Elizabeth his wife vs. Francis Tolson and John Lowe Jr. and John Baynes, exrs. of John Tolson. (MSA Vol. 12, p. 104).
20 Oct 1772. Docket. Thomas Barker and Mary his wife, John Thorpe, Ezekial Thorpe, John Curtis and Elizabeth his wife, William Clark, Joseph Cord and Martha his wife, reprs. of Edward Thorpe decd. vs. Rachel Thorpe, admx. of Edward Thorpe decd. (MSA Vol. 12, p. 105).
20 Oct 1772. Docket. Mary Norwood, widow and devisee of Edward Norwood decd; Samuel and John, Ruth, Elizabeth, and Mary Norwood, sons and daughters of Edward Norwood, infants by said Mary Norwood, their next friend vs. Edward Norwood, exr. of Edward Norwood decd. (MSA Vol. 12, p. 106).
8 Dec 1772. Docket. William Moore, John Bond and James Giles and Ann his wife vs. Isaac Few and John Deaver. (MSA Vol. 12, p. 118).
9 Feb 1773. Docket. Robert Ross vs. John Jessop and Nelly his wife. (MSA Vol. 12, p. 124).
9 Feb 1773. Docket. Elizabeth Caile vs. Jane Woolford and James Woolford, son of Levin. (MSA Vol. 12, p. 130).
9 Feb 1773. William Moore, John Bond, and James Giles of Baltimore Co., Gent. and Ann his wife vs. Isaac Few and John Deavor. The Bill of Complaint dated 27 Oct 1772 states that Ann Giles is extx. of Edward Fell, formerly of Baltimore Co. decd. The complainants wish to obtain a release from the defendants for payment made. (MSA Vol. 12, p. 130).
9 Feb 1773. Docket. William Goodwin, next friend of Elizabeth Goodwin Dorsey vs. Samuel Dorsey, son of Caleb. (MSA Vol. 12, p. 134).
9 Feb 1773. William Pratt by Christopher Cross Ruth, his next friend vs. Elizabeth Pratt. The Bill of Complaint dated 5 Feb 1773 states that William Pratt of Queen Anne's Co. is the eldest son and heir at law of John Pratt of said co. decd. and that he is 11 yrs. old. John Pratt intermarried with Mary Burk and had issue by her, namely William Pratt her

eldest son and several other children. Mary Pratt died before John Pratt, after which he intermarried with Elizabeth Griffith of Queen Anne's Co. John Pratt died leaving guardianship of William in the care of Elizabeth, his widow. The petitioner requests that William Pratt be removed from the guardianship of Elizabeth. Christopher Cross Routh is William Pratt's uncle. (MSA Vol. 12, p. 134).

9 Feb 1773. Joshua Clarke and William Hopper of Queen Anne's Co. vs. Edward Oldham of Talbot Co. The Bill of Complaint dated 7 Jun 1772 states that Edward Oldham is father-in-law of the petitioners, and for the last 9 months has lost his reason and can not manage his affairs. (MSA Vol. 12, p. 137).

4 Mar 1772. Deposition of Greenberry Goldsborough of Talbot Co. aged ca. 29 yrs. in above case. (MSA Vol. 12, p. 138).

6 Mar 1772. Deposition of William Thomas of Talbot Co. in above case states that Mr. Goldsborough, now decd., was father-in-law to Edward Oldham and Mr. Edge was brother-in-law to Edward Oldham. (MSA Vol. 12, p. 139).

10 Mar 1772. Deposition of Anne Oldham of Talbot Co. in above case that she has been married to Edward Oldham about 18 yrs. (MSA Vol. 12, p. 140).

Jurors found that Edward Oldham has 6 daughters now living-Ann wife of Joshua Clarke, Elizabeth wife of William Hopper, Hannah wife of Nicholas Martin, Sarah aged 16 yrs., Margaret aged 14 yrs., and Mary aged 10 yrs. He also has 3 grandchildren, the children of his eldest daughter Mary Markland decd., namely Mary aged ca. 15 yrs, Edward aged ca. 17 yrs., and Charles aged ca. 12 yrs. (MSA Vol. 12, p. 142).

18 May 1773. Thomas Sloss vs. William McIlvaine. Deposition of Samuel Sloss of Kent Co., Gent. aged ca. 50 yrs. that he knew David McIlvaine, brother of the defendant (9 Mar 1768). (MSA Vol. 12, p. 179).

9 Mar 1768. Depositions taken in above case (1) Edward Waters of Somerset Co. aged ca. 28 yrs. (2) William Geddes of Somerset Co. aged ca. 29 yrs. (MSA Vol. 12, p. 181).

10 Mar 1768. Deposition of Levin Ballard of Somerset Co. aged ca. 28 yrs. (MSA Vol. 12, p. 183).

10 Mar 1768. Depositions taken in above case (1) Levin Dashiell of Somerset Co. aged ca. 30 yrs. (2) William Walton of Somerset Co., taylor, aged ca. 30 yrs. (MSA Vol. 12, p. 185).

10 Mar 1768. Deposition of John Caren of Somerset Co., Gent. aged ca. 38 yrs. in above case. (MSA Vol. 12, p. 186).

10 Mar 1768. Deposition of Gowon Wright of Somerset Co., Gent. aged ca. 35 yrs. in above case. (MSA Vol. 12, p. 187).

11 Mar 1768. Deposition of John Webb of Somerset Co., mariner aged ca. 38 yrs. in above case. (MSA Vol. 12, p. 189).

11 Mar 1768. Depositions taken in above case (1) John Done of Somerset Co., Gent. aged ca. 53 yrs. (2) Levin Woolford of Somerset Co., Gent. aged ca. 35 yrs. (MSA Vol. 12, p. 191).

12 May 1768. Deposition of Robert Leatherbury of Somerset Co., ship carpenter aged ca. 37 yrs. in above case. (MSA Vol. 12, p. 194).

12 May 1768. Deposition of Richard Waters of Somerset Co., Gent. aged ca. 44 yrs. in above case. (MSA Vol. 12, p. 195).

12 May 1768. Depositions taken in above case (1) Stephen Horsey of Somerset Co., Gent. aged ca. 44 yrs. (2) Joseph Gillis of Somerset Co., Gent. aged ca. 62 yrs. (MSA Vol. 12, p. 196).
12 May 1768. Deposition of George Dashiell of Somerset Co., Gent. aged ca. 25 yrs. in above case. (MSA Vol. 12, p. 197).
12 May 1768. Deposition of John Jordan of Somerset Co., aged ca. 39 yrs. in above case. (MSA Vol. 12, p. 198).
19 May 1768. Depositions taken in above case (1) William Venables of Somerset Co., ship carpenter aged ca. 50 yrs. (2) Thomas Whitney of Somerset, ship carpenter aged ca. 50 yrs. (MSA Vol. 12, p. 199).
24 May 1768. Deposition of Robert Taylor of Somerset Co., planter aged ca. 48 yrs. in above case. (MSA Vol. 12, p. 200).
24 May 1768. Deposition of William Turpin of Somerset Co., Gent. aged ca. 62 yrs. in above case. (MSA Vol. 12, p. 201).
21 Sep 1768. Depositions taken in above case (1) William Miles of Somerset Co., planter aged ca. 46 yrs. (2) William Moore of Somerset Co., Gent. aged ca. 29 yrs. (MSA Vol. 12, p. 202).
18 May 1773. Docket. James Miller vs. Robert and John Beall, sons of John Alexander Beall and James Beale his brother. (MSA Vol. 12, p. 214).
19 Oct 1773. John Mackall Jr. of Calvert Co. and Margaret his wife vs. James Morsell and wife. The Bill of Complaint dated 29 Jan 1763 states that Margaret was the only daughter of John Gough of Calvert Co. who died ca 16 Mar 1743. Elizabeth Young, a widow, was appointed to care for the infant Margaret. Elizabeth Young took possession of John Gough's lands after his decease. She later intermarried with James Morsell of Calvert Co., planter. Margaret married John Mackall on 11 Mar 1758. (MSA Vol. 12, p. 215).
1 Sep 1763. The answer of James Morsell and Elizabeth his wife states that Rebecca Day was the daughter-in-law of John Gough. (MSA Vol. 12, p. 221).
27 Aug 1770. Depositions of (1) Rebecca Ward aged ca. 35 yrs. (2) Thomas Johnson aged ca. 67 yrs. in above case. (MSA Vol. 12, p. 231).
28 Aug 1770. Depositions of (1) Abigail Ivy aged ca. 31 yrs. (2) Edward Hall aged ca. 26 yrs. (3) James Ward aged ca. 35 yrs. in above case. (MSA Vol. 12, p. 232).
29 Aug 1770. Deposition of Parker Young aged ca. 55 yrs. in above case. (MSA Vol. 12, p. 233).
29 Aug 1770. Deposition of William Hillhouse aged ca. 53 yrs. in above case. (MSA Vol. 12, p. 234).
29 Aug 1770. Depositions of (1) Mary Brome aged ca. 39 yrs. (2) Joseph Dawkins aged ca. 42 yrs. in above case. (MSA Vol. 12, p. 235).
30 Aug 1770. Depositions of (1) John Pardoe aged ca. 28 yrs. (2) James John Mackall aged ca. 52 yrs. (3) Benjamin Day aged ca. 35 yrs. in above case. (MSA Vol. 12, p. 238).
30 Aug 1770. Depositions of (1) Jacob Bowen aged ca. 48 yrs. (2) James Somervell aged ca. 39 yrs. in above case. (MSA Vol. 12, p. 239).
31 Aug 1770. Depositions taken in above case (1) Benjamin

Blackburn aged ca. 39 yrs. (2) Richard Everit aged ca. 50 yrs. that he married Ann Pardo about 2 yrs. after the death of John Gough. (MSA Vol. 12, p. 240).

31 Aug 1770. Depositions of (1) Samuel Coe aged ca. 42 yrs. (2) John Ward aged ca. 26 yrs. (3) Joseph Conwell aged ca. 25 yrs. in above case. (MSA Vol. 12, p. 241).

31 Aug 1770. Depositions of (1) Edmund Clare aged ca. 25 yrs. (2) Alexander Somervell aged ca. 36 yrs.(3) Michael Culpepper aged ca. 32 yrs. in above case. (MSA Vol. 12, p. 242).

1 Sep 1770. Depositions taken in above case (1) James Dawkins aged ca. 44 yrs. that John Gough was courting Ann Pardo a short time before his death. (2) Samuel Gray aged ca. 33 yrs. (3) Hannah Mackall aged ca. 35 yrs. that John Mackall was born in 1738. (4) John Turner aged ca. 25 yrs. (MSA Vol. 12, p. 243).

22 Dec 1770. Depositions of (1) Samuel Parran aged ca. 53 yrs. (2) Dorcas Johnson aged ca. 36 yrs. in above case. (MSA Vol. 12, p. 244).

22 Dec 1770. Depositions taken in above case (1) Elizabeth Cook aged ca. 30 yrs. (2) Edward Gardner aged ca. 63 yrs. (3) Thomas Johnson aged ca. 67 yrs. that he saw a book in the possession of John Mackall where James Mackall, father of the complainant, wrote memorandums of births of his children among which was "My son John Mackall was born ye 22nd of Oct in ye year of our Lord God 1738 about sunrise..." (MSA Vol. 12, p. 245).

25 Mar 1771. Depositions of (1) Isabella Henly aged ca. 39 yrs. (2) William Harris Jr. aged ca. 48 yrs. in above case. (MSA Vol. 12, p. 246).

2 Apr 1771. Depositions of (1) John Ireland aged ca. 33 yrs. (2) Rachel Ward aged ca. 35 yrs. (3) James Somervell aged ca. 39 yrs. in above case. (MSA Vol. 12, p. 247).

15 May 1771. Depositions of (1) Benjamin Hall aged ca. 38 yrs. (2) Robert Freeland aged ca. 48 yrs. in above case. (MSA Vol. 12, p. 248).

15 May 1771. Deposition of William Allnutt aged ca. 60 yrs. in above case. (MSA Vol. 12, p. 249).

25 Jul 1770. Depositions of (1) William Ireland aged ca. 56 yrs. (2) John Lynch aged ca. 32 yrs. in above case. (MSA Vol. 12, p. 250).

25 Jul 1770. Deposition of Rebecca Dorsey aged ca. 34 yrs. in above case. (MSA Vol. 12, p. 251).

25 Jul 1770. Depositions taken in above case (1) John Grover aged ca. 80 yrs. (2) Samuel King aged ca. 53 yrs. (3) Thomas King aged ca. 68 yrs. (MSA Vol. 12, p. 252).

26 Jul 1770. Depositions taken in above case (1) Benjamin Hanco aged ca. 78 yrs. (2) Aaron Williams aged ca. 70. (3) Francis Hutchens aged ca. 50 yrs. (4) Ellis Slater aged ca. 71 yrs. (MSA Vol. 12, p. 253).

27 Jul 1770. Depositions of (1) Benjamin Grover aged ca. 38 yrs. (2) Mary Freeland aged ca. 63 yrs. (3) Mary Yoe aged ca. 57 yrs. in above case. (MSA Vol. 12, p. 254).

12 Sep 1770. Depositions of (1) Mary Hunt aged ca. 58 yrs. (2) Benjamin Sedwick aged ca. 39 yrs. (MSA Vol. 12, p. 255).

13 Sep 1770. Deposition of William Harris aged ca. 53 yrs. in above case. (MSA Vol. 12, p. 256).

13 Sep 1770. Depositions of (1) Aaron Williams Jr. aged ca. 36 yrs. (2) Edward Hatfield aged ca. 67 yrs. in above case. (MSA Vol. 12, p. 257).
13 Sep 1770. Deposition of John Dossey aged ca. 40 yrs. (MSA Vol. 12, p. 258).
14 Sep 1770. Depositions of (1) Daniel Ducey aged ca. 44 yrs. (2) Philip Dossey aged ca. 65 yrs. in above case. (MSA Vol. 12, p. 259).
15 Sep 1770. Deposition of Benjamin Hunt aged ca. 46 yrs. in above case. (MSA Vol. 12, p. 260).
15 Sep 1770. Depositions taken in above case (1) Thomas Norfolk aged ca. 60 yrs. (2) Joseph Gordin aged ca. 43 yrs. that about 30 yrs. ago Margaret Gough went to live with William Day. (3) Jacob Freeland aged ca. 39 yrs. (MSA Vol. 12, p. 261).
27 Jul 1770. Depositions of (1) Betty Clare aged ca. 64 yrs. (2) Mary Norfolk aged ca. 37 yrs. in above case. (MSA Vol. 12, p. 262).
28 Jul 1770. Depositions of (1) John Norfolk aged ca. 45 yrs. (2) John Norfolk aged ca. 85 yrs. (3) William Allnutt aged ca. 59 yrs. in above case. (MSA Vol. 12, p. 263).
18 Sep 1770. Depositions of (1) Elizabeth Slater aged ca. 49 yrs. (2) Richard Young aged ca. 46 yrs. in above case. (MSA Vol. 12, p. 264).
19 Sep 1770. Depositions of (1) James Dorsey aged ca. 35 yrs. (2) Charles Grahame aged ca. 49 yrs. in above case. (MSA Vol. 12, p. 265).
19 Sep 1770. Depositions of (1) Sarah Fowler aged ca. 38 yrs. (2) Elizabeth Lawrence aged ca. 30 yrs. (3) Joshua Sedwick aged ca. 53 yrs. in above case. (MSA Vol. 12, p. 267).
20 Sep 1770. Deposition of Loraina Hatfield aged ca. 48 yrs., in above case, states that she lived with John Gough for 2 yrs. and was there at the time of his death. (MSA Vol. 12, p. 268).
13 May 1771. Depositions of (1) Jeremiah Watson aged ca. 30 yrs. (2) Samuel Slater aged ca. 34 yrs. (3) James Norfolk aged ca. 39 yrs. (MSA Vol. 12, p. 269).
14 May 1771. Depositions taken in above case (1) Sarah Stevens aged ca. 50 yrs. (2) Joseph Gosdin aged ca. 43 yrs. (3) Joseph Ireland aged ca. 26 yrs. (4) Molly Wood aged ca. 33 yrs. (MSA Vol. 12, p. 270).
16 May 1771. Deposition of Mary Poor aged ca. 55 yrs. in above case. (MSA Vol. 12, p. 271).
27 Aug 1770. Deposition of Rebecca Ward aged ca. 35 yrs. in above case. (MSA Vol. 12, p. 273).
15 May 1771. Deposition of William Ireland 3rd aged ca. 29 yrs. in above case. (MSA Vol. 12, p. 284).
15 May 1771. Deposition of John Campbell aged ca. 47 yrs. in above case. (MSA Vol. 12, p. 285).
26 Jul 1770. Deposition of Daniel Fibbens aged ca. 39 yrs. in above case. (MSA Vol. 12, p. 289).
15 Sep 1770. Deposition of Michael Catterton aged ca. 48 yrs. in above case. (MSA Vol. 12, p. 295).
18 Sep 1770. Depositions of (1) Elizabeth Slater aged ca. 19 yrs. (2) Elizabeth Lawrence aged ca. 30 yrs. in above case. (MSA Vol. 12, p. 299).

14 May 1771. Deposition of Joseph Ireland aged ca. 26 yrs. in above case. (MSA Vol. 12, p. 301).
19 Oct 1773. James Kent and Elijah Bishop and wife and John Shoebrook and wife vs. John Emory. The Bill of Complaint dated 14 Jun 1762 brought by Matthew Hawkins of Queen Anne's Co., planter, admr. de bonis non of Robert Hawkins of Queen Anne's Co., decd., Dorothy [sic] and Juliana Hawkins vs. John Emory. Juliana Hawkins is the widow and extx. of Robert Hawkins and Deborah and Juliana Hawkins are his only children, both infants under 21 yrs. Deborah is aged 7 yrs. and Juliana is 5 yrs. Matthew Hawkins is their uncle. Juliana, widow, later intermarried with John Emory of Queen Anne's Co., planter, alias John Emory Register. Juliana died 1 Nov 1761. (MSA Vol. 12, p. 314).
Feb 1763. Above case abated due to death of Matthew Hawkins. (MSA Vol. 12, p. 319).
13 Jun 1764. Bartholomew Jacobs was appointed admr. de bonis non of Robert Hawkins, and Deborah and Juliana Hawkins in above case. (MSA Vol. 12, p. 319).
Feb 1765. Above case abated due to death of Bartholomew Jacobs. (MSA Vol. 12, p. 322).
27 Feb 1765. William Jacob was appointed admr. de bonis non of Robert Hawkins and Deborah and Juliana Hawkins in above case. (MSA Vol. 12, p. 322).
29 Jul 1769. Deposition of Valentine Thomas Honey aged ca. 49 yrs. in above case states that Robert Hawkins died ca. 8 Oct 1756. (MSA Vol. 12, p. 334).
29 Jul 1769. Deposition of William Carman aged ca. 62 yrs. in above case. (MSA Vol. 12, p. 338).
Dec 1769. Above case abated due to the death of William Jacobs. (MSA Vol. 12, p. 346).
21 Jul 1770. James Kent of Queen Anne's Co., planter, admr. de bonis non of Robert Hawkins; Elijah Bishop and Deborah his wife; and Juliana Hawkins brought their Bill of Complaint. Deborah, wife of Elijah Bishop, is the daughter of Robert Hawkins. Juliana Hawkins is an infant under 21 yrs. (MSA Vol. 12, p. 346).
May 1773. John Shoebrook and Juliana his wife exhibited their supplemental Bill of Complaint against John Emory alias John Emory Register. John Shoebrook is a minor under 21 yrs. and Elijah Bishop is his guardian. John Shoebrook intermarried with Juliana Hawkins, one of the daughters of Robert Hawkins, decd. (MSA Vol. 12, p. 354).
May 1773. Docket. John Cole and Dianah his wife vs. George Cole and John Macnemara. (MSA Vol. 12, p. 354).
May 1773. Docket. Richard Willis vs. Robert Roberts and Mary his wife. (MSA Vol. 12, p. 355).
May 1773. Docket. John Cooke vs. Thomas Pindell and Mary his wife. (MSA Vol. 12, p. 355).
May 1773. Docket. Thomas Lawson, Lancelot Jacques, and Robert Conden vs. Elizabeth Dorsey, extx. of Henry Dorsey. (MSA Vol. 12, p. 355).
14 Dec 1773. Richard Moale and Francis Halton his wife and Jeremiah Chase vs. Dr. John Stevenson. The Bill of Complaint dated 11 Jan 1762 states that Francis is 17 yrs. and Jeremiah Chase is 13 yrs. and they are the only children of Richard

Chase, late of Baltimore Co., Gent. decd. Richard Chase died in 1757, leaving John Stevenson his admr. (MSA Vol. 12, p. 363).

14 Dec 1773. Answer of John Stevenson states that Richard Chase appointed the Rev. Thomas Chase and Rev. Hugh Dean his exrs. (MSA Vol. 12, p. 367).

[pages 396-819 were blank and were removed from the book]

22 May 1780. John Cockey of Baltimore Co. vs. Charles Hammond, exr. of Philip and Rezin Hammond. The Bill of Complaint dated 20 Oct 1772 states that Charles Hammond was the son of Philip Hammond. (MSA Vol. 12, p. 819).

25 Jan 1775. Deposition of Lancelot Todd Sr. of Anne Arundel Co. aged ca. 59 yrs. in above case. (MSA Vol. 12, p. 830).

14 Feb 1775. Depositions taken in above case (1) Thomas Dorsey of Anne Arundel Co., planter aged ca. 39 yrs. (2) John Dorsey of Anne Arundel Co., merchant aged ca. 39 yrs. (MSA Vol. 12, p. 831).

10 Jan 1775. Deposition of Robert Davis of Anne Arundel Co., planter aged ca. 55 yrs., in above case, states that Philip Hammond was the father of the defendants. Alexander Wharfield, son of Richard; Henry Howard; Samuel Owings of Baltimore Co.; Henry Pierpoint; Nicholas Gassoway, son of Nicholas; Adam Shipley and others were present when Philip Hammond sold his Negroes. (MSA Vol. 12, p. 837).

10 Jan 1775. Deposition of Richard Shipley of Anne Arundel Co., planter aged ca. 66 yrs. in above case. (MSA Vol. 12, p. 838).

19 Jan 1775. Deposition of Philip Hammond of Anne Arundel Co., planter aged ca. 35 yrs., in above case, states that his father was Philip Hammond and that John Hammond was brother to Charles Hammond, the defendant. (MSA Vol. 12, p. 841).

11 Jan 1775. Deposition of Robert Hudson of Anne Arundel Co., planter aged ca. 40 yrs. in above case. (MSA Vol. 12, p. 842).

12 Jan 1775. Deposition of Alexander Todd of Anne Arundel Co., planter aged ca. 38 yrs. in above case. (MSA Vol. 12, p. 843).

12 Jan 1775. Deposition of Joshua Young of Anne Arundel Co., planter aged ca. 55 yrs. in above case. (MSA Vol. 12, p. 844).

3rd Tues of Oct 1784. Michael Pue, William Goodwin and Milcah his wife, and Eleanor Dorsey, surviving exrs. of Caleb Dorsey of Anne Arundel Co. vs. Edward Dorsey, son of Samuel. The Bill of Complaint dated 9 June 1784 shows a codicil of the will of Caleb Dorsey which lists 2 sons, Samuel and Edward Dorsey. Samuel Dorsey died in 1777 intestate and greatly in debt, leaving a son Edward a minor of 2 yrs. Margaret Dorsey is the widow of Samuel. The will of Caleb Dorsey also lists daughters-Rebeccah Ridgeley, Mary Pue, Milcah Dorsey, Eleanor Dorsey, Peggy Hill Dorsey, and Priscilla Dorsey. (MSA Vol. 12, p. 846).

Edward Dorsey, son of Caleb, was appointed the guardian of Edward Dorsey, son of Samuel. (MSA Vol. 12, p. 853).

21 Dec 1790. Report of the Committee regarding the Chancery Office concluded that the Records of Decrees and Proceedings are made up to 1773. From Dec 1773 to 1786 no record is

made. (MSA Vol. 12, no page number).

19 Jan 1791. The General Assembly contracted Samuel Harvey Howard, Register in Chancery, to transcribe and record in a proper manner the proceedings of the Court of Chancery from 1773 to December 1786. (MSA Vol. 12, no page number).

8 Feb 1774. John Elgar of London Merchant vs. Francis Rawlings. The Bill of Complaint dated 27 Jul 1763 states that John Elgar entered into an agreement with Jehosaphat Rawlings, mariner decd. for the purchase of a cargo of goods from London. Before the goods arrived in Maryland, Johasaphat Rawlings died intestate and his brother Francis Rawlings was appointed admr. (MSA Vol. 13, p. 2).

25 Feb 1768. Deposition of Bruce Thomas Beale Worthington of Anne Arundel Co. aged ca. 39 yrs. in above case. (MSA Vol. 13, p. 19).

25 Feb 1768. Deposition of Thomas Sprigg of Anne Arundel Co., Gent. aged ca. 52 yrs. in above case. (MSA Vol. 13, p. 20).

25 Feb 1768. Depositions taken in above case (1) Nicholas Worthington of Anne Arundel Co., Gent. aged ca. 33 yrs. (2) John Rawlings of Kent Co., son of Francis Rawlings, aged ca. 25 yrs. (MSA Vol. 13, p. 22).

8 Feb 1774. Thomas Browning of Kent Co. vs. John Lambert Wilmer and William Geddes and wife. The Bill of Complaint dated 2 Aug 1771 states that Thomas Pryer late of Kent Co., decd. was seized in fee of a tract called *Angels Lot* and mortgaged the same to Simon Wilmer and his heirs. Thomas Pryer died and left issue John Pryer his son and heir at law. Simon Wilmer died and devised the land to William Geddes and Mary his wife, and appointed John Lambert Wilmer his exr. (MSA Vol. 13, p. 35).

28 Sep 1773. The answer of John William Geddes and Mary his wife states that they purchased the right of dower belonging to the widow of mortgagor of William Ellias and Sarah his wife, formerly Sarah Prior. (MSA Vol. 13, p. 39).

28 Sep 1773. The answer of John Lambert Wilmer states that he was left exr. by his father. (MSA Vol. 13, p. 40).

7 Sep 1773. Depositions taken in above case (1) John Clayton Sr. that he believes John Pryor is the son of Thomas and Sarah Pryor of Kent Co. This deponent heard that John Pryor had sold his right of redemption on *Angels Lot* to Thomas Browning. (2) Joseph Clayton that he saw the mother of John Pryor married to a William Ellis of New Castle Co. (3) Margaret Clayton that John Pryor is the eldest son of her brother Thomas Pryor and Sarah his wife of Kent Co. (MSA Vol. 13, p. 43).

28 Oct 1773. Deposition of George Browning in above case states that he is the brother of Thomas Browning. (MSA Vol. 13, p. 45).

8 Feb 1774. Michael Tom of Frederick Co., farmer vs. William Gaither and Elizabeth his wife and Thomas Davis. The Bill of Complaint dated 21 Dec 1773 states that Ephraim Davis of Frederick Co. was seized in fee of a tract called *Stoney Ridge* and entered into an agreement of sale for the same with Michael Tom dated 21 Mar 1766. Michael Tom paid full consideration money, but Ephraim Davis died intestate before conveyance was executed. Admin. was granted to Elizabeth,

widow of Ephraim Davis who since intermarried with William Gaither and land descended to Thomas Davis, a minor of 4 yrs. as the eldest son and heir at law of Ephraim Davis. (MSA Vol. 13, p. 52).

19 May 1774. Samuel Chew, John Clayton and John Chew of Philadelphia, Merchants vs. Rizdon Moore and Mary his wife of Dorchester Co. The Bill of Complaint dated 15 Feb 1769 states that an unpaid debt exists between the parties. (MSA Vol. 13, p. 56).

19 May 1774. Benjamin Ogle vs. Ann Ogle, Robert Carter and wife and Christopher Lowndes and wife. The Bill of Complaint dated 11 Feb 1771 states that Benjamin Ogle of Annapolis is the only son and heir at law of Samuel Ogle Esq. late of Annapolis. Samuel Ogle died leaving Benjamin Tasker Esq. and Col. Benjamin Tasker as exrs. Col. Benjamin Tasker died in Oct 1760 leaving his lands to his father, Benjamin Tasker Esq, his sister Ann Ogle (widow of Samuel), his sister Elizabeth Lowndes (wife of Christopher), and his sister Frances Carter (wife of Hon. Robert Carter of VA). Benjamin Tasker Esq. died in 1768, appointing Ann Ogle, Christopher Lowndes, and Robert Carter his exrs. Benjamin Ogle arrived at age 21 in 1770. (MSA Vol. 13, p. 59).

A copy of Samuel Ogle's will mentions his wife, Ann Ogle; son Benjamin; daughters Mary and Meliora Ogle. (MSA Vol. 13, p. 65).

A copy of Benjamin Tasker's Esq. will mentions daughters Ann Ogle, Rebecka Dulany, Elizabeth Lowndes, and Frances Carter; 4 grandsons-Benjamin Ogle, son of late Governor Ogle; Daniel Dulany, son of Daniel Dulany Esq; Benjamin Lowndes, son of Christopher; and Benjamin Carter, son of Robert Carter Esq. of VA. Also mentions Benjamin Benson, under 21 yrs. (MSA Vol. 13, p. 71).

4 Jul 1768. Ann Tasker, widow and relict of Benjamin Tasker Esq. swore this was the only last will and testament. (MSA Vol. 13, p. 73).

27 Oct 1773. Deposition of Christopher Souther of Prince George's Co., planter aged ca. 49 yrs. in above case. (MSA Vol. 13, p. 97).

27 Oct 1773. Deposition of Jacob Green of Prince George's Co., planter aged ca. 40 yrs., in above case, states that he lived with Samuel Ogle at the time of this death. (MSA Vol. 13, p. 98).

28 Oct 1773. Deposition of Upton Scott of Annapolis, Physician aged ca. 45 yrs. in above case. (MSA Vol. 13, p. 99).

28 Oct 1773. Deposition of John Ridout of Annapolis Esq. aged ca. 40 yrs., in above case, states that he married Mary, daughter of Samuel Ogle. (MSA Vol. 13, p. 101).

28 Oct 1773. Deposition of George Stewart of Annapolis Esq. aged ca. 65 yrs. in above case. (MSA Vol. 13, p. 102).

14 Jan 1774. Deposition of Charles Carroll of Anne Arundel Co. Esq. aged ca. 71 yrs., in above case, states that Benjamin Ogle is the son of Ann Ogle, whose father is the late Benjamin Tasker Esq. Sr. Benjamin Ogle is the nephew of Col. Benjamin Tasker. (MSA Vol. 13, p. 106).

14 Jan 1774. Deposition of Nicholas Maccubbin of Annapolis, merchant aged ca. 65 yrs. in above case. (MSA Vol. 13, p.

107).

19 Jan 1774. Depositions taken in above case (1) John Duckett of Annapolis aged ca. 39 yrs. (2) Joseph Sprigg of Prince George's Co. aged ca. 38 yrs. (MSA Vol. 13, p. 111).

14 Feb 1775. Jeremiah Townley Chase of Annapolis, Gent. vs. Dr. John Stevenson. The Bill of Complaint dated 13 Oct 1769 states that Jeremiah Townley Chase is the son and heir of Richard Chase, late of Baltimore Co. Gent. Jeremiah's sister, Frances Halton intermarried with Richard Moale of Baltimore, merchant; and his uncle was Rev. Thomas Chase. Frances arrived at 21 yrs. 11 Jan 1766 and Jeremiah arrived at age 21 on 3 Jun 1769. (MSA Vol. 13, p. 130).

28 Apr 1773. Deposition of Samuel Chase of Annapolis Esq. aged ca. 32 yrs., in above case, states that he is the son of Rev. Thomas Chase. (MSA Vol. 13, p. 142).

28 Apr 1773. Deposition of Rev. Thomas Chase, Rector of St. Paul's Parish in Baltimore Co. aged ca. 70 yrs. in above case. (MSA Vol. 13, p. 148).

28 Apr 1773. Deposition of Robert Alexander of Baltimore, attorney at law, aged ca. 33 yrs. in above case. (MSA Vol. 13, p. 149).

28 Apr 1773. Depositions taken in above case (1) Benjamin Howard of Anne Arundel Co. aged ca. 29 yrs. (2) Rev. Hugh Dean, Rector of St. John's Parish in Baltimore Co., aged ca. 69 yrs. (MSA Vol. 13, p. 150).

10 Dec 1778. Docket. Samuel Howell by Sarah Wirchwaist his mother vs. Jacob Giles. (MSA Vol. 13, p. 194).

10 Dec 1778. Docket. Stephen Gartrell vs. John Penn, son and heir at law of Anne Penn one of the daughters of S. Gartrell. (MSA Vol. 13, p. 197).

11 Feb 1779. Docket. Richard Dale, son and heir at law of John Dale vs. John Roberts and Robert Saunders. (MSA Vol. 13, p. 202).

11 Feb 1779. Thomas Browning of Kent Co. vs. Mary Balthrope and Edward Smoot. The Bill of Complaint dated 2 Mar 1775 states that Thomas Browning agreed with Boles Tyer Balthrop late of Charles Co. on 13 Jul 1767 to purchase a tract of land which Balthrop's wife had as a right of dower. At his death, Balthrop left only a child, Mary Balthrop, who is a minor under the guardianship of Edward Smoot. (MSA Vol. 13, p. 203).

20 Apr 1775. The answer of Edward Smoot states that Balthrop's wife was Anne, since decd. (MSA Vol. 13, p. 205).

11 Feb 1779. Thomas Jenings of Annapolis, Attorney at Law vs. Mary Hesselius and John Hesselius the infant heir at law of John Hesselius decd. The Bill of Complaint dated 25 Jan 1779 states that Jenings contracted with the late John Hesselius of Anne Arundel Co. decd. for the purchase of the following tracts:*Alcot's Triangle*, *Hog Neck* otherwise called *Davis' Lot* and *Bennet's Park*. Before the deed of conveyance was executed, John Hesselius died, leaving John Hesselius his only son and heir at law, an infant of about 1 yr. and his widow, Mary Hesselius, mother and natural guardian of John Hesselius. (MSA Vol. 13, p. 208).

11 Feb 1779. William Goodwin of Baltimore Co., merchant vs. Margaret Dorsey, admx. of Edward Dorsey, heir at law of

Samuel Dorsey decd. late of Anne Arundel Co. The Bill of Complaint dated 25 Jan 1779 states that Samuel Dorsey was indebted to William Goodwin by a legacy left to Milcah Dorsey, now Goodwin, wife to William Goodwin, by Caleb Dorsey, her father. Margaret Dorsey is the widow and relict of Samuel Dorsey, and Edward Dorsey is about 6 yrs. of age. (MSA Vol. 13, p. 213).

11 Feb 1779. John Wells of Anne Arundel Co. vs. Margaret Dorsey, admx. and Edward Dorsey, heir at law of Samuel Dorsey decd. The Bill of Complaint is dated 25 Jan 1779. (MSA Vol. 13, p. 216).

11 Feb 1779. The answer of Margaret Dorsey, admx. and Edward Dorsey states that Samuel Dorsey died Sep 1777. (MSA Vol. 13, p. 219).

11 Feb 1779. John Dorsey vs. Margaret Dorsey admx. and Edward Dorsey, heir at law of Samuel Dorsey. The Bill of Complaint is dated 25 Jan 1779. (MSA Vol. 13, p. 222).

11 Feb 1779. Michael Pue and Mary his wife vs. Margaret Dorsey, admx. and Edward Dorsey, heir at law of Samuel Dorsey decd. The Bill of Complaint dated 25 Jan 1779 states that Mary Pue is the daughter of Caleb Dorsey of Anne Arundel Co. decd. in Jun 1772 and a sister of Samuel Dorsey, decd. (MSA Vol. 13, p. 229).

May 1780. A note in the book stating that it is out of order. (MSA Vol. 13, p. 257).

10 Dec 1780. Docket. Charles Greenbury Griffith vs. Ebenezer Davis, exr. and Forrest Davis, son and heir at law of Lodowick Davis, decd (Montgomery Co.). (MSA Vol. 13, p. 296).

10 Dec 1780. Docket. Samuel Chase vs. John Welsh and Susannah his wife, extx. of Samuel Mansell and George Mansell, exr. of Samuel Mansell (Anne Arundel Co.). (MSA Vol. 13, p. 298).

11 Feb 1781. Enoch Morgan vs. James Kendrick. The Bill of Complaint dated 31 Aug 1768 brought by Henry Morgan of Talbot Co. states that on 29 Jul 1681 John Wootters, decd. had a tract in Talbot Co. called *Coventry* laid out for him of 350 ac. On 31 Mar 1684 he assigned the land to John Jadwin of Talbot Co. decd. who took possession of the land. In his will, John Jadwin left *Coventry* to his daughter, Sarah Jadwin. If she were to die without issue the land would descend to his daughter Elizabeth Jenkinson's children and his grandson, Jeremiah Jadwin's children. About 18 Feb 1707, Sarah Jadwin intermarried with Philip Morgan, now decd, by whom she had issue her eldest son Enoch Morgan, now decd. He married and had issue, his eldest son Henry Morgan. After Philip Morgan's death, his widow Sarah (now decd.) intermarried with James Kendrick ca. 1734, who died ca. 1747 and by whom she had issue James Kendrick, the defendant. (MSA Vol. 13, p. 301).

4 Jun 1772. Deposition of Michael Kirby of Talbot Co. aged ca. 74 yrs., in above case, states that Enoch Morgan married Sarah Neall. Sarah Jadwin is buried on the plantation where the defendant now lives. He heard that Philip Morgan was married in Carolina. Enoch Morgan died in Talbot Co. (MSA Vol. 13, p. 307).

4 Jun 1772. Depositions taken in above case (1) Sarah Booth of

Talbot Co. aged ca. 69. (2) Elizabeth Kirby of Talbot Co. aged ca. 60 yrs. (MSA Vol. 13, p. 308).
4 Jun 1772. Depositions taken in above case James Wilson of Talbot Co. aged ca. 78 yrs, a Quaker. (2) Keziah Burgess of Talbot Co. aged ca. 51 yrs. that she knew James Kendrick from his marriage with her mother. She did not know Sarah Jadwin before her marriage with Philip Morgan. (MSA Vol. 13, p. 309).
5 Jun 1772. Deposition of James Benny of Talbot Co. aged ca. 64 yrs. in above case. (MSA Vol. 13, p. 310).
5 Jun 1772. Deposition of Sarah Morgan, a Quaker, mother of the complainant of Talbot Co. aged ca. 51 yrs., in above case, states that she was Sarah Neall and married Enoch Morgan on 3 Jul 1742. Enoch died about 6 yrs. ago. (MSA Vol. 13, p. 311).
5 Jun 1772. Deposition of Saban Morgan of Talbot Co. aged ca. 49 yrs., in above case, states that he heard his mother was before her marriage Sarah Jadwin, and he does not remember his father Philip Morgan. Philip Morgan left these parts. (MSA Vol. 13, p. 311).
5 Jun 1772. Deposition of John Thornton of Talbot Co. aged ca. 58 yrs. in above case. (MSA Vol. 13, p. 312).
5 Jun 1772. Deposition of Margaret Kirby of Talbot Co. aged ca. 63 yrs., in above case, states that she heard the defendant's father had a girl by his intermarriage with Sarah Morgan. (MSA Vol. 13, p. 314).
5 Jun 1772. Depositions taken in above case (1) Joseph Callahan of Talbot Co. aged ca. 38 yrs. (2) Sabin Morgan of Talbot Co. aged ca. 49 yrs. that he believes the defendant James Kendrick will be 35 next July and the daughter of the marriage of the defendant's father and Sarah Morgan would be 4 or 5 yrs. older than the defendant. (MSA Vol. 13, p. 315).
9 Sep 1772. Deposition of Thomas Turner of Talbot Co. aged ca. 51 yrs., in above case, states that the daughter of James Kendrick decd. and Sarah his wife was named Sarah. (MSA Vol. 13, p. 316).
15 Sep 1772. Deposition of John Kirby of Talbot Co. aged ca. 40 yrs. in above case. (MSA Vol. 13, p. 317).
Oct 1773. Above case was abated due to the death of the complainant, Henry Morgan. Case continued in Dec Court 1773 by Enoch Morgan, infant brother of Henry Morgan decd. by Francis Baker, his next friend. (MSA Vol. 13, p. 318).
19 May 1781. Thomas Gantt Denwood of Somerset Co., mariner vs. Thomas Denwood's adms., Ephraim Wilson, James Wilson and William Winder. The Bill of Complaint dated 23 Feb 1770 states that Thomas Denwood late of Somerset Co. was the father of the complainant and was indebted to Ephraim Wilson as exr. of David Wilson decd. Thomas Denwood died intestate in Mar 1760 leaving Thomas Gantt Denwood, his eldest son an infant, and Mary his widow. Said Mary intermarried with William Winder of Somerset Co. (MSA Vol. 13, p. 343).
A copy of a grant of Ephraim Wilson mentions his brother James Wilson; three sisters Ann, Betty, and Esther; and his father David Wilson. (MSA Vol. 13, p. 348).
25 May 1781. The answer of William Winder and Mary his wife states that Thomas Denwood died intestate leaving 8 children,

5 of which were infants. Thomas Denwood, the son, was of full age in 1759. One of the children was Priscilla Denwood, now Jones. (MSA Vol. 13, p. 349).

10 Jun 1772. Deposition of William Gilliss of Somerset Co., Gent. aged ca. 41 yrs. in above case. (MSA Vol. 13, p. 357).

20 Jul 1772. Deposition of Samuel MClemmy of Somerset Co., Gent. aged ca. 27 yrs. in above case. (MSA Vol. 13, p. 358).

20 Jul 1772. Deposition of John Denwood of Somerset Co., Gent. aged ca. 24 yrs., in above case, states that he was a son of Thomas Denwood. (MSA Vol. 13, p. 359).

20 Jul 1772. Depositions taken in above case (1) John McGrath of Somerset Co., planter aged ca. 43 yrs. that John Jones intermarried with Priscilla Denwood. (2) Levin Woolford of Somerset Co., planter aged ca. 38 yrs. (MSA Vol. 13, p. 360).

17 Aug 1772. Deposition of William Waters of Somerset Co., Gent. aged ca. 32 yrs. in above case. (MSA Vol. 13, p. 363).

17 Aug 1772. Deposition of Joseph Gilliss of Somerset Co., Gent. aged ca. 67 yrs. in above case. (MSA Vol. 13, p. 364).

17 Aug 1772. Deposition of Levin Ballard of Somerset Co., Gent. aged ca. 65 yrs. in above case. (MSA Vol. 13, p. 365).

13 Oct 1772. Depositions taken in above case (1) Edward Waters of Somerset Co., Gent. aged ca. 65 yrs. (2) Peter Waters of Somerset Co., Gent. aged ca. 27 (1 Jul 1772). (MSA Vol. 13, p. 366).

17 Aug 1772. Deposition of John Jordan of Somerset Co., planter aged ca. 43 yrs. in above case. (MSA Vol. 13, p. 367).

17 Aug 1772. Deposition of Mary Ann Woolford of Somerset Co., widow aged ca. 25 yrs., in above case, states that one of the children of Thomas and Mary Denwood, Betsey Denwood, left her mother and went over the bay. This deponent has not received her distributive share. (MSA Vol. 13, p. 368).

17 Aug 1772. Depositions taken in above case (1) Arnold Elzey of Somerset Co., Gent. aged ca. 48 yrs. (2) Matthias Miles of Somerset Co., surveyor aged ca. 26 yrs. (MSA Vol. 13, p. 369).

17 Aug 1772. Depositions taken in above case (1) William Skirvin of Somerset Co., planter aged ca. 52 yrs. (2) Thomas Prior of Somerset Co., planter aged ca. 45 yrs. (3) Ephraim Wilson of Somerset Co., planter aged ca. 46 yrs. (MSA Vol. 13, p. 370).

17 Aug 1772. Deposition of Thomas Holbrook of Somerset Co., Gent. aged ca. 48 yrs. in above case. (MSA Vol. 13, p. 371).

13 Oct 1772. Depositions taken in above case (1) William Haley of Somerset Co., planter aged ca. 31 yrs. (2) John Malcomb of Somerset Co., blacksmith aged ca. 28 yrs. that he served his time as apprentice with John Jones. (3) John Jones, son of Robert, of Somerset Co. planter aged ca. 33 yrs. (MSA Vol. 13, p. 372).

17 Aug 1772. Depositions taken in above case (1) Robert Ebzey of Somerset Co., Gent. aged ca. 45 yrs. (2) William Miles of Somerset Co., planter aged ca. 51 yrs. (MSA Vol. 13, p. 373).

17 Aug 1772. Deposition of David Wilson of Somerset Co., planter aged ca. 35 yrs. in above case. (MSA Vol. 13, p. 374).

17 Aug 1772. Deposition of Mary Winder of Somerset Co.,

spinster aged ca. 48 yrs. in above case. (MSA Vol. 13, p. 375).

17 Aug 1772. Deposition of Denwood Wilson of Somerset Co., planter aged ca. 32 yrs. in above case. (MSA Vol. 13, p. 376).

17 Aug 1772. Deposition of Rev. Hamilton Bell of Somerset Co., Gent. aged ca. 61 yrs. in above case. (MSA Vol. 13, p. 377).

13 Oct 1772. Depositions taken in above case (1) Thomas Sloss of Somerset Co., Gent. aged ca. 50 yrs. (2) Samuel Wilson of Somerset Co., Gent. aged ca. 37 yrs. (MSA Vol. 13, p. 378).

17 Aug 1772. Depositions taken in above case of (1) Robert Elzey of Somerset Co., Gent. aged ca. 45 yrs. (2) David Wilson of Somerset Co., planter aged ca. 35 yrs. (MSA Vol. 13, p. 379).

In the Records of Somerset Co., admin. papers list representatives of Thomas Denwood-Mary Denwood, Thomas Sloss and Charles Woolford of Somerset Co. bound unto Thomas Denwood, Priscilla Jones, Elizabeth Denwood, John Denwood, Leah Denwood, Mary Denwood, Mary Ann Woolford, and Levin Denwood, repr. of Thomas Denwood decd. (MSA Vol. 13, p. 388).

19 Oct 1781. James Townley Rigby of Annapolis vs. William Noke, William Waller and Jane his wife formerly Neilson, Henry Stephenson, and Thomas Brereton. The Bill of Complaint dated 7 Aug 1768 states that the complainant on 10 Jan 1774 on the island of Jamaica intermarried with Ann Molden of Jamaica, milliner. In March following, Elizabeth Molden now wife of John Harvey of London Mariner and sister of Ann, arrived in Jamaica from England. James Rigby and Ann his wife were at that time preparing to settle in Maryland, and Elizabeth agreed to accompany them. Margaret Molden, formerly of London, milliner, was another sister of Ann, who resided in French Netherlands. James Rigby and Ann his wife and Elizabeth Molden were to be transported to Maryland by Abraham Vanbibber on his Brigg, John. However, James and Ann missed the boat and paid for passage on another vessel. The John arrived in Baltimore in June, and James and Ann arrived in July. Elizabeth sold possessions of James and Ann which arrived by the Brigg, John to the defendants without the knowledge of James and Ann. (MSA Vol. 13, p. 424).

10 Feb 1782. Allen Quynn of Annapolis vs. Moses Maccubbin. The Bill of Complaint dated 17 May 1779 states that William Maccubbin late of Anne Arundel Co. decd. was seized in fee of part of a tract called Wadrop in Anne Arundel Co. On 14 Aug 1777 he agreed with Allen Quynn for the purchase and sale thereof. William Maccubbin died leaving Moses his only son and heir at law who at the time of his father's death was an infant, and is now an infant of 4 yrs. Mary Maccubbin, widow of William, is the mother and natural guardian of Moses. (MSA Vol. 13, p. 473).

10 Feb 1782. Deposition of Keziah Monroe of Annapolis, widow, in above case. (MSA Vol. 13, p. 477).

10 Feb 1782. Deposition of William Harrison of Annapolis aged ca. 50 yrs. in above case. (MSA Vol. 13, p. 479).

10 Feb 1782. Depositions taken in above case (1) Thomas Sparrow of Annapolis aged ca. 36 yrs. (2) William Gordon of Annapolis aged ca. 40 yrs. (MSA Vol. 13, p. 480).

10 Feb 1782. Depositions taken in above case (1) Westal Meek of Anne Arundel Co. aged ca. 37 yrs. (2) Benjamin Fairbairn of Annapolis aged ca. 27 yrs. (MSA Vol. 13, p. 483).

10 Feb 1782. Depositions taken in above case (1) Mary Maccubbin, wife of William Maccubbin, aged ca. 26 yrs. that William died about 2 yrs. ago leaving her with 2 children, Moses and a girl. (2) Moses Maccubbin, brother of William, father of the defendant, of Anne Arundel Co. aged ca. 25 yrs. (MSA Vol. 13, p. 489).

A copy of the will of William Maccubbin mentions son Moses and daughter Elizabeth. (MSA Vol. 13, p. 493).

19 Oct 1782. Thomas and Rebecca Hanson of Prince George's Co. vs. John Addison, trustee and Walter, John, Thomas, Mary and Henry Addison, infant children of Thomas Addison decd. of Prince George's Co. The Bill of Complaint dated 20 May 1782 states that Thomas Addison died ca. 23 Sep 1774 leaving his widow Rebecca and children-Walter, John, Thomas, Mary and Henry. Rebecca intermarried with Thomas Hanson ca. 1 Apr 1778. (MSA Vol. 13, p. 515).

A copy of the will of Thomas Addison mentions sons Walter and John, father John, uncle Thomas, and wife Rebecca. Codicil 1 dated 12 Jun 1772 mentions another child, Thomas Grafton Addison. Codicil 2 dated 13 May 1773 mentions another child, Mary Grafton Addison, and sisters Eleanor Boucher and Ann Addison. (MSA Vol. 13, p. 549).

INDEX

-A-

ABBINGTON, John, 93
  Mary, 93
ABBOTT, Ann, 77
  Jane, 26
  John, 77
  Samuel, 26, 28, 77
ABESTON, William, 8
ABIGALL, 66
ABINGTON, 70
  John, 69
  Mary, 69
ACHESON, Hannah, 6
  Robert, 6
  Vincent, 6
ACKWORTH, Samuel, 104
ACTON, Henry, 79
  John, 79
ADAIR, Alexander, 61, 63
  Christian, 61, 63
ADAMS, 61
  Alexander, 60, 61, 70, 72
ADDERSON, John, 18
ADDERTON, Jeremiah, 17
  Jerome, 18
  Joseph, 16
  Mary, 16, 17, 18
ADDISON, Ann, 127
  Eleanor, 65
  Henry, 127
  John, 14, 127
  Mary, 127
  Mary Grafton, 127
  Thomas, 14, 65, 127
  Thomas Grafton, 127
  Walter, 127
ADKEY, John, 42
ALCOT'S TRIANGLE, 122
ALEXANDER, Amos, 112
  Dan, 112
  Daniel, 112
  Henry, 27, 28
  Mark, 112
  Moses, 112
  Nathaniel, 112
  Robert, 67, 78, 80, 122
  Theophilus, 112
  William, 60, 72, 78, 80
ALING, James, 19
ALLEN, Francis, 88
  George, 100
  James, 20
  William, 105
ALLINGE, William, 22
ALLISON, Charles, 62
  Elizabeth, 88, 89
  John, 69
  Patrick, 88
  Robert, 88
  Thomas, 62
ALLMAN, Thomas, 41
ALLNUTT, William, 116, 117
ALMODINGTON, 18
ALVEY, Pope, 2
ANCTILL, Elizabeth, 39
ANDERSON, John, 11, 44, 57
ANDREWS, Christopher, 1
  John, 101
  Mary, 1
  Patrick, 75
  Sarah, 75, 104
ANGELS LOT, 120
ANGLE, James, 61
ANSELL, Ann, 95
  William, 95
APSLY, William, 108
AQUOUSOCK, 22
ARCHER, Thomas, 107
ARDING, John, 5
ARENOLD, Ann, 2
  Lawrence, 2
ARMSTRONG, Francis, 48, 77
ARNOLD, David, 113
  Rebecca, 113
  William, 58
ARNOLL, Thomas, 18
ASBRITON, William, 46
ASCOMBE, John, 7
  Winifred, 7
ASHCOMB, Benjamin, 11
  Charles, 11
  Lawrence, 11
  Mary, 11
  Nathaniel, 11
  Samuel, 11
ASHCOME, Charles, 23
  Martha, 23
ASHCROFT, Thomas, 43
ASHLEY, William, 51
ASHMAN, George, 111
ASPINALL, Henry, 2
ASSISTOR, William, 38
ATCHINSON, Hannah, 10
  Robert, 10
  Vincent, 10
ATCHISON, William, 70
ATHEY, George, 14
ATHORPE, Catherine, 80
  Thomas, 80
ATKINSON, Ann, 106
  George, 103
  John, 34, 106
  Robert, 20
ATKOW, Mary, 73
  Thomas, 73
ATTHOW, Thomas, 73
ATTWOOD, George, 91
ATWICKS, Elizabeth, 9
  Humfrey, 9
ATWOOD, John, 16
AULD, James, 27
AVERY, James, 4
  John, 4

-B-

BACON, Anthony, 92
  Elizabeth, 92
BAILEY, George, 86
  John, 111
BAILLY, George, 86
  Sarah, 86
BAKER, Elizabeth, 13, 46
  Francis, 124
  Henry, 109
  Isaac, 25
  John, 6, 13, 46
  Maurice, 57

129

BALDEN, 57
  Thomas, 57
  William, 57
BALDWIN, John, 61
  Mary, 85
BALDWYN, John, 84
BALE, Anthony, 68
  Mary, 68
  Sarah, 68
  Thomas, 68
  Urah, 68
BALLARD, Charles, 45
  Levin, 114, 125
  Sarah, 45
BALLIN, Margery, 12
  William, 12
BALTHROP, Anne, 122
  Boles Tyer, 122
  Mary, 122
BALTHROPE, Mary, 122
BALTIMORE'S GIFT, 53
BARBAR, Luke, 33
BARBER, Edward, 29
  John, 75
  Thomas, 29, 32
BARBIER, Elizabeth, 8
  Luke, 8
BARCLAY, Isabella, 96
  Thomas, 96
BARELY HILLS, 63, 64
BARHAM, John, 66
BARKER, Mary, 113
  Thomas, 113
BARKETT, 18
BARLEY, Anne, 17
BARNES, Frances, 77
  Francis, 28, 29
  Henry, 69
BARNES NECK, 20
BARNES NECK ADDITION, 20
BARON, Benjamin, 86
  Elizabeth, 86
BARREN ISLAND, 102, 112
BARRETT, John, 5
BARTLETT, Thomas, 48
BARTON, Sarah, 19
  William, 12, 16, 18, 19
BASHFORDE MANNOR, 39
BATCHELLORS DELIGHT, 5

BATCHELOR'S REST, 64
BATEMAN, Christopher, 49
  Henry, 61
  John, 2
  Mary, 2
  William, 34, 61
BATH'S ADDITION, 14
BATSON, Ann, 16
  Edward, 16
BATTEN, Margery, 1
  William, 1
BATTERSHALL,
  Elizabeth, 33
  Willliam, 33
BAVINGTON, John, 42, 55, 56
BAYLEY, John, 22
BAYLY, John, 34
  William, 34
BAYNE, Ann, 13
  Elsworth, 39, 43
  John, 13
BAYNES, John, 113
BEACH NECK, 7
BEALE, Ann, 68
  Anthony, 68
  Charles, 36, 69, 76
  Col., 35
  Elizabeth, 21, 97
  James, 76
  John, 21, 75, 76
  Ninian, 10, 14, 16, 18, 19, 20, 21, 23, 28, 29, 35, 76
  William, 76
BEALES CAMP, 38
BEALES CHANCE, 28
BEALL, Ann, 104
  James, 115
  John, 115
  John Alexander, 115
  Ninian, 28
  Robert, 115
  Samuel, 95
  Thomas, 82
  William, 82, 91
BEAMONT, John, 3
BEANE, Ellinor, 9
  Walter, 9
BEAN'S CREEK, 39
BEARCROFT, John, 11

BEARD, 18
  John, 42, 43, 47
BEARDS, Richard, 16, 17
BEASLY, Abraham, 26
BECK, Elizabeth, 5, 10
  John, 5
  Margaret, 5, 10
  Mary, 5, 10
  Richard, 5, 8
BECKETT, Humphrey, 44
BECKWITH, Ann, 13
  Basil, 74
  Charles, 13, 74
  Frances, 3
  George, 3, 74
  William, 74
BEDDOE, Griffith, 79
BEEDLE, Henry, 1
  Sophia, 1
BEETLE, John, 47
BELL, Anthony, 64
  Charles, 61
  George, 64
  Hamilton, 126
  Isaac, 64
  John, 12
  Thomas, 64
BELT, Joseph, 36
BEN, 66
BENNET'S PARK, 122
BENNETT, 63
  Disborah, 4
  Richard, 63, 65, 72, 108, 110
  Thomas, 44
BENNY, James, 124
BENSON, Benjamin, 121
  Elizabeth, 91
  Nicholas, 91
  Perry, 77
  Pery, 91
BENSTON, George, 89
BENTLEY, Stephen, 31, 32
BENTON, Francis, 28
BERRY, Ann, 59
  David, 59
  Elizabeth, 58
  William, 10, 52
BESON, Thomas, 3
BESS, 66

BETTERSOY, Edward, 61
　Lydia, 61
BETTY, 62
BICKERTON, John, 84
　Mary, 84
BIDDYSON, Thomas, 32
BIGGER, John, 18, 19, 24
BIGGIN, John, 13
BIGGS, Ambrose, 10
BIRCHFIELD, Maurice, 38, 51
BIRD, Charles, 3
　Margaret, 3
BISCOE, John, 81
BISHOP, Deborah, 118
　Elijah, 118
BISSETT, Ann, 106
　David, 106
　James, 106
BITTENSON, Edward, 61
　Lydia, 61
BLACK, 85
　Alexander, 85
　William, 85
BLACKBURN, Benjamin, 115, 116
BLACKISTON,
　Ebenezer, 108
　Sarah, 108
BLACKISTONE,
　Elizabeth, 59
　Nathaniel, 59
BLACKSTONE, Sarah, 108
BLADE, William, 16
BLADEN, Thomas, 53
　William, 21, 51
BLAKE, Charles, 62
　Dorothy, 62
　Henrietta Maria, 62
　John, 62
　Philemon, 62
BLAKES HOPE, 27
BLAND, Damaras, 5
　Damoras, 10
　Damoris, 10
　Demoras, 4
　Thomas, 3, 4, 5, 10
BLANFORD, Tobitha, 9
BLANGY, Lewis, 1, 4

　Mary, 1, 4
BLAY, Isabella, 72
　Rachel, 72
　William, 72
BLEAKES HOPE, 27
BLIZARD, Giles, 11
　Susanna, 11
BLOMFIELD,
　Elizabeth, 8
　John, 8
BLOOMER, Elizabeth, 53
　Thomas, 53
BLOOMFIELD, James, 84
　Mary, 84
BLUE PLAIN, 14
BOARMAN, James, 88
　William, 9, 27, 88
BOBT, Charles, 47
BODIE, Peter, 80
BODKIN, Dominick, 12
　James, 12
BODLE, 41
BODLE ATS KNIGHT, 41
BOHEMIA MANNOR, 42
BOHEMIA MANOR, 56
BOHEMIA RIVER, 54
BOND, John, 107, 113
　Thomas, 71
BONNER, Elizabeth, 1
　Henry, 1, 17
BOOMER, John, 39
BOOMGARDIAN, John, 55
BOON, Humphrey, 99
　Robert, 83
BOONE, Humphrey, 101
BOOTH, Basil, 43
　Basill, 43
　John, 43
　Mrs., 43
　Sarah, 123
BORDLEY, Ariana, 70, 78
　Beale, 79
　Elizabeth, 79
　John, 79
　John Beale, 110
　Margaret, 110
　Matthias, 79
　Rachel, 42, 43, 47
　Sarah, 96
　Stephen, 78, 79, 96

Thomas, 42, 43, 47, 70, 78, 79
　William, 79
BORMAN, William, 27
BORROUGH, 43, 44
BOSEMAN, William, 13
BOSMAN, Risdon, 69
BOTELER, Charles, 16
BOUCHELL, Catherine, 104
　Samuel, 55
BOUCHELSE, Peter, 54
BOUCHER, Eleanor, 127
BOUKY, 50
BOULDING, William, 55
BOWDLE'S CHOICE, 43, 44
BOWEN, Benjamin, 106
　Jacob, 115
BOWLES, James, 67
　John, 1, 57
　Margery, 1
　Tobias, 67
BOWLING, James, 11
　Mary, 11
　Robert, 54
BOYCE, Alexander, 26
　Roger, 51, 87, 88
BOYD, Adam, 57
BOYER, Richard, 47
　Thomas, 47
　William, 19, 47
BOYETH, Thomas, 42
BOZMAN, John, 18
　Risden, 91
　Risdon, 69
　Rizdon, 43
　Thomas, 77
BRACCO, John, 104
BRADFORD, Catherine, 107
　John, 36, 76, 87, 88, 89, 97
　Joice, 76
　Joyce, 36, 63, 89, 96, 97
　William, 95
BRADLEY, Anne, 17
　Elizabeth, 44
BRADON, James, 107
BRADSHAW, John, 52
BRANNOCK, John, 40, 45, 63, 65

131

Johon, 77
Thomas, 42, 45
BRANT, Randolph, 30
BRASHEAR, Benjamin, 24
BRASHEARS, Benjamin, 24
  Robert, 24
BRASHEER, Mary, 63
  Robert, 63
BRATZ, Bernard, 112
BRAWNOR, Edward, 69
BRAYFORD, John, 19
BRAYNE, Benjamin, 66
BREED, John, 5
BRENT, Ann, 12
  George, 12
  Giles, 1
  Henry, 12
  Margarett, 39
  Mary, 39
  William, 39
BRERETON, Thomas, 126
BREWER, William, 64
BREWERTON, 61
  Dianna, 60
  Hannah, 61
  William, 60, 61
BRICE, John, 30, 98
  Sarah, 29
BRIDGES, Charles, 20
BRISCOE, John, 81
  Philip, 40, 83
BRITE, Thomas, 4
BROCKSON, Elizabeth, 55
BROME, Mary, 115
BRONACK, Bettingly, 64
BROOK, 73
  Henry, 87
  William, 10
BROOKE, Basil, 106
  Clement, 73
  John, 8, 18
  Katherine, 8
  Leonard, 39
  Lucy, 93, 103
  Mrs., 73
  Roger, 10
  Thomas, 51, 93, 102, 103
BROOKE ADVENTURE, 18
BROOKS, Baker, 11

  Grace, 43
  Robert, 10
  William, 10
BROOK'S PARTITION, 11
BROOME, 49
  John, 43
  Martha, 43
BROUGHTON, John, 112
  Mary, 112
BROUGHTON ASHLEY, 32
BROUTON, John, 25
BROWN, Ann, 111
  Benjamin, 106
  Daniel, 32
  George, 88
  James, 10, 12
  Jane, 102
  John, 9, 10, 102
  Joseph, 54
  Peregrine, 54
  Philip, 8
  Rachel, 72
  Thomas, 26
BROWNE, Derrick, 49
  Thomas, 28
BROWNING, George, 120
  John, 4, 7
  Thomas, 56, 113, 120, 122
BRUCE, Thomas, 112
BRUFFE, Thomas, 16
BRYMER, William, 34
BRYON, Daniel, 67
BUCHANAN, Andrew, 111
  George, 63, 65, 86
  Margaret, 63, 65
  Margarett, 65
BUCK NECK, 38
BULLEN, John, 78, 97
  Sarah, 97
  Thomas, 69
BULLEY, John, 61
BULLOCK, Francis, 20, 37
BUNCLE, Alexander, 105
BURDUS, Mary, 97, 98
  Richard, 97, 98, 103
BURGES, ---, 14
  Amy, 6
  John, 6

BURGESS, Keziah, 124
BURGESSE, Col., 17
  John, 44
  Richard, 44
BURK, John, 108
  Mary, 113
BURNEAT, John, 27
BURROSS, John, 30
BURROUGHS, John, 22, 23, 29, 35
BURTON, Samuel, 68
BUSBY, Elizabeth, 78
  Margaret, 79
  Robert, 78, 79
  Thomas, 79
BUSH MANNING, 73
BUSHWOOD, 50
BUTLER, James, 36, 76
  Joice, 76
  Thomas, 76, 96, 97
BUTTON, Cecilus, 13
  Margaret, 13
BUTTRAM, Elizabeth, 7
  Nicholas, 7
BYARD, Samuel, 42, 47

-C-

CADES, Thomas, 31
CAHILL, Amos, 52
CAHOON, Cornelius, 86
  Humphrey, 54
  Sarah, 86
CAILE, Elizabeth, 113
CALDER, James, 95
CALDWELL, 61
  James, 104, 105
  John, 60, 70
  Martha, 105
  Rachel, 104, 105
CALF PASTURE, 21
CALLHAN, Joseph, 124
CALVERT, Cecilius, 53
  Charles, 17, 18, 46, 50, 53, 62, 72, 78
  Dorothy, 62
  Elizabeth, 53, 54
  Mary, 53, 54
  Rebecca, 72

Richard, 17, 18, 53
William, 17, 50, 53, 54
CALVERTON MANOR, 3
CAMBERWELL, 52
CAMPBELL, Alexancer, 11
Duncan, 108
Frances, 101
Francis, 51
John, 101, 117
Walter, 14
CAMPER, Mary, 16
CANIDEY, Cornelius, 22
CANN, James, 95
CANNON, Thomas, 40
CAPLIN, Elizabeth, 6
Henry, 6
CAREN, John, 114
CAREY, Ann, 113
Mary, 113
CARLINE, Henry, 7
CARLISLE, David, 109
Mary, 109
CARLYLE, Alexander, 14
William, 14
CARMAN, William, 118
CARMICHAEL, William, 104
CARNELL, Urah, 68
CARNEY, Robert, 71
CARPENTER, John, 34
CARR, John, 52
William, 33
CARRINGTON, Elizabeth, 17
Timothy, 87
CARROL, Charles, 67, 70, 82
Daniel, 67
James, 65, 72
CARROLL, Annastasia, 85
Charles, 63, 65, 66, 74, 83, 84, 85, 86, 96, 97, 103, 109, 111, 113, 121
Daniel, 63, 66, 76, 82
Dominick, 85
Elenor, 82

Elinor, 85
Elizabeth, 109
Henry, 111
James, 109
John, 86
Julian, 85
Mary, 82, 85, 96
Mary Clare, 96, 98
Susannah, 85
CARSLAKE, John, 91
CARTER, Benjamin, 121
Darby, 44
Elizabeth, 1
Frances, 121
John, 1, 80
Robert, 121
William, 30, 93, 94
CARVILE, Jane, 96
CARVILLE, Jane, 96
John, 96
CASH, Elizabeth, 7
CATTERTON,
Catherine, 16, 17
Michael, 117
CATTLINS PLAINS, 26, 28
CATTO, Araminta, 104
George, 104
CAUSEEN, Ignatius, 48
John, 48
CAUSOON, Ignatius, 48
Nicholas, 48
CEADER BRANCH, 18
CEADOR BRANCH, 18
CEDARPOINT, 43
CESAR, 66
CHADBORNE, Susanna, 3, 9
William, 3, 9
CHAFFE, John, 8
Mary, 8
CHALMERS, Walter, 99
CHAMBERLAIN, Thomas, 41, 57
CHAMBERLAINE, John, 95
Mary, 95
Thomas, 95
CHAMBERLEY, 35
CHAMPINGHAM, 12
CHANDLER, Job, 8

William, 47, 67
CHANDLEY, Drewcilla, 104
John, 104
CHAPLAIN'S LAND, 18
CHAPMAN, Edward, 37
Mary, 37
Robert, 1
William, 68, 80, 85, 86, 92
CHAPPELL, John, 19, 20
CHASE, Frances
Halton, 112
Jeremiah, 112, 118
Jeremiah Townley, 122
Richard, 91, 112, 119, 122
Samuel, 112, 122, 123
Thomas, 112, 119, 122
CHATHAM, Edward, 48
CHECK, John, 55
CHEEK, John, 54
CHENY, Elizabeth, 34
John, 34
CHESELDINE, Dryden, 94
Kenelinn, 94
Mary, 94
Susanna, 94
CHESELDYNE, Kenelyn, 39, 62, 63
CHESTERFIELD, 38
CHEW, Ann, 96, 112
Bennett, 113
Francis, 104, 110, 112
Henrietta Maria, 96, 110
Henry, 88
John, 121
Joseph, 24
Margaret, 110
Mary, 96, 110, 112
Richard, 96, 104, 110, 112
Samuel, 54, 63, 96, 110, 112, 121
Samuell, 1
William, 14
CHILD, Abraham, 79
CHILDE, Francis, 42

133

CHISELDINE,
   Keneline, 103
CHOCKE, George, 66
   Rachel, 66
CHRISTIAN, John, 18
   Thomas, 55
CHRISTIAN TEMPLE
   MANOR, 53, 62
CHRISTOPHER, John,
   70
CHUNN, Andrew, 112
   Peregrine, 112
CHURCH, Thomas, 56
CHURNELL, Joseph, 30
CHURNELLS NECK, 30
CHURTSY, 14
CLAGETT, Charles, 78
   Mary, 4
   Sarah, 52
   Thomas, 4, 52, 67
CLAGGETT, Thomas, 67
CLAPHAM, Josiah, 113
   Sarah, 113
CLARE, Betty, 117
   Edmund, 116
   Hannah, 77
   John, 77
CLARK, George, 39
   Jane, 91
   John, 48
   Neale, 49
   Robert, 48
   Thomas, 91
   William, 113
CLARKE, Ann, 114
   Henry, 22
   Joshua, 114
   Neale, 37
   Neall, 46
   Robert, 49
CLAUGH, Sarah, 2
   William, 2
CLAW, William, 4
CLAWE, Sarah, 4
   William, 4
CLAYLAND, Anne, 28
   William, 28, 49
CLAYTON, John, 120, 121
   Joseph, 120
   Margaret, 120
   William, 60
CLEAR DOUBT, 32
CLEAVE, Josie, 40
   Joyce, 40

Nalley, 40
Nathaniel, 40
Neddy, 40
CLEMENTS, John, 22, 23, 44, 45, 51
CLIFF, John, 27
CLOCKE, Daniel, 9
CLOCKER, Alice, 46
   Daniel, 46
CLOUDS, Nicholas, 30, 31
CLUB, John, 43
CLYDE, Robert, 69
COADE, John, 15
   William, 15
COATES, Leonard, 10
   Martha, 10
COCKEY, John, 84, 119
   Thomas, 84
COCKSHUTT, John, 48
CODD, Ann, 77
   Berkley, 77
   Mary, 63, 77
   St. Ledger, 63, 77
COE, Samuel, 116
COFFER, John, 23
COLCHESTER, 10
COLE, Charles, 72
   Dianah, 118
   Edward, 86, 87
   Elizabeth, 50, 59
   Francis, 31
   George, 118
   Hannah, 84
   John, 65, 84, 118
   Richard, 49
   Robert, 9
   Valentine, 31
COLEMORE, Thomas, 65
COLE'S CAVES, 65
COLLIER, Francis, 21
   Peter, 66
COLLINS, James, 40
   Richard, 44
   Thomas, 44
COLMORE, Thomas, 75
COLVILLE, John, 103
COLWELL, Thomas, 92
COMBES, Elizabeth, 54
   George, 111
   Richard, 62
   William, 54
COMBE'S ADVENTURE,

111
COMBS, William, 50
COMEGYS, Cornelius, 28, 96
   Edward, 96
   Nathaniel, 28
   William, 28, 49
COMPTON, William, 22
CONDEN, Robert, 111, 118
CONGO, Ann, 14
CONLEE, Mary, 51
CONNANT, Charles, 106
   Sarah, 105, 106
CONNAWAY, Phillip, 13
CONNELL, Daniel, 14
   William, 53
CONNER, John, 96
   Richard, 23
CONTEE, Alexander, 57, 58, 76
   Francis, 58
   John, 57, 58
   Mary, 58
   Peter, 57, 58
CONWELL, Joseph, 116
COOD, Ann, 56
   Elizabeth, 56
   John, 13, 56
   Mary, 56
   Richard, 56
   Winifred, 56
COODE, John, 59
   Susanna, 59
COOK, Ann, 71
   Elizabeth, 116
   John, 96
   Thomas, 14, 71
COOKE, John, 118
COOKSEY, Susanna, 50
COOP, Nicholas, 31
COOPER, Edward, 91
   John, 20
   Mary, 48
   Nathaniel, 33
   Nicholas, 20
   Richard, 48, 58
   Susannah, 20
   Thomas, 58, 64
COPSON, John, 92
CORBETT, Hutton, 24
CORD, Joseph, 113
   Martha, 113

CORDEN, Thomas, 10
CORKSHUTT, Ann, 48
  Jane, 48
  Jeane, 48
  Mary, 48
CORNELIUS, Mathias, 9
CORNWALLIS, Captain, 46
COSTIN, Henry, 40, 42, 29, 39
COTTER, John, 68
COTTINGHAM, Charles, 64
COTTMAN, Benjamin, 70
COTTON, Edward, 22
COULER, Robin, 23
COURSEY, Elizabeth, 36
  Henry, 36, 37, 102
  James, 34, 36, 101, 102
  Jane, 36
  John, 101
  Julliana, 102
  Thomas, 36
  William, 36, 101
COURSEY'S CHOICE, 36
COUSEEN, Jane, 48
COUTTS, Hercules, 96
  Mary, 96
COVENTRY, 123
COVERTHOUGHT, Robert, 18, 38
COW QUARTER, 28
COWARD, Sibilla, 55
COWLEY, George, 23
COX, Anthony, 26
  Benjamin, 40, 42, 47
  Guisbert, 56
  Henry, 23, 31
  John, 26, 40, 47, 67
  Thomas, 40, 47
COYNE, 66
CRABB, Ralph, 67
CRANE, John, 53
CRAWFORD, David, 76
CRAXSON, Thomas, 31
CRAYCROFT, Charles, 93
  Ignatius, 93
CREAGH, Frances, 97

  Patrick, 97
CRESSY, Samuel, 3
  Susanna, 3
CROKER, Rachel, 88
CROMWELL, John, 57
  William, 57
CROOK, Robert, 40
CROOME, 29
CROP MANNOR, 49
CROSS DOOR, 25
CROSS DOWER, 25
CROSS NECK, 46
CROSSE DOYER, 25
CROW, Garney, 73
  Gurney, 73
CROXALL, Charles, 97
CUFFIN, David, 80
CULPEPPER, Michael, 116
CUMING, William, 78
CUMMING, William, 82, 95, 97
CUMMINGS, Elizabeth, 102
  William, 101, 102, 63
CUNNINGHAM, Daniel, 16
CURRANT, James, 77
  Susannah, 77
CURRE, Thomas, 4
CURTIS, Elizabeth, 113
  John, 113
  Michael, 52, 83
  Sarah, 83
CURTISS, Michael, 83
  Sarah, 83

-D-
DABB, John, 2
DAFFORN, Thomas, 11
DALE, John, 122
  Richard, 122
DALE TOWN, 72
DALLAM, William, 107
DALLY, Thomas, 14
DALTON, Richard, 9
DANIEL, John, 22
DANSEY, John, 22
DANZEY, John, 15
  Martha, 23
DAR, Oswald, 41
DARBY, John, 27
DARE, Gideon, 82

  Nathaniel, 43
DARNAL, Henry, 65
DARNALL, 85
  Edward, 104
  Elinor, 108
  Elizabeth, 108
  Henry, 33, 76, 85, 86, 91, 108
  John, 113
  Thomas, 104
DARROLL, Daniel, 76
DARRUMPLE, Elenor, 78
  John, 78
DASH, John, 57
  Oswald, 57
DASHIEL, Thomas, 60
DASHIELL, George, 115
  Levin, 114
  Michael, 105
DAVIS, Allen, 93
  Ebenezer, 123
  Elizabeth, 120
  Ephraim, 120, 121
  Forrest, 123
  James, 93
  John, 15, 51, 93, 98
  Jonathan, 82, 93
  Lodowick, 123
  Morris, 57
  Robert, 119
  Sarah, 57
  Thomas, 30, 120, 121
  William, 51, 56
DAVIS' LOT, 122
DAVISON, John, 91
DAWKINS, James, 116
  Joseph, 115
DAWSEY, Elizabeth, 42
  William, 42
DAWSON, Ann, 90
  Anthony, 26
  James, 59, 63
  John, 90, 91
  Mary, 63
  Robert, 60
  Sarah, 60
  William, 90
DAY, Ann, 84
  Avarilla, 82
  Benjamin, 115

Edward, 10, 82, 84
Elizabeth, 84
Rebecca, 115
William, 117
DEACON, Mary, 61
William, 61
DEALE, Alexander, 62
Thomas, 109
William, 61, 62
DEAN, Hugh, 119, 122
DEAVER, Hannah, 85
John, 85, 107, 113
DEAVOR, John, 113
DEAVOUR, Gilbert, 18
Richard, 72
DEERY, Ellinor, 9
John, 9
DELMORE END, 31
DEMELL, John, 44
DENNY, Ann, 52
Anne, 36
Christopher, 36, 52
DENT, Elizabeth, 57
Jane, 40
Jane Pitman, 56
Major, 43, 47
Mary, 22
Peter, 40, 43, 56, 57
Thomas, 9, 58, 103
William, 12, 14, 103
DENTON, Henry, 12, 54
John, 112
Mary, 12
Vachel, 12, 76, 79
Vachell, 54, 66
DENWOOD, Betsey, 125
Elizabeth, 126
John, 125, 126
Leah, 126
Levin, 18, 126
Livin, 23
Mary, 124, 125, 126
Priscilla, 125
Thomas, 124, 125, 126
Thomas Gantt, 124
DEPOST, Martin, 72
DERMOTT, Edmond, 9
DICK, 66
DICKENSON, John, 25

Walter, 25
DICKINSON, Walter, 31
DICKS, John, 13
DICKSON, George, 70
Obed, 78
DICKSON'S NECK, 40
DIGGES, Charles, 67
Edward, 67
Ignatius, 91
John, 67
Mary, 67
Nicholas, 91
William, 67, 70, 91
DIGGS, Charles, 18
Edward, 18
Elizabeth, 18
Mr., 53
William, 18
DINAH'S BEVERDAM, 39
DINIARD, Thomas, 6
DISHROOM, Lewes, 70
DOCURA, John, 61
Thomas, 61
DODSON, Daniel, 102
DOLIOMIOSIA, Alexander, 13
DOMALL, John, 14
DONALDSON, James, 78
DONE, John, 114
DORCHESTER, 72
DORRINGTON, Mary, 58
Sarah, 8
William, 8, 58
DORSEY, Basil, 103, 108
Basill, 92
Caleb, 108, 109, 110, 113, 119, 123
Comfort, 76
Edward, 3, 5, 10, 13, 16, 21, 34, 92, 108, 110, 119, 122
Eleanor, 119
Elijah, 110
Elizabeth, 75, 76, 118
Elizabeth Goodwin, 113
Greenbury, 76
Henrietta Maria, 110

Henry, 118
James, 117
John, 13, 21, 76, 119, 123
Joseph, 16
Joshua, 76
Margaret, 21, 119, 122, 123
Mary, 119
Michael, 16
Milcah, 119, 123
Peggy Hill, 119
Priscilla, 119
Rebecca, 116
Rebeccah, 119
Richard, 75, 76, 92, 98, 110
Samuel, 21, 113, 119, 123
Sarah, 5, 10
Thomas, 108, 109, 119
Thomas Beale, 110
DOSSEY, John, 117
Philip, 117
DOUGHERTY, Ann, 94
Walter, 94
DOUGLAS, James, 111, 112
John, 7
Joseph, 97
Mary, 111, 112
Susannah, 85
William, 111, 112
DOUGLASS, George, 105
DOWDALL, John, 57
DOWDEL, Christopher, 70
DOWLING, Robert, 46
DOWN, Robert, 45
DOYNE, Joshua, 53
DOYNES, William, 23
DREW, Anthony, 104
Mary Ann, 104
DRIVER, Martin, 78
DROUGHED, Agnes, 64
DRURY, Christian, 7
William, 7
DUCEY, Daniel, 117
DUCKETT, John, 122
Richard, 44
DUCKWORTH, Ann, 50
DUFF, Simon, 78
DUKE, James, 81

DULANY, Ann, 113
  Benjamin, 113
  Daniel, 63, 75,
    78, 86, 96, 97,
    111, 113, 121
  Henrietta Maria,
    96, 108, 110, 112
  Rebecka, 121
  Walter, 111, 113
DURANT, Eagle, 5
DURHAM, 9
DUVALL, Marreen, 44
  Marren, 44
DWANE, Dennis, 23
  Mary, 23

-E-
EAGLE, Mary, 71
EARLE, Anne, 36, 37
  Carpenter, 102
  James, 37, 52, 102
  Michael, 36, 37
EASON, John, 33
EASTGATE, Caleb, 23
EATON, Jeremiah, 2
  Jeremy, 2
  Mary, 2
EBDONS REST, 5
EBZEY, Robert, 125
ECCLESTON, John, 63,
    105, 106
  Sarah, 105, 106
  Susanna, 63
EDELEN, Richard, 3
EDELIN, Ann, 94
  Edward, 70
  Richard, 94
EDGE, Mr., 114
EDGERTON, Charles,
    16, 17, 53, 54
  Mary, 17, 53, 54
EDLEN, Richard, 19
EDLINGTON, 14
EDLOE, Barnaby, 8
  Joseph, 8
EDMONDS, Thomas, 22,
    38
EDMONDSON, James,
    21, 76
  John, 21
  Thomas, 21
ELGAR, John, 120
ELIZABETH MANOR, 53
ELLENOR, Andrew, 2
  Ann, 2

Sarah, 2
ELLIAS, Sarah, 120
  William, 120
ELLIOT, Edward, 15
ELLIOTT, Edward, 27
  Elizabeth, 27
  Henry, 5
  Jane, 5
  Robert, 63
ELLIS, William, 120
ELZEY, Armond, 45
  Arnold, 125
  Peter, 18
  Robert, 126
EMERSON, Elizabeth,
    5
  Nicholas, 5
EMISON, Elizabeth,
    112
  Tobias, 112
EMORY, Ann, 112
  Arthur, 112
  John, 118
  Juliana, 118
END OF CONTROVERSIE,
    42
ENFIELD CHASE, 14
ENNALLS, Henry, 51
  Thomas, 17, 44,
    51, 58
ERICKSON, Elizabeth,
    82
  Gunder, 82
  Mary, 82
ESSINGTON, 26
EVANS, Ann, 38, 77
  David, 33
  Edmond, 38, 39
  Elizabeth, 7, 39
  Francis, 39
  James, 109
  Job, 19
  Joseph, 99, 100
  Katherine, 38
  Lewis, 38, 39
  Lois, 38
  Philip, 47
  Sarah, 38
  Susan, 39
  Susannah, 99, 100
  Walter, 36
  William, 7
EVAN'S RANGE, 35
EVERIT, Ann, 116
  John, 107

Richard, 116
EVET, John, 54
EVITT, John, 55, 72
EVITTS, Joseph, 72
EWING, John, 109

-F-
FAIR PLAY, 28
FAIRBAIRN, Benjamin,
    127
FAIRPLAY, 27, 28
FALCONER, Gilbert,
    57
FARFARR, William, 40
FARIMBO, 66
FARTHING, James, 44
  John, 44, 93
  William Maria, 44
FAULKNER, Ralph, 95
FEAUDRY, Elizabeth,
    84
  Moses, 84
FEDDEMAN, Richard,
    27
FELL, Edward, 113
FENDALL, Benjamin,
    109
FENTON, William, 48
FENWICK, Ignatius,
    106
  Richard, 33
  Sarah, 106
FENWICK MANNOR, 33
FENWICKS, Ellen, 25
  Ignatius, 25
FERNLEY, Henry, 43
FETTEREL, Anne, 63
  Edward, 63
FEW, Isaac, 113
FIBBEN, 34
FIBBENS, Daniel, 117
FIBNEE, 34
FIELD, Edward, 38,
    50
FINLEY, Jane, 17
  Robert, 17
FINN, Francis, 95
FISH, Henry, 35
FISHER, Archibald,
    109
  Elizabeth, 75
  Francis, 80
  John, 75
FITZ, Joseph, 47
FITZHUGH, William,

137

110
FLEMING, Elizabeth, 88
 John, 88
 Sarah, 88
 William, 88
FLEMMING, William, 89
FLETCHALL, Thomas, 61
FLETCHER, Michael, 77
FLORA, 66
FLOYD, Thomas, 5
FODERGILL, William, 100
FONDALE, Robert, 18
FORBES, Alexander, 57
 Dryden, 94
 George, 84, 94
 James, 94
 John, 94
 Mary, 94
FORD, Edward, 62
 Jane, 82
 John, 82
 Richard, 47
 Robert, 34
 William, 37, 66
FOREST, Richard, 39
FORREST, James, 49
 Richard, 46
FORWARD, Jonathan, 66, 71
FOSIEG, John, 22
FOTTRELL, Achsah, 92
 Acksah, 86
 Edward, 86, 92
FOWKE, Ann, 8
 George, 8
 Gerrard, 8
FOWLER, Elizabeth, 99
 Sarah, 58, 117
FOXON, Richard, 9
FOXUM, Richard, 3
FRANCH, James, 50
FRANKLIN, Robert, 66
FRANTON, Elizabeth, 32
 John, 32
FRAZER, Alexander, 61, 62
 John, 58

Sarah, 61, 62
FREE SCHOOL FARM, 20
FREEHOLD OF LAND, 49
FREELAND, Jacob, 117
 Mary, 116
 Robert, 87, 116
 Sarah, 87
FREEMAN, George, 82
 John, 16
 Margarett, 16
 William, 47, 55
FRENCH, James, 59
FRENCH WOMAN'S, 44
FRENCH WOMAN'S BRANCH, 57
FRESH POND NECK, 4
FRIENDSHIP, 36
FRILEY, Jane, 15
 Robert, 15
FRISBY, Ann, 51
 Ariana, 51
 Elizabeth, 85
 James, 51
 Mary, 85
 Nicholas, 85
 Peregrine, 51, 71, 85
 William, 51, 57, 85
FRITH, Elizabeth, 27
 Henry, 27
FRY, Edward, 28
 Elizabeth, 28
FULLER, John, 20
FURLEY, John, 61

-G-
GADHILL, 19, 20
GADSBY, John, 57
GAITHER, Elizabeth, 120
 John, 37, 101
 Rebecca, 101
 William, 120, 121
GAITRELL, John, 37
GALE, Dorothy, 50
 Levin, 70, 86, 89, 92
GALERBY, 40
GALLAWAY, Richard, 11
 Samuel, 37
GALLOWAY, Elizabeth, 102
 John, 75, 76

Richard, 102
 Samuel, 13
 Sophia, 102
GAMES, Frances, 81
 John, 78, 81
GANT, Jon, 89
 Thomas, 89
GARDINER, William, 84
GARDNER, Edward, 116
 Jeremiah, 102
 Joseph, 34
 Luke, 21
 Matthew, 53
 William, 3
GARLAND, Ann, 87
 Elizabeth, 87
 Mary, 87
 Randal, 87
 Randall, 87
GARNETT, George, 110
GARNISH, 17
 Jane, 16, 17
 John, 16
GARRET, Amos, 86
 Mary, 86
GARRETT, Amos, 42, 43, 47, 104
 Frances, 104
 John, 108
 Sarah, 108
GARTRELL, Stephen, 122
GARY, William, 12
GASSAWAY, John, 106
 Thomas, 68
GASSOWAY, Nicholas, 119
GATRELL, Jane, 49
 John, 49
GAY, Nicholas Ruxton, 111
GEDDES, John William, 120
 Mary, 113, 120
 William, 113, 114, 120
GEORGE, Sampson, 54
GERARD, Justinian, 9, 83
 Sarah, 83
 Thomas, 9
GERLING, Simon, 33
GERRARD, Elizabeth, 59

John, 16, 50, 59
Justinian, 50, 59, 83
Sarah, 83
Susanna, 50, 59
Thomas, 50, 59
GIBSON, Ann, 90
Elizabeth, 91
Richard, 91
Woolman, 90
GILCHREST, Robert, 110
GILES, Ann, 113
Jacob, 104, 122
James, 113
Joannah, 104
John, 66
Rachel, 66
William, 105
GILL, Jane, 64
John, 64
GILLESPIE, William, 109
GILLIS, Joseph, 115
Thomas, 60
GILLISS, Joseph, 125
Thomas, 70
William, 125
GILL'S LAND, 22
GILPIN, Thomas, 105, 106
GINN, Elizabeth, 71, 86
GIORSLEAD, Joakim, 13
GIROSLEAD, Joakim, 13
Margaret, 13
GIST, Richard, 65
Thomas, 111
William, 111
GITTINGS, Thomas, 74
GIVEN, Mary, 112
Thomas, 112
GLADMAN, Michael, 111
GLADSTONE, James, 44
John, 14
GLASSINGTON, John, 63, 64
GLENT, Peter, 58
GLEVIN, Bartholomew, 1, 2
GLOVER, Elizabeth, 24

Giles, 24
William, 14, 24
GOATLEY, Mary, 95
GODDARD, George, 60
GODFREY, George, 5, 10, 29
GODLINGTON'S, 72
GODSGRACE, John, 22
GODSHALL, John, 67
GOFF, John, 34
GOLD, Mary, 23
GOLDER, John, 112
GOLDSBERRY, John, 39
GOLDSBOROUGH, Greenberry, 114
GOODLUCK, 23
GOODRICK, Francis, 87
Margaret, 14
Robert, 14
GOODWIN, Milcah, 119, 123
William, 113, 119, 122, 123
GOODWYN, John, 66
GORDIN, Joseph, 117
GORDON, Ann, 54
Anne, 57
George, 92, 94
James, 65
Robert, 78
William, 126
GORSUCH, Charles, 31
GOSDIN, Joseph, 117
GOSTWICK, Joseph, 31
GOUGH, Elizabeth, 20
John, 115, 116, 117
Margaret, 115, 117
GOULD, James, 52
GOULDEN, Gabriel, 26
Gabriell, 25
Mary, 25
GOVANE, Ann, 98, 100
William, 98, 100
GRAFTY, Samuel, 15
GRAHAME, Charles, 110, 117
GRAINGER, Mary, 95
William, 95
GRAMMER, John, 8
GRANGER, Benjamin, 4
Mary, 4
GRAY, Ann, 98
George, 13

Jane, 52
Jane Pitman, 56
John, 98
Margaret, 13
Samuel, 116
William, 78
GREAS---, John, 41
GREAT BOHEMIA MANNOR, 47
GREAVES, John, 41, 59
GREEN, George, 16, 17
Henry, 16
Jacob, 121
John, 38
Jonas, 97
Leonard, 67
GREENBERRY, Charles, 32
Rachel, 32
GREENBURY, Anne, 36
Charles, 36
Rachel, 36
GREENFIELD, Ann, 94
Col., 81
Kenelinn Trueman, 94
Susanna, 94
Thomas, 23, 54
Thomas Trueman, 23, 94
Trueman, 82
Truman, 87
William, 54
GREEN'S DELIGHT, 35
GREENWELL, John, 49
GREMMER, Henry, 8
GREY, Andrew, 72
Thomas, 72
GRIFFIN, Charles, 49
Orlando, 49
Samuel, 81
GRIFFITH, 22
Anthony, 90
Charles Greenbury, 123
Elizabeth, 114
Jane, 90
Luke, 107
Orlando, 113
Samuel, 38
Sarah, 38
GRINDALL, Christopher, 103

139

GRINGOE, Mary, 31
  William, 31
GROOM, William, 5
GROONIFF, John, 13
  Ruth, 13
GROVER, Benjamin, 116
  Catherine, 53
  John, 116
GRUNDY, Robert, 17, 61, 65
GUIBEL'S CHANCE, 57
GUIBERT, Thomas, 65
GUICHARD, Samuel, 19, 84
GUILSCHARD, Ann, 84
GUITCHARD, Samuel, 35
GUITHER, Nicholas, 46
  William, 46
GULICK, Nicholas, 39
GUNBY, Francis, 14
GUNDRY, Robert, 13
GUNMAT, 51
GURCHAM, Ann, 14
  Samuel, 14
GUYBERT, Joshua, 15
GUYTHER, Mary, 9
  Nicholas, 9
  Sarah, 97
  William, 9

-H-

HACKER, John, 37, 40, 44, 59
  Richard, 80
HACKETT, Nicholas, 5
  William, 30
HACKWORTH, Samuel, 105
HADAWAY, George, 20
HADDOCK, James, 18, 19, 67
  Sarah, 19, 75
HADDORF, James, 16
  Sarah, 16
HADEN, William, 38
HAEKINS, Rachel, 98
HAGAN, Thomas, 34
HAGAR, Thomas, 27
HAGATHE, John, 30
HAGEN, James, 30
  Thomas, 30
HAGER, Mary, 27

HAGGERTY, Dennis, 71
HAGON, James, 93
HALEY, William, 125
HALFHEAD, Jane, 5
  John, 5, 8
HALL, Alexander, 60
  Aquila, 113
  Benjamin, 16, 116
  Christopher, 6, 78
  Dorothy, 108
  Edward, 66, 115
  Elisha, 32
  Elishar, 54
  Elizabeth, 6, 54, 78
  Francis, 108
  Henry, 103
  Jasper, 20, 25
  Joanah, 68
  John, 19, 21, 33, 54, 66, 73, 103
  Richard, 29, 32
  Thomas, 6, 78
HALLEY'S MANNOUR, 74
HALL'S CRAFT, 57
HALL'S HARBOUR, 106
HALL'S LAND, 6
HALTON, Frances, 122
  Francis, 118
HAMBLETON,
  Alexander, 67
  Edward, 15
  William, 1, 15, 27
HAMILTON, George, 94
  John, 66, 84
  Sarah, 60
  William, 60
HAMMOND, 101
  Ann, 98, 99
  Charles, 36, 78, 98, 101, 102, 119
  Daniell, 2
  Frances, 48, 98, 102
  John, 76, 102, 119
  Lawrence, 99
  Mary, 84, 106
  Mordecai, 48, 102
  Nicholas, 84, 99, 106
  Philip, 119
  Rachel, 36
  Rebecca, 99
  Rezin, 119
  Wealthy, 98

  Wealthy Ann, 99
  William, 86, 99
HAMOUR, John, 44
HAMPLETON, 44
HAMPTON, Richard, 79
HANCO, Benjamin, 116
HANDY, John, 70
HANKIN, Edward, 112
HANNAH, 66
HANNAT, John, 22
HANSON, John, 69
  Rebecca, 127
  Robert, 93
  Thomas, 127
  William, 93
HANT, Susanna, 10
HAP, 53
HAP AT A VENTURE, 53
HAPPY LOTT, 46
HARBERT, Alexander, 14
  Charles, 32
  William, 20
HARBOUR ROUSE, 90
HARD TRAVEL, 19, 20
HARD TRAVELL, 19
HARDESTY, Francis, 49
  Thomas, 57
HARDING, John, 5
HARISON, Frances, 12
HARMAN, Ephraim, 47
  Ephraim Augustine, 47
HARPER, Thomas, 56
HARRAHAVE, John, 28
  Mary, 28
HARRIS, Ariana Margaritta, 96
  Benton, 105
  Edward, 110
  Elizabeth, 110
  George, 8
  Jackaline, 10
  James, 96
  John, 39, 89
  Mary, 38, 110
  Richard, 37, 38
  Sarah, 8, 62, 89, 110
  Thomas, 90, 110
  William, 10, 96, 110, 116
HARRISON, Frances, 74, 75

James, 109
Richard, 12
Thomas, 110
William, 74, 75, 126
HARRY, 66
HART, Mary, 45
 Morgan, 45
HARVEY, Elizabeth, 126
 Frances, 3
 John, 126
 Nicholas, 3
 William, 111
HARWOOD, Richard, 44
 Thomas, 44
HASELER, Levin, 33
HASELWOOD, Ann, 4
 John, 4
 Mary, 4
HASTINGS, Samuel, 72
HATCHMAN, Thomas, 63
HATFIELD, Edward, 117
 Loraina, 117
HATHAWAY, George, 48
 Kowland, 48
HATTON, Ann, 9
 John, 2
 Richard, 9
 Thomas, 2
HAWKINGS, Elizabeth, 12
 Howard, 12
HAWKINS, Augustine, 15
 Deborah, 61, 63, 118
 Dorothy, 118
 Enault, 69
 Ernault, 69
 Henry, 39
 John, 61, 63, 69, 94, 34
 Juliana, 118
 Matthew, 118
 Robert, 118
 Susanna, 15
HAWOOD, Raphael, 18
HAYDEN, George, 34
HAYDON, William, 57
HAYES, James, 49
 Mary, 94
HAYMOND, William, 60
HAYS, Thomas, 58

HAYWOOD, Raphael, 18
HEAD, Adam, 33
 Anne, 33
 Edward, 41, 44
 Elizabeth, 7
 William, 7
HEALLY, John, 56
HEARD, Bridgett, 7
 John, 49
 William, 7
HEATH, Daniel Charles, 113
 James, 15, 16, 17, 71
 James Paul, 100
HEATH'S LANDING, 35
HEBB, Thomas, 23, 24
HEBDEN HOLE, 25
HEDGES, Rebecca, 100
 William, 100
HELLEN, James, 78
HEMSLEY, Elizabeth, 15
 Jane, 15
 Mary, 51
 Philemon, 15, 51
 Philip, 38, 41
 William, 15, 42
HEMSLY, Capt., 12
 Judith, 12
HEMSON, Jonathan, 54
HENDALL, John, 23
HENDERSON, Jacob, 90
HENDRICK, John, 53
HENDRIX, John, 22
HENLEY, Daniel, 59
 Danniell, 50
HENLY, Isabella, 116
HENRY, John, 35
HEPBURN, John, 112
 Mary, 112
HEPBURNE, Elizabeth, 70
 John, 104, 112
 Mary, 104, 112
 Patrick, 52, 70
HERBERT, Vitus, 61
HERCULES, 66
HERMAN, Augustine, 54, 55
 Casparius, 55, 56
 Casparius Augustine, 54
 Casparus A., 11
 Ephraim, 56

 Ephraim Augustine, 54
 Ephraim Augustus, 16
 Franciana, 56
 Judith, 56
 Thompson, 56
HESSELIUS, John, 122
 Mary, 122
HEWETT, Robert, 49
HEWITT, Mr., 7
HICKS, Thomas, 35, 80
HIGGINSON, Gilbert, 71, 80
HILL, Clement, 49, 67, 76
 Elizabeth, 13, 105, 106
 Giles, 13, 16
 Henry, 61, 79
 Joseph, 79, 103, 105, 106
 Mathew, 9
 Richard, 5, 78, 79
HILLHOUSE, William, 115
HILLYLEE, 29
HINDERSON, Andrew, 7
 Elizabeth, 7
HINDS, Thomas, 30
HINESLEY, Thomas, 40
HINEY, William, 44
HINTON, Thomas, 11, 14
HITCH, Elijah, 104
HITCHINSON, John, 3
HITCHMAN, William, 109
HLINTIFSO, Elizabeth, 44
HOCKETY, 37
HODGES, Robert, 89
HODGSON, Thomas, 103
HODSON, John, 37, 53, 65
HOG ISLAND, 52
HOG NECK, 122
HOGGINS, Peter, 82, 93
HOGGNECK, 49
HOIGH, Robert, 14
HOLBROOK, Thomas, 125
HOLDSWORTH, Joshua,

29
HOLEINGS, John, 25
HOLLAND, Francis, 66
  Otho, 17
  Thomas, 87
  William, 66
HOLLANDSHEAD, Francis, 62
HOLLAWAYS INCREASE, 6
HOLLENGER, Phillip, 55
HOLLIDAY, James, 57
  Sarah, 57
HOLLINGS, Mary, 26
HOLLINGSWORTH, Charles, 12, 49
  John, 30, 31
HOLLINS, John, 25
  Mary, 25
HOLLIS, Elizabeth, 8
  Henry, 8
HOLLOWAY, Dianah, 6
  Oliver, 6
HOLLYDAY, James, 63
  Sarah, 63
HOLMES, Mary, 86
  Richard, 25
HOLY, Ann, 54
HOLYDAY, James, 63
  Sarah, 63
  William, 14
HOMEWOOD, Ann, 98, 100, 101
  Charles, 100, 101
  Rebecca, 100, 101
  Thomas, 84, 98, 99, 100
HOMMOND, Rachel, 100
HONEY, Valentine Thomas, 118
HOOD, Gasper, 72
  Sarah, 72
HOOK, Elizabeth, 56
  William, 56
HOOKE, William, 64
HOOPER, Elinor, 4
  Henry, 4, 5, 17, 23
  Mary, 56, 73
  Richard, 4, 5, 23
  Ruth, 4
  Sarah, 4
HOPEWELL, Hugh, 8
HOPKINS, Bennett, 48

Francis, 58
Gerard, 37
Joseph, 38
Richard, 111
Thomas, 91
William, 58, 71, 91
HOPKIN'S FORBEARANCE, 71
HOPKINSON, Joshua, 86
HOPPER, Elizabeth, 114
  William, 114
HORSEY, Stephen, 115
HORSLEY, Joseph, 3
  Rosamond, 3
HOSKINS, Bennett, 48
  Oswald, 48
  Philip, 48
HOULDSWORTH, Helena, 11
  Samuel, 11
HOULSTON, Joseph, 105
HOWARD, Benjamin, 109, 110, 122
  Ephraim, 76
  Frace, 51
  Gideon, 95, 103
  Henry, 119
  John, 95, 103, 109
  Joseph, 76
  Luke, 51
  Mary, 40
  Michael, 77
  Philip, 84
  Phillip, 103
  Richard, 22
  Samuel, 103
  Samuell Harvey, 120
HOWARD'S CHANCE, 63, 64
HOWARD'S RANGE, 103
HOWARTON'S RANGE, 14
HOWELL, John, 24, 66, 72
  Margarett, 24
  Nathaniel, 72
  Samuel, 122
  Thomas, 66, 72
HOWES, Owen, 11
HUBBARD, Elizabeth, 84

John, 84
HUDSON, John, 10, 40, 80
  Robert, 119
HULLER, John, 38
HUMBERS, John, 42
HUMPHREY, Thomas, 36
HUNGERFORD, Edmund, 78
HUNT, Benjamin, 117
  Mary, 116
  Michael, 36
  Morgan, 45
  Thomas, 35
  Woolfren, 12
  Wornell, 36
HURD, John, 112
HURDLE, Rachel, 94
HUTCHENS, Charles, 80
  Francis, 116
HUTCHINS, Charles, 80
  Elizabeth, 22
HUTCHINSON, Ann, 69
  Elizabeth, 69
  Mary, 69
  William, 69
HUTTON, Barbara, 13
  John, 13
  William, 9
HYDE, Herbert, 96
  John, 96
  Samuel, 96
HYDES, John, 61
HYLAND, John, 11
HYNSON, James, 113
  John, 39, 42, 95
  Mary, 42
  Nathaniel, 38, 39, 42, 71
  Thomas, 7, 101, 113
  William, 108

-I-
IAGOE, Richard, 30
ILGATO, Caleb, 48
IMBERT, Andrew, 59
INDIAN TOM, 65
INGRAM, Hannah, 8
  John, 8, 12
  Peasly, 100
  Thomas, 2, 87
IOCE, Pasco, 108

IRELAND, John, 116
  Joseph, 117, 118
  Thomas, 82
  William, 116, 117
IRELLAND, Elizabeth, 58
ISAACK, Richard, 37
ISRAEL, John, 16, 21
IVY, Abigail, 115
  Anne, 21
  Anthony, 21, 49

-J-

JACK, 66
JACKSON, John, 94
JACOBS, Bartholomew, 118
  William, 118
JACOBSON, Jeffrey, 9
  Peter, 9
JACQUES, Lancelot, 112, 118
JADWIN, Elizabeth, 123
  Jeremiah, 123
  John, 123
  Sarah, 123, 124
JAGOE, Richard, 30
JAMES, Charles, 2
  Elizabeth, 2
  Joseph, 12, 25, 44
  Richard, 7
  Samuel, 80
JAMESON, Thomas, 39
JAMEY, 66
JANART, John, 55, 56
JENIFER, Ann, 56
  Daniel, 56, 103
  Daniel of St. Thomas, 56
  Daniell, 8, 47
  Elizabeth, 47
  Jacob, 56
  Mary, 8
  Miss, 46
JENIFER'S GIFT, 103
JENINGS, Ariana, 70, 78
  Arriana, 70
  Edmond, 78
  Edmund, 70
  Joseph, 91
  Mary, 91
  Mrs., 111
  Thomas, 122

JENKINS, Edward, 86, 87
  Enoch, 80
  John, 53
  Thomas, 87
JENKINSON, Elizabeth, 123
JENNINGS, Thomas, 111
JERMAN, Stephen, 70
JERRY, Thomas, 47
JESSOP, John, 113
  Nelly, 113
JOBSON, Ann, 71
  John, 71
  Thomas, 71
JOCE. See Ioce.
JOE, 66
JOFFS, William, 19, 20
JOHNS, Kinsey, 109
  Richard, 36, 109
  Susanna, 109
JOHNSON, Anne, 112
  Cornelius, 72
  Daniell, 8
  Donnell, 1
  Dorcas, 116
  Elizabeth, 8
  James, 1
  John, 94
  Peter, 1
  Randolph, 82
  Robert, 112
  Thomas, 112, 115, 116
  Whittington, 105
  William, 46
JOLLY, Edward, 4
  Margaret, 4
  Richard, 108
JONES, 90
  Ann, 45, 54, 58, 101
  Anne Greenbury, 100
  Daniel, 64, 65
  Edward, 45, 55
  Elizabeth, 17
  Francis, 79
  Hugh, 52
  John, 79, 98, 99, 100, 101, 125
  Jonathan, 15, 16, 35

  Joshua, 101
  Leonard, 80
  Martha, 15
  Mary, 65
  Morgan, 105, 106
  Philip, 83
  Priscilla, 106, 125
  Priseilla, 126
  Richard, 28, 65
  Robert, 31, 53
  Solomon, 81
  Thomas, 15
  William, 7, 46, 81
JONE'S ADVENTURE, 7
JONES'S WOODS, 31
JOPHS, Mary, 20
JORDAIN, Elizabeth, 7
  John, 7
JORDAN, Elizabeth, 83
  John, 115, 125
  Justinian, 52, 56, 62, 83
  Mary, 56, 83
JOWLES, Dryden, 94
  Henry, 5
  Henry Peregrine, 94
  Kenelinn Greenfield, 94
  Sibel, 5
  Sybill, 5
JOY, Peter, 33
JOYNER, Sarah, 2
  William, 2
JUDITH, 36
JURST, Joseph, 59

-K-

KANBURY, John, 67
KEDGER'S BITE, 41
KEECH, Elizabeth, 23
  James, 22, 23
KEEN, John, 56
  Samuel, 110
KEENE, Martha, 10
  Richard, 92, 97
  Susanna, 10
KEITH, Alexander, 40
  George, 50
KELHAM, John, 64
KELLAM, John, 105
KELLEY, Rachel, 92

KELLOM, Thomas, 105
KEMP, John, 20
  Matthew, 104
  Richard, 57
KENDRICK, James, 123, 124
  Sarah, 123
KENKIE, Herman, 54
KENNARD, Philip, 38
KENNERLY, Joseph, 42
KENT, James, 118
KERNEY, Dennis, 23
  Mary, 23
KEWELLIRIN, Richard, 64
KEY, Phillip, 67
KEYS, Elizabeth, 47
KILBORNE, Elizabeth, 1
  Francis, 1
  Margaret, 1
KILBURNE, Charles, 21, 34
  Elizabeth, 21
KILLAM, John, 105
KING, Robert, 45, 57
  Samuel, 116
  Thomas, 116
KING'S NECK, 6
KINWARD, Nathaniel, 77
KIRBY, Elizabeth, 124
  John, 124
  Margaret, 124
  Matthew, 77
  Michael, 123
KIRK, John, 64, 65
  Margarett, 65
KIRKE, John, 73
  Sarah, 73
KIRK'S PURCHASE, 64
KITELY, Mrs. William, 109
KNIGHTON, Dorothy, 19, 21
  George, 19
  James, 19
  John, 19
  Millicent, 21
  Sarah, 19
  Thomas, 19, 20, 21
KNOWLES, James, 69
  John, 69
  Lawrence, 69

KONIFER, Elizabeth, 53
KOSS, John, 41

-L-

LACHIA MANNOR, 87
LADD, Richard, 3
  Rosamond, 3
LADY BALTIMORE, 65
LADY'S DELIGHT, 19
LAMB, John, 99, 100
  Katherine, 36
  Sarah, 99
LANCASTER, Abraham, 27
  Richard, 54
  Thomas, 89, 107
LANE, John, 67, 89
  Walter, 27
  William, 96
LANGLEY, 48
LANKASHIRE, 27
LANKESTER, 27
LANTARNAM, 34
LANTERUM, 27
LARKIN, John, 13
  Thomas, 13, 35, 72, 51
LARNER, Edmund, 72
  Elizabeth, 72
LARRAMORE, Honnor, 71
LARRIMORE, Margaret, 100
  Roger, 100
LARRIMORE'S ADDITION, 100
LASH, Hugh, 71
LAWFELL, John, 23
LAWRENCE, Benjamin, 102
  Elizabeth, 102, 117
  Levin, 102
  Rutter, 77
LAWSON, Alexander, 92
  Hans, 46
  John, 66
  Mary, 104
  Thomas, 30, 118
  William, 30
LAYFIELD, George, 65, 66
  Priscilla, 65

  Samuel, 66
  Thomas, 65
LEACH, John, 23
LEATHERBURY, Robert, 114
LEATHERWOOD, Samuel, 34
LECKIE, John, 51
LECOMPT, Nehemiah, 45
  Philemon, 64
LEE, Francis, 41
  James, 72
  Lewis, 109
  Mary, 41
  Philip, 43, 91
  Phillip, 67
  Richard, 76, 91
  Sarah, 41
LEEDS, Edward, 15
  John, 15
  William, 15
LEEKY, Alexander, 46
LEGATT, Bridget, 9
  John, 9
LEGET, John, 2
LEGG, Daniel, 102
LEMASTER, Abraham, 34
LEMON, Hickford, 70
LETCHWORTH, Elizabeth, 9
  Joseph, 9
  Thomas, 9, 35
LEVETT, Elizabeth, 65
  Robert, 65
LEWIS, Ann, 73
  Elizabeth, 98
  William, 2, 8, 83
LEWIS'S NECK, 8
LIGET, Bridgett, 2
LILLINGSTONE, Carpendor, 48
  Frances, 48
LINDON, James, 56
  Margaret, 56
LINDOW, James, 40, 43
  Margaret, 40, 43
LINDSEY, Edmund, 8
  James, 7
LINN, John, 16
LITTLE, John, 3
  Mary, 3

Thomas, 113
LIVINGSTON, Francis, 20
LLOYD, Alice, 62
  Ann, 54
  Col., 12
  Edward, 39, 41, 42, 63, 110
  James, 51, 54
  Madam, 12
  Phil, 40
  Philemon, 12, 40, 41, 45, 48, 62, 67
  Sarah, 42, 63
LLOYDE, Anne, 61
LOCH, William, 66
LOCKWOOD, Elizabeth, 13
LOCKYEAR, John, 107
LOCUST THICKET, 12
LOMAS, John, 92, 97
LOMAX, Cleoburn, 12
  John, 78
  Margaret, 78
LONDON, 66
LONG, Ann, 112
  Jeremiah, 3
  John, 1
  Mary, 99
  Sewell, 99, 112
LONG ACRE, 7
LONGMAN, Daniel, 12, 13
  Stephen, 13
  Steven, 12
LORD, James, 26, 27
LORD BALTIMORE, 65
LOUISE, Samuel, 10
LOUTHIS, William, 16
LOVE, Dorothy, 112
  Thomas, 29, 112
LOWDER, Charles, 52
LOWE, Anne, 25
  Henry, 33
  John, 113
  Nicholas, 22
  Vincent, 19
LOWING, Phillip, 23
LOWNDES, Benjamin, 121
  Christopher, 121
  Elizabeth, 121
LOWRY, Hester, 11
  William, 11

LOWTHER, Col., 52
  Madam, 52
  Maria Johannah, 52
LOYDALE, John, 52
LOYDALL, John, 52
LOYDE, Lyonel, 91
LUCKLAND, 40
LUCY, 66
LUMBARD, Francis, 7
LUMLEY, Alexander, 14
  Sarah, 14
LUNN, Dianah, 6
  John, 16
  Thomas, 6
LURKE, John, 6
  Mary, 6
  Nicholas, 6, 7
LUSBY, Aaron, 92, 93
  Eleanor, 92, 93
  Jacob, 93
  John, 92, 93, 100
  Margaret, 100
  Mary, 93
  Rachel, 93
  Samuel, 93
  Susannah, 104
  Thomas, 93
LYDALL, John, 52
LYDIA'S REST, 61
LYNCH, John, 116
LYNE, George, 18
LYNES, Ann, 40, 51
  Philip, 40, 51
LYNTHICUMB, George, 82
  Jane, 82
LYON, William, 111

-M-

MCALLEN, Arthur, 105
MCCART, John, 41
MACCLAINE, Amy, 86
  Hector, 86
  William, 86
MCCLANE, Amy, 86
  Ann, 86
  Catherine, 86
  Hector, 86
  John, 86
  Sarah, 86
  William, 86
MACCUBBIN,
  Elizabeth, 127
  John, 79

  Mary, 126, 127
  Mary Clare, 98
  Moses, 126, 127
  Nicholas, 121
  William, 126, 127
MACCUBBINS, Samuel, 35
MCCUDDY, John, 88, 89
  Mary, 88, 89
MACDANIEL, Bryan, 24
MCDONALD, Angus, 113
  Ann, 113
MACE, Josias, 43
  Nicholas, 43
MCFADDEN, Angus, 105
MCFEDDING, Angus, 105
MCGILL, David, 54
MCGRATH, John, 125
MACGREGORY, Hugh, 90
  James, 90
MCILVAINE, David, 114
  William, 114
MCILVANE, David, 109
  William, 109
MACKALL, Barbara, 78
  Benjamin, 78
  Hannah, 116
  James, 116
  James John, 115
  John, 74, 81, 82, 115, 116
  Margaret, 115
  Susannah, 41, 81
MACKARTEE, John, 32
MACKEY, James, 24
MACKLEFISH, David, 68
MACKMORRIE, James, 70
MACLEAN, James, 95
MCLEMMY, Samuel, 125
MACLEOD, Elizabeth, 79
MCLEOD, Elizabeth, 97
MACLEOD, Robert, 79
MCLEONE, Turlow, 64
MACLOUGHLLIN,
  Elizabeth, 24
  Kenelm, 24
MCNAMARA, Margarett, 15

Thomas, 15
MACNEMARA, John, 118
  Margaret, 42, 43, 47, 63, 96, 97, 98
  Michael, 47, 96, 103
  Thomas, 42, 43, 47, 63, 96, 103
MCWILLIAMS, Thomas, 65
MADDOX, James, 23
MAGGATEE, Patrick, 22
MAGRUDER, 24
  John, 74, 90
  Samuel, 67, 74
MAHONEY, Elizabeth, 50
MAIDEN POYNT, 12, 13
MALBURY, Francis, 23
MALCOMB, John, 125
MALLIKIN, James, 14
MALSON, Mary, 17
MANDERS, Sarah, 83
MANING, John, 10
  Nathaniel, 10
MANLESTER, Joseph, 60
MANNER, John, 12
  Lydia, 12
MANNING, Elizabeth, 9
  John, 73
  Nathaniel, 74
  Richard, 74
  Thomas, 8, 73, 74
MANSELL, George, 123
  Samuel, 123
MANWARING, 34
MANYING, Richard, 73
MARBURY, Luke, 91
MARIARTE, Daniel, 65
  Ninian, 65
MARIARTEE, Ninian, 90
MARIATEE, Jane, 90
  Ninian, 90
MARINX, Hugh, 6
  Katharine, 6
MARKLAND, Charles, 55, 114
  Edward, 114
  Mary, 55, 114
MARKLIN, Richard, 48

MARKS, James, 12
  John, 12
MARLEY, Cornelius, 33
MARLO, John, 30
MARSH, Richard, 23, 86
  Thomas, 7, 94
MARSHALL, Ann, 16
  Anne, 52
  Charles, 16
MARSHAM, Ann, 12
  Richard, 12, 18
MARSHAM'S POINT, 21
MARSHES POINT, 21
MARSHES SEAL, 19, 20
MARTEN, John, 87
  Michael, 87
MARTIN, Hannah, 114
  James, 16
  John, 95
  Michael, 38, 40, 51
  Nicholas, 114
  Thomas, 26
  William, 27
MARTINI, Abdelo, 3
  Thomas, 27
MARY'S MOUNT, 47
MASCALL, Richard, 6
MASH, Elizabeth, 17
MASK, John, 57
MASON, Ann, 89
  George, 89
  Robert, 11
MASSEY, Mr., 50
  Samuel, 95
  Sarah, 95
MATHEWS, Hugh, 85
  Ignatius, 5, 6, 9
  James, 106, 107
  John, 106, 107
  Levin, 106
  Roger, 107, 68
  Sarah, 46
  Thomas, 9
MATHIS, Ignatius, 48
  William, 48
MATTHEW, Jonathan, 67
  Mary, 67
MATTHEWS, Thomas, 93
MATTINGLY, Cezar, 41
MATTINGSLY, Cezar, 41

MATTOX, Samuell, 4
MATTUCKS, Alexander, 27
MAULDIN, Elizabeth, 43
MAURFORD, Edward, 31
MAYNING, Richard, 73
MEARSGATE, 39
MECALL, George, 9
MECOTTER, Alexander, 32, 33
MEDCALF, Elizabeth, 20
  George, 20
MEDLEY, John, 6
  Thomas, 10
  William, 6
MEEK, Francis, 24
  Mary, 24
  Westal, 127
MEER'S GATE, 40
MEER'S GATE ADDITION, 40
MEHENNY, Macom, 2
MELLOR, John, 43
  Mary, 43
MELTON, Thomas, 40
MENIGER, Michael, 82
  Susannah, 82
MERCER, Thomas, 42, 47
MERCHANT, James, 58
MEREDITH, Samuel, 111
MERIKEN, Christian, 7
  John, 7
MERRIKEN, John, 98, 99
  Joshua, 98
MERRIKIN, Hugh, 7, 96
  Jacob, 96
  John, 95
MERRIMAN, John, 111
MERRIOT, Elizabeth, 101
MERRIT, William, 113
MERRYKIN, Hugh, 83
  John, 83
MERRYMAN, Charles, 13
MERYDITH, Robert, 52
MESSICK, Nehemiah, 80

MIDDLE NECK, 54
MIDDLETON, Hugh, 87
  John, 14
  Robert, 14, 58, 87
  Samuel, 87
  William, 86, 87
MIDFORD, John, 65
MIDLETON, John, 67
  William, 69
MILE END, 74
MILES, Elizabeth, 75
  Frances, 75
  John, 47, 75
  Mary, 75
  Matthias, 125
  Tobias, 75
  William, 115, 125
MILES END, 20
MILL RUN, 74
MILLARD, Richard, 57
MILLER, Alice, 51
  Ann, 51, 74
  Arthur, 38, 51
  James, 115
  Jane, 18
  John, 74
  Michael, 38, 51
MILLERNE, 29
MILLIGAN, Robert, 105
MILLS, Elizabeth, 42
  Frances, 59
  John, 54
  Peter, 83
  William, 10, 42, 85
MING, Edward, 32
MINSKIE, Samuel, 72
MIRAX, Margaret, 59
MITCHELL, Grace, 25, 73
  Henry, 73, 74
  Peter, 95
MOALE, Frances, 122
  John, 71
  Richard, 118, 122
MOBERLY, John, 44
MOCAL, James, 76
MOCCAL, James, 75
MOGBEE, Jane, 44
  Matt, 44
MOLDEN, Ann, 126
  Elizabeth, 126
MOLL, 66
  John, 45

MOLLINGTON, Samuel, 16
MOLLINGTON HAPP, 16
MOLLISSTON, Henry, 89
MONK, Mary, 82
MONROE, Keziah, 126
MOON, Richard, 20
MOOR, Joseph, 11
MOORE, Ann, 95
  Cassandra, 113
  James, 16
  John, 75, 104, 113
  Mary, 121
  Matthew, 104
  Priscilla, 104
  Rizdon, 121
  Roger, 7
  William, 113, 115
MORGAN, Abraham, 22, 90
  David, 24, 51
  Enoch, 123, 124
  Grace, 51
  Henry, 92, 123, 124
  Philip, 123, 124
  Saban, 124
  Sarah, 123, 124
  William, 51
MORLEY'S CHOICE, 57
MORRIS, John, 22
MORSELL, Elizabeth, 115
  James, 115
MOSS, Richard, 83
MOUNT HOPE, 21
MOUNTS, Peter, 4
MOY, Richard, 44
MOYE, Richard, 44
MT. HARMOUR, 2
MT. HOPE, 22
MUDD, Barbary, 49
  Henry, 30, 49
  Thomas, 13, 49
MUDD'S REST, 49
MULLAKIN, John, 25, 26, 28
  Patrick, 25
MUMFORD, James, 71
  Thomas, 71
MUNDAY, 66
MUNSE, Peter, 4
MURDOCK, William, 89
MURPHEY, Ann, 87

  William, 87
MURROE, Anguish, 80
MUSSHETT, John, 95
  Penelope, 95

-N-
NANNY, 66
NANSONUM WOODS, 21
NATHANIEL'S POINT, 15, 39, 40, 42
NATIONS, Ann, 53
NEALE, Ann, 54
  Anthony, 22, 30, 67
  Elizabeth, 17, 53
  Francis, 22
  James, 16, 17, 18, 22, 53, 54
  Mary, 17, 53
  Raphael, 67
NEALE'S GIFT, 22
NEALL, Sarah, 123, 124
NEILSON, George, 70
  Jane, 126
NELL, 66
NELSON, Arthur, 36
  John, 36
NEWALL, Peter, 58
NEWBURY, William, 39
NEWCOMB, Ann, 90
  Robert, 90
NEWMAN, George, 12, 22
  John, 11, 12, 22, 39, 42
  Lydia, 12
  Rebecca, 11
NICHOLS, William, 11
NICHOLSON, Beale, 75
  Elizabeth, 75, 76
  Governor, 34
  William, 75, 76
NICKSON, Richard, 60
NOAKES, George, 18
  Rebecca, 18
NOBLE, George, 69
  Isaac, 60
  Joseph, 70
NOE, John, 29
NOKE, William, 126
NONE SO GOOD IN FINLAND, 88
NORFOLK, James, 117
  John, 117

Mary, 117
Thomas, 117
NORMAN, George, 57
NORRIS, Edmund, 38
  John, 14
NORTON, John, 13, 32
  Mary, 13
NORWOOD, 29
  Andrew, 21
  Edward, 110, 111, 112, 113
  Elizabeth, 21, 113
  John, 113
  Mary, 113
  Ruth, 113
  Samuel, 113
NOVETT, John, 20
  Richard, 20
NOWELL, Ellinor, 64
  John, 64
NUNAM, John, 14, 29
NURDOCK, William, 89
NUTHALL, Barbara, 46
  Brent, 39, 49, 50, 61
  John, 46, 50
NUTT, Job, 5
NUTTHALL, John, 39
  Mary, 39
NUTTWELL, James, 30

-O-

OATLEYS CHOICE, 6
OBENCE, Obediance, 47
OCANE, Jane, 11
  John, 11
O'DOUGHERTY, Federa, 71
OFFUTT, Nathanial, 90
OGDEN, Mary, 95
  Nehemiah, 95
OGG, George, 82
OGLE, Ann, 121
  Benjamin, 121
  Governor, 121
  Mary, 121
  Meliora, 121
  Samuel, 121
O'HIGGERTY, Dennis, 71
OKAINE, Martha, 4
  Rickart, 4
OLD TOWNE, 23

OLDFIELD, George, 4, 11, 54
OLDHAM, Ann, 114
  Anne, 114
  Edward, 114
  Elizabeth, 114
  Hannah, 114
  John, 55, 59, 60, 65
  Margaret, 114
  Mary, 114
  Sarah, 114
OLIVERS NECK, 6
OMEHA, Bryan, 91
OMELY, Bryant, 91
ONION, Stephen, 55
  Zacheus, 110
ORCHARD, John, 82
ORGAN, Matthewe, 64
ORIN, Robert, 19
ORME, Robert, 16
ORRICK, Caroline, 113
  Charles, 113
  Elizabeth, 113
  James, 71
  John, 57
  Susannah, 113
ORSLER, Edward, 110
OSBORNE, James, 106, 107
OTHOSON, Herman, 55
OTTOSEN, Otto, 42
OTTOSON, Otto, 55
OULCHERLONY, John, 54
OUTCHTERLONY, John, 80
OVERMARSH, 64
OVERSEE, Elizabeth, 1, 8
  Simon, 1
  Symon, 8
OWEN, John, 72
  Thomas, 96
OWING, Henry, 101
  Michal, 101
OWINGS, Henry, 100
  Michal, 100
  Samuel, 119

-P-

PACA, Aquila, 72
  John, 107, 112
  Mary, 110

Rachel, 72
William, 110
PACKER, Edward, 4
  Elizabeth, 4
PADGETT, 18
PAGE, George, 101
  Margaret, 101
PAGETT, Amy, 5
  Sarah, 5
  William, 5
PAGGETT, Thomas, 5
  William, 5
PAINTER'S RANGE, 72
PAINTER'S REST, 71
PAKE, Walter, 2
PALMER, Thomas, 109
PARDOE, Ann, 116
  John, 115
PARKER, Ann, 69
  Edward, 4
  Elizabeth, 4, 41, 81, 90
  Gabriel, 69, 81, 82
  Gabrielle, 41
  George, 41, 81, 82, 90
  Judith, 10
  Mary, 41
  Nicholas, 10
  Robert, 111
  Sarah, 41
  Susannah, 41, 81, 82
PARPOINT, Mahitable, 44
PARR, John, 77
PARRAN, Alexander, 65, 66
  John, 66
  Mary, 66
  Samuel, 116
PARRATT, Henry, 6
PARROTT, Benjamin, 10
  Elizabeth, 10
  Gabriel, 13, 41, 81
  Gabriell, 13
  Henry, 1
  Susanna, 13
  William, 1
PARSLOW, Helena, 11
  Thomas, 11
PARSONS, Elizabeth,

PARTRIDGE, Daubigny
  Buckler, 111
PASCALL, George, 5
  J, 5
  James, 5
  Sarah, 5
PASCALL'S PURCHASE,
  15, 35
PASCAL'S PURCHASE,
  16
PATRICKS PLAINS, 27
PATTERSON, Mary, 77
  Thomas, 77
PATTISON, James, 22,
  56
  Jane, 77
  Jeremiah, 77
  John, 72
  Mary, 72, 73, 77,
  95
  Thomas, 77
PAYN, John, 14
  Mary, 14
PEACOCK, Paul, 33
PEAK, Christopher,
  23
PEARCE, Benjamin,
  42, 71
  Col., 56
  Daniel, 49
  Mary, 42
  William, 38, 42
PEARL, William, 31
PEARLE, Robert, 82
  William, 31, 32
PEARSON, Symon, 38
PEEKE, Thomas, 45
PEEL, Samuel, 36
PEELE, John, 102
  Robert, 102
  Samuel, 66, 102
  William, 102
PEGG, 66
PEIRCE, Daniel, 28
  John, 1
PEIRCY, Thomas, 3
PEIRPOINT,
  Mahitable, 17
PEIRSON, Robert, 20
PEMBERTON, Benjamin,
  60
PENN, Anne, 122
  John, 122
  Mark, 67

PENNINGTON,
  Elizabeth, 47
  Henry, 47
PENROY, John, 10
  Thomas, 10
PERIGOY, Sarah, 31
PERKINS, William,
  110
PERRY, Daniel, 31
  Ignatius, 74
  James, 74
  Richard, 2
  Samuel, 75
  Sarah, 75
PETER, 66
PETERS, Abraham, 15
PETERSON, Andrew, 4,
  56
PETTIBONE, Philip,
  101
PHELPS, Walter, 16,
  17, 34, 39, 81
PHIGGETT, Daniel, 25
PHILIPS, Bar-
  tholomew, 41
  Daniel, 73, 74
  James, 88
  Margaret, 41
  Mitchell, 74
PHILLIPS, Mitchell,
  73
PHILLIP'S BORROUGH,
  17
PHILPOT, Bryan, 61
PHIPARD, Ann, 84
PHIPPARD, Mary, 94
PIERCE, Daniel, 55
  William, 55
PIERPOINT, Henry,
  119
PILE, Elizabeth, 90
  Francis, 29
  Mary, 90
  Richard, 90
  William, 90
PILES, Elizabeth, 69
  William, 69
PINDELL, Mary, 118
  Thomas, 118
PINDER, Jane, 64
PINDOR, Alexander,
  52
  Christopher, 52
  Edward, 64
PINNELL, Katherine,
  21
  Michael, 21
PINY NECK, 71
PIPER, Christopher,
  104, 105
  Job, 104
  Rachel, 104
PIPER'S HILL, 50
PIRKINS, John, 27
PISSCATTAWAYS, 53
PITSTOE, Philip, 31
PLAITER, George, 51
PLATER, Ann, 75
  George, 72, 74,
  75, 91
PLOWDEN, Edmund, 39
  George, 39
  Margaret, 39
PLUMMER, Mary, 60
PLUNKETT, Richard,
  71
POCOSON, 88
POLK, David, 104
POOR, Mary, 117
POPE, John, 105
POPLAR NECK, 52
POPLAR'S NECK, 45
POPPINGAY, 1
PORTER, Andrew, 109
  Francis, 28
  James, 106
  Jane, 106
  John, 105, 106
  Laurence, 28
  Sarah, 106
PORTEUS, Edmund, 93
PORTLAND MANNOR, 108
POSEY, John, 39, 43
  Mary, 39
POTTER, John, 6
POTTS GIFT, 28, 29
POWELL, Thomas, 37
POWER, Richard, 64
POWERS, Nicholas, 41
PRATHER, William, 36
PRATT, Elizabeth,
  113, 114
  John, 113, 114
  Mary, 113, 114
  Sarah, 99, 100
  Thomas, 99, 100
  William, 113, 114
PRESTON, Anne, 25
  Daniel, 107
  James, 102

Joan, 26
John, 25
PRICE, Ann, 9, 90
  Edward, 40
  Henry, 20
  Jenkin, 6, 13
  John, 9
  Mary, 45
  Matthew, 6
  William, 45
PRICHARD, Catherine, 89
  John, 89
PRIOR, Catherine, 17
  Edmond, 17
  Sarah, 120
  Thomas, 42, 125
PRITCHARD, Catherine, 89
  John, 89, 103
PRITCHETT, John, 2
  William, 2, 18
PROBART, William, 96
PROCTOR, Elizabeth, 16
PROVIDENCE, 84
PRYER, John, 120
  Thomas, 120
PRYOR, Edmond, 21
  John, 120
  Katherine, 21
  Sarah, 120
  Thomas, 120
PUE, Mary, 119, 123
  Michael, 119, 123
PULLEN, Ellinor, 64

-Q-
QUEEN, John, 70
QUIGLEY, John, 9
  Owen, 9
QUINCEY, Edmund, 89
QUYNN, Allen, 126

-R-
RALPHO, 46
RAMSEY, John, 38
RANDALL, Catherine, 76
  Christopher, 68, 76
RASIN, Sarah, 107, 108
  William, 107, 108
RATTCLIFF, Richard, 13
RAWBONE, Elizabeth, 78, 79
  James, 78
RAWLEIGH, William, 80
RAWLES, William, 7
RAWLINGS, Aaron, 72
  Aron, 34
  Francis, 120
  Jehosaphat, 120
  John, 11, 120
RAYMOND, Jonathan, 60, 70, 71
  Judith, 60
RAZOLINI, Onorio, 72
READ, David, 7
READER, Benjamin, 41
REARDON, Sarah, 108
RECORD, Elizabeth, 6
REED, George, 51
  Hannah, 25
  John, 25
  Walter, 28
REEVES, Thomas, 32
REGISTER, John Emory, 118
REID, James, 51
  Lydia, 51
REIGNOLDS, John, 4
RENFRO, John, 54
RENSHAW, Anne, 61
  William, 61
RESBROOKE, William, 7
RESERVE, 38
RESTON, Edward, 76
  Jane, 25
  John, 25
RESURRECTION MANOR, 2
REVELL, Catherine, 45
  Randall, 45
  Sarah, 45
REVES, Thomas, 32
  Ubgal, 83
REVILL, 33
REYNOLDS, Thomas, 49, 87
  William, 98
RICARTON, 64, 65
RICH, Ann, 58
  Stephen, 20
RICH NECK, 26, 27

RICHARDS, Edward, 52
RICHARDSON, Anthony, 92
  Elizabeth, 92
  James, 29
  John, 8, 11, 29
  Mary, 8
  Richard, 102, 103
  Samuel, 103
  Thomas, 92, 111, 112
  William, 47, 68
RICHARDSONS RIGDE, 37
RIDBY, 48
RIDDLE, George, 95
RIDER, John, 80
RIDGELEY, Ann, 65
  Henry, 79
  Nicholas, 57, 65
  Rebeccah, 119
  Robert, 102
RIDGELY, John, 110
RIDGLEY, 43, 44
  Henry, 14
RIDLEY, Rebecca, 52
RIDOUT, John, 121
  Mary, 121
RIGBY, Ann, 126
  James, 2, 126
  James Townley, 126
  John, 78
RILEY, Hugh, 35, 37
RILEY'S RANGE, 35, 37
RINGGOLD, Rebecca, 95
  Sarah, 108
  William, 59, 108
RINGOLD, James, 59
RIOLY, Hugh, 43, 44
RIPPON, 91
RIVERS, Charles, 71
ROBERTS, John, 85, 122
  Mary, 118
  Robert, 118
ROBIER, George, 52
  Thomas, 52
ROBIN, 66
ROBINS, George, 57
  Henry, 70
ROBINSON, Charles, 113
  David, 51

Elizabeth, 113
George, 3
Grace, 51
John, 37, 51
Judith, 51
Susanna, 3
William, 3
ROBINSONS FARME, 37
ROBSON, John, 56
ROBY, John, 87
  Richard, 87
  Sarah, 87
  Thomas, 87
ROCK, George, 92
  Mary, 92
ROCKY POINT, 20
RODD, Lance, 79
  Thomas, 79
RODE, Abraham, 50
  Mrs. Francis, 50
ROE, Edward, 5
  John, 55
  Mary, 2, 5
ROGERS, John, 15, 48
  Mary, 58
  William, 58
ROIZER'S REFUGE, 20
ROOK, John, 21
ROSE, 66
ROSS, Robert, 113
  Thomas, 107
ROTTERDAM, 31
ROUSBY, Ann, 75
  Christopher, 1, 14
  Elizabeth, 1
  John, 51, 73, 74, 75
ROUTH, Christopher Cross, 114
ROWSE, Bridgett, 6
  Gregory, 6
ROZER, Benjamin, 8, 14
  Notty, 14
RUFF, Mary, 82
RULE, Peter, 45, 46
RULEY, anthony, 61
RUMNEY, Edward, 97
RUNN, Nicholls, 34
RUSHOON, Stephen, 44
RUSSELL, Abraham, 51
  John, 27, 51
  William, 10
RUTH, Christopher Cross, 113

Moses, 107
RUTLAND, Thomas, 109
RUTTER, Alice, 17
  John, 17
  Ralph, 54
RYAN, John, 17
RYE, Charles, 14
  John, 14
RYLAND, Allice, 55
  John, 55
RYLEY, Hugh, 14, 22, 38
RYLEY'S RANGE, 38

-S-
ST. AUGUSTINE'S MANOR, 55
ST. AUGUSTINE'S MANNOR, 56
ST. BRIDGETT'S, 67
ST. JOHN'S FREEHOLD, 1
ST. JOHN'S MANNOR, 54
ST. JOSEPH'S MANOR, 3
ST. LAURENCE'S FREEHOLD, 49
ST. LAWRENCE, 40, 41
ST. MARY'S HILL, 46, 47
SALLERS, Ann, 6
  John, 6
SALSBURY, Elizabeth, 49
  William, 49
SAM, 66
SAMBO, 66
SAMPSON, 36
SAMUEL, Peter, 80
  Richard, 80
SANDERS, John, 13, 46, 48
  Matthew, 15
SANDFORD, Cornelius, 95
SANDS, Robert, 20
SANFORD, Alice, 2
SANGO, 66
SANNER, Thomas, 81
SATT, Robert, 52
SATTLE, John, 41
SAUNDERS, Edward, 11
  Elizabeth, 32
  Jane, 11, 50

Joseph, 32
Robert, 122
William, 60
SAWELL, Anne, 33
  James, 88
  John, 18, 33
  Peter, 18
SAXTON, Sarah, 57
SAYOR, Col., 12
SCARBOROUGH, Henry, 2
  John, 105
SCHERTILIFE, Ann, 22
  John, 22
SCHOOL HOUSE, 8
SCOT, Ann, 56
  William, 56
SCOTLAND, 28
SCOTT, Andrew, 93
  Cuthbert, 7
  Daniel, 38
  Day, 84, 104
  Edward, 51, 58, 59
  Elizabeth, 7
  James, 107
  Jane, 43, 56
  Jane Pitman, 56
  John, 40, 43, 56, 104
  Mary, 93
  Robert, 62
  Upton, 121
  Walter, 47, 54, 55
SCRIVOUS, Phillip, 53
SCUTT, Mary, 111
SEAERTON, Marquis, 9
SECTAR, 35
SEDWICK, Benjamin, 116
  Joshua, 19
  Thomas, 19
SEICHE, 66
SELBY, William, 18
SELLMAN, William, 68
SERGENT, John, 37
SEWALL, Henry, 46
  Susannah, 46
SEWARD, William, 35
SEWELL, Charles, 31
  Elianor, 31
  Henry, 100
  Nicholas, 46, 50, 100
  Peter, 22

SEWELLIN, John, 109
SEYMOUR, John, 58
SHAPLEY, Phillip, 17, 23
SHATTELESS, John, 22
SHAW, Margaret, 41
SHEALE, Bridgett, 6
  Robert, 6
SHEFFIELD, 40
SHELBY, Evan, 112
SHEPBUSH MANNING, 74
SHEPPARD, John, 69
SHERMAN, Peter, 61
SHERREDINE,
  Jeremiah, 43
  Martha, 43
SHERRY, Job, 64
SHERWOOD, Daniel, 59, 60, 61
  Hugh, 15
  Philip, 43
SHIELD, Briant, 36
SHIPLEY, Adam, 119
  Richard, 102, 119
SHOEBROOK, John, 118
  Julliana, 118
SHOREDITCH, 27
SHULIVANT, Ann, 6
  Jeremiah, 6
SIKES, Thomas, 59
SIM, Mary, 93
  Patrick, 93
SIMMES, John, 78
SIMMONS, Elizabeth, 19
SIMON READER'S, 18
SIMONS, Elizabeth, 19, 21
  George, 19, 21
SIMPSON, Patrick, 54
  Thomas, 53
SINCLAIR, Priscilla, 13
  Robert, 13
SINGLETON, John, 95
SIRMAN, Peter, 70
SIVICK, John, 15
  Susanna, 15
  William, 15, 19
SKIDMORE, Edward, 3, 9
SKILLINGTON, Mary, 48
SKINNER, Adderton, 81, 82

  Andrew, 30
  Ann, 36
  William, 60, 81
SKIRVIN, William, 125
SLATER, Elizabeth, 117
  Ellis, 116
  Henry, 47
  Samuel, 117
SLOSS, Samuel, 114
  Thomas, 114, 126
SLUYTER, Peter, 55
SLYE, Charles, 50
  Gerard, 13
  Gerrard, 13, 50, 52, 59, 62
  John, 15
  Robert, 29, 32, 50, 59
  Susanna, 50, 59
  Susannah, 59
SLYTER, Henry, 42
SMALLPIECE, John, 4
SMALLWOOD, Bayne, 84, 89
  Elizabeth, 87
  James, 53
  Leadston, 87
  Prior, 53, 67, 84, 89
  Pryor, 67
SMALLWOOD'S PARK, 89
SMITH, Ann, 16, 77
  Anthony, 109
  Arthur, 45
  Charles Somerset, 52
  Deborah, 110
  Edward, 5, 16, 51
  Elizabeth, 82
  Emporer, 3
  Esquire, 21, 49
  Francis, 9, 43
  James, 8, 71, 104, 112
  John, 21, 29, 38, 40, 46, 51, 54, 55, 58, 73, 77, 82, 109, 111
  Joseph, 110
  Margarett, 65
  Maria Johanna, 52
  Mary, 51, 58, 82
  Peter, 12

  Philip, 80
  Rachel, 92
  Richard, 11, 52
  Robert, 12, 17, 21, 49, 61
  Samuel, 68
  Thomas, 5, 29, 32, 51
  Walter, 10
  Widow, 56
  William, 8, 17, 26, 40, 51, 85, 107
SMITH'S NECK, 61
SMITH'S RIDGE, 20
SMITHSON, Thomas, 22, 52
SMOOT, Edward, 122
SMOOTE, Grace, 9
  Richard, 9
  William, 9
SNOWDEN, Richard, 91, 96, 103
SNUGGS, John, 14
SOCKWELL, Mary, 40
  Thomas, 22, 53
SOMERVELL,
  Alexander, 116
  James, 115, 116
SOMERVILLE, James, 77
SOPEAR, Eleanor, 55
  Simon, 55
SOUTH ISLANDS, 59
SOUTH MARSHES, 59
SOUTHER, Christopher, 121
SOUTHES, Jane, 16
SPARROW, Thomas, 68, 102, 126
SPEAK, Bowling, 49, 58
SPEAKE, John, 62
SPEAR, Eleanor, 55
  Simon, 55
SPENCER, Archibald, 111
  James, 28
SPERNON, Joseph, 11
SPIKERNALL, Abraham, 78
SPINCK, Henry, 22
SPINK, Henry, 34
SPRIGG, Edward, 63, 65, 67, 90

Elizabeth, 90, 112
Joseph, 122
Margery, 69
Osborn, 90, 96
Rachel, 96
Richard, 90
Thomas, 9, 69,
  102, 112, 120
SQUIRES, John, 46
STALLONS, Jacob, 23
STANDLEY, Mary, 1
  William, 1
STANFILL, john, 84
STANLEY, John, 12
STANTON, Mary, 51
STARLING, Thomas, 63
START, Ephraim, 91
STEELE, Ann, 105
  Henry, 105
STEPHENSON, Henry,
  126
STERLING, Christian,
  63
  Thomas, 63
STEUART, George, 100
  William, 100
STEVENS, Ann, 14
  Elizabeth, 65
  John, 4, 14
  Katherine, 8
  Robert, 8
  Sarah, 117
  William, 65
STEVENSON, Anna, 49
  Edward, 49
  James, 109
  John, 111, 112,
    118, 119, 122
STEWARAD, Thomas, 87
STEWARD, Alexander,
  84
  Daniel, 87
  James, 39, 42
  Thomas, 87
STEWART, Anthony,
  112
  George, 99, 121
  James, 107
  John, 108
  Patrick, 88
STINCHCOMB, John,
  110
STINNETT, John, 38
STOAKES, Peter, 22
  William, 42

STOCKELEY, 22
STOCKETT, Elizabeth,
  72
  Thomas, 72
STOCKLEY, Woodman,
  22
STODDART, James, 53,
  82
  Sarah, 82
STODDERT, 70
  Elizabeth, 69
  James, 69
  John, 69
STOKES, George, 76,
  80
  Humphrey Wells,
    76, 80
  John, 76, 80, 81
  Susannah, 76, 80
STONE, William, 47,
  57, 62, 63
STONESTREET, Edward,
  53
  Thomas, 53, 69
STONEY RIDGE, 120
STOOPE, John, 42
  Mary, 42
STOOPLEY GIBSON, 2
STOPKINS, John, 17
STOREY, Mary, 92
  Robert, 92
  Walter, 1, 40, 51,
    53
STOTT'S LOTT, 16
STOUT, Ann, 77
  James, 77
STRICKLAND, Joseph,
  23
STRINGER, James, 2,
  3
STRINGFELLOW, Hen-
  rietta
  Maria, 62
STRONG, Elizabeth, 2
  Leonard, 2
STUMP, John, 109
STURGIS, William,
  105
SUDLER, Emory, 112
SUE, 66
SUNDERLAND, John, 11
  Josias, 81
  Margaret, 11
SUTTON, John, 49
SUTTON GRANGE, 32

SWANN, Robert, 111
SWANSONS LOTT, 21
SWEATNAM, Edward, 51
SWIFT, William, 52
SWORNIFLED, Chris-
  tian, 14
SYKES, Thomas, 56
SYLE, Jane, 50
SYMPSON, Patrick, 71

-T-
TAGGART, Samuel, 109
TAILLOR, John, 80
  Margaret, 80
TAILLOUR, John, 71
TALBOT, Edward, 102
TAMAN, John, 51
TANEY, Margaret, 13
  Michael, 13, 33
TANIHILL, Andrew, 36
TANMAN, John, 31
TANNEHILL, William,
  14
TANNER, Henry, 23,
  30, 31
TANNYHILL, Ninian,
  90
TANT, James, 33
  Margarett, 33
TASKER, Ann, 121
  Benjamin, 72, 73,
    79, 86, 111, 121
  John, 29, 31, 73
  Thomas, 29, 73
TATE, Hannah, 48
TATTERSHALLS GIFT,
  31
TAUMAN, John, 22
TAVERNS, William, 22
TAYLARD, Audry, 39
  William, 16, 39
TAYLOR, Ann, 68
  Avarilla, 82
  Catherine, 105
  John, 54, 80
  Jonathan, 81
  Joseph, 106
  Margaret, 97
  Michael, 63, 68,
    71
  Peter, 80, 89
  Robert, 14, 43,
    69, 115
  Samuel, 82
  Thomas, 10, 44,

45, 80, 82
  Wealthy, 37
  William, 105
TAYLOR'S FOLLEY, 22
TAYLOR'S PRIDE, 44
TEAGUE, John, 37
TENEHILL, Andrew, 10
TENNY, 66
TENT, Abigail, 76
TERRY, Thomas, 42
THE DESERTS, 11
THE FIELD, 40
THE GROVE, 72
THE MISTAKE, 58
THE ORDINARY, 31
THE PLAINES, 59
THOMAS, Ann, 96, 110
  Elizabeth, 104
  Griffin, 65
  Henry, 84
  John, 96
  Macum, 6
  Philip, 85, 96,
    104, 110, 112
  Thomas, 12, 108
  William, 46, 84,
    104, 114
THOMPSON, Andrew,
    112
  Charles, 80
  Christopher, 70
  Col., 47
  Cornelius, 113
  George, 8, 14
  John, 67, 113
  Margaret, 8, 14
  Margarett, 24
  Mary, 11
  Robert, 11
  William, 48, 113
THORLEY, Benjamin,
    15
  Edward, 5
  Mary, 5
THORNTON, John, 124
THORPE, Edward, 113
  Ezekial, 113
  John, 113
  Rachel, 113
THRIMBY GRANGE, 40
THURLEY, Benjamin,
    15
TIBBALLS, Rebecca,
    51
TILDEN, John, 72

Marmaduke, 104
TILGHMAN, Edward,
    101
TILLEY, Joseph, 10
  Mary, 10
  Rebecca, 89, 103
  Rebeccah, 103
TILLY, Charles, 34
  Joseph, 3
  Mary, 3
TIMBER NECK, 34
TIMBERWELL, 88
TINBULL, Elizabeth,
    101
  William, 101
TIPPETT, Philip, 39
TIPTON, Jonathan, 37
  Samuel, 111
TOBSON, Thomas, 79
TOD, Ann, 13
  James, 13
TODD, Alexander, 119
  Charles, 100
  Lance, 84
  Lancelot, 100, 119
  Lancelott, 78
  Margaret, 100
  Richard, 84
  Thomas, 78, 79
TODD'S HARBOUR, 78,
    79
TOFT, Ann, 56
TOLSON, Francis, 113
  John, 113
TOM, Michael, 120
TOMOSON, Elizabeth,
    13
  Justinian, 13
TOMSON, Charles, 45
TONGUE, John, 41
TOVEY, Samuel, 10
  Samuell, 6
TOWER, William, 106
TOWNENECK, 23
TOWNEY, Michael, 5
TOWNSEND, Amy, 86
  John, 86
TRACY, Susanna, 15
  Thomas, 15
TRAIL, David, 95
TRANT NECK, 23
TRAVERS, Mathew, 73
TRAVERSE, Elizabeth,
    56
  John, 112

Matthew, 112
TRENT NECK, 23
TRINDON, Sarah, 14
TRIPP, Henry, 63
TROTT, Thomas, 19
TROTTMAN, Thomas, 29
TRUEMAN, Nathaniel,
    9
  Thomas, 9, 23, 29
TRUMAN, Thomas, 22
TRUNDEL, Mary, 15
TUCKER, Amy, 6
  John, 6, 66, 67
  Robert, 67
  Thomas, 19, 20
TULL, George, 65
TUNSTALE, John, 59
TURAH, 66
TURBUTT, Foster, 60
  William, 101
TURBUTTON, William,
    102
TURLEY, Robert, 105
TURNER, John, 35,
    116
  Margaret, 41
  Robert, 3
  Thomas, 124
  William, 84
TURPIN, Solomon, 60
  William, 115
TWISDEN, Levina, 50
TYLER, Robert, 26,
    35, 49
TYLER'S CHANCE, 43,
    44
TYLER'S DISCOVERY,
    43, 44

-U-
UNGLE, Robert, 60
UPPER BENNETT, 24
UPPER SPRING NECK,
    31, 32
URINSON, 42
UTIE, Coll.
  Nathaniel, 1
UTRECK, 49

-V-
VADRY, John, 29
VALENTINE, George,
    34
VAN BIBBER, James,
    56

154

VAN BURKELO, Harman, 47
　Herman, 54
VAN SWERINGEN, Mary, 53
VANACK, Sarah, 72
VANBIBBER, Abraham, 126
　Mathias, 16
VANBURKELOE, Herman, 42
VANDERFORD, Michael Paul, 17
　Paul, 21
VANDIVER, Jane, 64
VANSANT, John, 113
VANSWEARINGEN, Mary, 16
VANSWERINGEN, Garret, 10
　Mary, 39
VEDGBY, Frances, 79
VENABLES, William, 115
VENALL, John, 7
VERMULEN, Giles, 70
VERNON, Ann, 67
　Christopher, 15, 19, 21, 38, 67
　Lois, 38
　William, 38, 67
VINCENT, Richard, 104
VINTON, Ann, 95
VORSMAN, Peter, 55
VOWLES, Richard, 20

-W-
WADE, George, 38
　Mary, 24
　Richard, 24
WADE'S POINT, 15
WADNIOR, John, 25
WADROP, 126
WADSWORTH, Richard, 7
　Susan, 7
WAIDE, George, 24
WALDRIDGE, 49
WALKER, 26
　Charles, 35
　Elizabeth, 79, 92
　James, 79
　Mary, 20
　Philip, 92

Thomas, 10
William, 19, 20
WALLACE, David, 89
WALLER, Jane, 126
　William, 126
WALLINGFORD, John, 82
WALLINGSFORD, Benjamin, 82
WALLS, Alice, 93
　George, 93
WALNUTT RIDGE, 57
WALTHAM, Hannah, 61
　John, 61
WALTON, Elizabeth, 4
　William, 114
WANKINS, John, 14
WARCOPE, Thomas, 95
WARD, James, 115
　John, 39, 42, 47, 55, 61, 71, 116
　Rachel, 116
　Rebecca, 115, 117
　Richard, 105
　Thomas, 44
　William, 42
WARFIELD, Alexander, 49
　Richard, 49
WARING, Richard Marsham, 75
WARMAN, Hester, 34
WARREN, Augustinian, 22
　John, 22, 83
　Rebecca, 83
　Thomas, 41, 83
WARRENS, Bazill, 18
　Marsham, 18
WARSCOPE, Thomas, 94
WASHINGTON, Philip, 32
WATERS, Edward, 114, 125
　Mary, 104
　Nicholas, 104
　Peter, 125
　Richard, 114
　William, 125
WATKINS, Ann, 111
　Elizabeth, 6
　Joseph, 111
　Mary, 92
　Thomas, 6, 61
WATKINSON, Cor-

nelius, 23
WATSON, Jeremiah, 117
　William, 109
WATTERS, Jacob, 98
WATTS, Peter, 41
　Thomas, 39, 41, 45, 46
　William, 46
WATT'S LODGE, 45
WATTS LODGE, 46
WAUGHOP, John, 103
　Thomas Palmer, 103
WAYMAN, Leonard, 34, 80
WEBB, Edmund, 20
　Humphrey, 19
　Jane, 99
　John, 114
　William, 20
WEBSTER, Isaac, 107
　John Lee, 113
WEEKS, Alice, 51
　Joseph, 16
　Samuel, 16
WEEMS, David, 66, 84
　James, 66
WEER, Robert, 64
WELCH, Thomas, 57
WELLS, Charles, 64
　Eleanor, 93
　George, 1
　Humphrey, 52
　John, 123
　Mary, 1
　Thomas, 93
　Tobias, 1, 4
WELSH, John, 123
　Peirce, 37
　Susannah, 123
　William, 37
WENDELL, Jacob, 89
WEST ST. MARY'S, 6
WESTBURY MANNOR, 39
WESTGARTH, George, 36
WESTHAM, 32, 33
WESTMORELAND, 12
WESTWOOD LODGE, 19
WESTWOOD MANNOR, 109
WETHERAL, Henry, 107
WETHERALL, Henry, 95
　Mary, 95
WHARFIELD, Alexander, 119

Richard, 119
WHARTON, Henry, 83
  Jane, 83
WHEELER, Christian, 34
  Edward, 106
  Francis, 70
  John, 34
  Richard, 69
  Sarah, 106
  William, 52
WHERELL, William, 46
WHICHALEY, Thomas, 62
WHICHCOTE, Mary, 108
WHITE, Cornelius, 16
  James, 19, 81
  John, 105
  Joseph, 49, 58
  Priscilla, 65
  Richard, 25, 28
  Samuel, 26, 99
WHITE HALL, 37
WHITECLIFTS, 2
WHITEHAVEN, 43
WHITEHEAD, Ann, 85
  Hannah, 85
  William, 85
WHITELY, Arthur, 65. See also Wrightly.
WHITES FORD, 22
WHITNEY, Thomas, 115
WHITTENTON, William, 23
WHITTINGTON, John, 31
  William, 28
WICCOMICO, 100
WIDOW'S PURCHASE, 49
WIGG, Richard, 47
WILKINS, William, 97
WILKINSON, Elizabeth, 102
  Rosamond, 78
  Thomas, 78, 102
WILKINSON SPRING, 31
WILL, 66
WILLIAM PEARLE'S LAND, 32
WILLIAMS, Aaron, 116, 117
  Christopher, 71
  David, 7
  Ennion, 20
  Henry, 20
  Jacob, 47
  John, 36, 72, 77
  Lodowick, 2
  Mary, 2
  Matthew, 57
  Morgan, 8
  Robert, 109
  William, 22
WILLIAMS HOPE, 27
WILLIAMSON, David, 7
  John, 91, 94
  Samuel, 29, 32, 83
  Thomas, 98
WILLIS, Richard, 80, 118
WILLLIAMSON, Samuel, 62
WILLOUGHBY, William, 20, 21, 22
WILLOWBY, Willliam, 16
WILLS, Eleanor, 92
WILLSON, John, 15
  Josiah, 67
WILMER, Blackiston, 108
  Blackstone, 108
  Dorcas, 108
  John, 113
  John Lambert, 120
  Lambert, 94
  Rose, 108
  Sarah, 108
  Simon, 94, 120
  William, 108
WILMOT, Avarilla, 106
  John, 106
WILMOTT, John, 68, 111
WILSON, Ann, 124
  Betty, 124
  David, 124, 125, 126
  Denwood, 126
  Elizabeth, 16
  Ephraim, 56, 124, 125
  Esther, 124
  James, 124
  Jane, 57
  John, 16, 53, 80
  Josiah, 52, 67
  Margaret, 56, 57
  Samuel, 126
  Thomas, 40, 43, 56, 57, 80
WILTSHIRE, 72
WIMPLE, Mindert, 89
  Sarah, 89
WINDER, Mary, 124, 125
  William, 124
WINDSOR, Elizabeth, 59
  John, 59
WINNALL, John, 22, 53
WINSETT, Richard, 64
  Teresa, 64
WIRCHWAIST, Sarah, 122
WISE, Abigail, 52
  Abilail, 23
  Christopher, 23
WISELY, John, 63
WITTING, John, 44
WOBLEY, 20
WOLFCOMB, Edward, 14
  Rachel, 14
WOLFORD, Roger, 23
WOLFSFORD, 23
WOLLENBROUGH, 58
WOLLINSBROUGH, 58
WOLPLY, Andrew, 21
  Elizabeth, 21
WOOD, Franciana, 56
  James, 56
  Joseph, 56
  Molly, 117
WOODALL, James, 38
WOODEN, Elizabeth, 106
  Priscilla, 106
  Sarah, 106
  Solomon, 106
WOODIN, John, 47
WOODLAND NECK, 45
WOODS, Ambrose, 52
  William, 52
WOODWARD, Achsah, 92
  Acksah, 86
  Amos, 86, 92
  Mary, 71, 86
  William, 86
WOODWARDS, Eleanor, 92
  Elizabeth, 92
  Mary, 92

WOOLCHRUCH,
  Elizabeth, 3
  Henry, 3
WOOLFORD, Charles,
  126
  James, 65, 113
  Jane, 113
  Levin, 113, 114,
    125
  Mary Ann, 125, 126
  Roger, 14, 59, 80
WOOLISTON MANNOR, 22
WOOLMAN, Gibson, 91
  Richard, 42
WOOLMAN'S HERMITAGE,
  40
WOOLMAN'S
  INHERITANCE, 40,
    42
WOOLMANS
  INHERITANCE, 29
WOOLSEY MANNOR, 33
WOOTEN, Mary, 68
WOOTTERS, John, 123
WOOTTON, Turner, 68,
  89
WORLD'S END, 42
WORLEY, John, 57
WORTHINGTON, Bruce
  Thomas Beale, 120
  John, 85
  Nicholas, 120
  Thomas, 49, 75,
    76, 85
WRENCH, William, 57
WRIGHT, Gowon, 114
  Henry, 89
  John, 1
  Mary, 1
  Samuell, 34
  Solomon, 37
  Thomas Hynson, 101
WRIGHTLY, Arthur, 45
WYATT, Damoras, 10
  Damoris, 10
  Nicholas, 3, 4, 10

      -Y-
YATES, Martin, 33
YERBERRY, Thomas, 55
YOE, Mary, 116
YORBERRY, Thomas, 55
YOUNG, Ann, 97
  Benjamin, 97
  Elizabeth, 4, 75,
    115
  George, 16, 20,
    24, 75
  John, 79
  Joshua, 119
  Mary, 75
  Michaell, 31
  Parker, 115
  Philemon, 113
  Richard, 117
  Williiam, 53

www.ingramcontent.com/pod-product-compliance
Lightning Source LLC
Chambersburg PA
CBHW070444090426
42735CB00012B/2461